WONDER'S CHILD

BOOKS BY JACK WILLIAMSON:

THE LEGION OF SPACE—(1947)

DARKER THAN YOU THINK—(1948)

THE HUMANOIDS—(1949)

THE GREEN GIRL—(1950)

THE COMETEERS—(1950)

ONE AGAINST THE LEGION—(1950)

SEETEE SHOCK—(1950)

SEETEE SHIP—(1950)

DRAGON'S ISLAND—(1951)

THE LEGION OF TIME—(1952)

UNDERSEA QUEST—(with Frederik Pohl, 1954)

DOME AROUND AMERICA—(1955)

STAR BRIDGE—(with James Gunn, 1955)

UNDERSEA FLEET—(with Frederk Pohl, 1955)

UNDERSEA CITY—(with Frederik Pohl, 1956)

THE TRIAL OF TERRA—(1962)

GOLDEN BLOOD—(1964)

THE REEFS OF SPACE—(with Frederik Pohl, 1964)

STARCHILD—(with Frederik Pohl, 1965)

THE REIGN OF WIZARDRY—(1965)

BRIGHT NEW UNIVERSE—(1967)

TRAPPED IN SPACE—(1968)

THE PANDORA EFFECT—(1969)

ROGUE STAR—(with Frederik Pohl, 1969)

PEOPLE MACHINES—(1971)

THE MOON CHILDREN—(1972)

H. G. WELLS: CRITIC OF PROGRESS—(1973)

TEACHING SF—(1975)

THE FARTHEST STAR—(with Frederik Pohl 1975)

THE EARLY WILLIAMSON—(1975)

THE POWER OF BLACKNESS—(1976)

THE BEST OF JACK WILLIAMSON—(1978)

BROTHER TO DEMONS, BROTHER TO GODS—(1979)

THE ALIEN INTELLIGENCE—(1980)

TEACHING SCIENCE FICTION: EDUCATION FOR TOMORROW—(1980)

THE HUMANOID TOUCH—(1980)

THE BIRTH OF A NEW REPUBLIC—(with Miles J. Breuer), 1981

MANSEED—(1982)

WALL AROUND A STAR—(with Frederik Pohl), 1983

THE QUEEN OF THE LEGION—1983

WONDER'S CHILD: MY LIFE—(an autobiography, 1984)

LIFEBURST—(in progress)

LAND'S END—(with Frederik Pohl, in progress)

WONDER'S CHILD:

My Life in Science Fiction

JACK WILLIAMSON, *1908–*

BLUEJAY BOOKS INC.

Manufactured in the United States of America
First Bluejay printing: May 1984

LIBRARY OF CONGRESS CATALOGING IN PUBLICATION DATA

Williamson, Jack, 1908–
Wonder's child.

Includes index.
1. Williamson, Jack, 1908–   —Biography. 2. Authors,
American—20th century—Biography. 3. Science fiction—
Authorship. I. Title.
PS3545.I557Z477   1984   813'.52 [B]   84-11099
ISBN 0-312-94454-3

To Blanche

CONTENTS

WONDER

The word is Germanic, but the old Greeks understood it. Aristotle saw it in the "pity and terror" of classic tragedy, although even then it had begun to fade as men ceased to dread the old, implacable gods. Sophistication kills it. The author of Ecclesiastes denies any natural wonder in his time. Longinus, exploring its rhetoric in *On the Sublime,* seems wistful for its return. Closer to our time, Thomas Carlyle declares that "the reign of wonder is done." Others, down to Sam Moskowitz, have deplored its death.

Yet we're all born to it. In childhood we find it everywhere, our strange new worlds brightly alluring, brimming with puzzle and peril and hope. Growing older, we commonly let it slide away. We solve some of the puzzles, toughen ourselves to what we can't escape, lose too much of the hope. Or, too often now, we let it turn into a dull gray dread of worse things waiting.

This book is about my own life, most of all about the times of wonder I've treasured and clung to—found here and there in literature, where it lent life to the romantics and the transcendentalists; discovered more often in science and the splendors of our cosmos as science reveals them. Best of all in science fiction, wonder in its purest state.

Science fiction remade my life when I found it long ago in those early pulp magazines where it was being invented. Its name was strange at first to nearly everybody. Not that many cared to know. Not then, because the magazines looked like trash. They were cheaply printed "pulps" with queer machines

1

and horrid monsters on their covers, but for the few of us who dug them, even their names were drenched and dripping with wonder. *Amazing Stories, Astounding Stories, Astonishing* and *Startling* and *Marvel;* even *Wonder Stories*.

The sophisticates were not impressed. But to me—the green farm kid I was then, hungry for life and ignorant of nearly everything—and to a whole generation of wondering young Americans, those disdained publications came to reflect our awe at the strangeness of the universe, our readiness to challenge all we didn't understand, our hope of better worlds to come.

Most of those once-beloved beloved magazines are gone now, and all of us have changed. Yet I think we need wonder more than ever now, because we've lately come to share so much with those ancient Greeks. Though their dreaded gods have vanished, Zeus with his thunderbolts to hurl, we have our own more dreadful missiles ready. We can all feel terror again, and pity for a world in peril.

The message of Aeschylus and Sophocles and Euripides was never despair. Greek tragedy began as worship, evolved from temple rituals meant to attune us with our cosmos. Its theme was human nobility. In our own bleak-seeming present, those old gods dead and our own new technologies grown more awesome than they ever were, we need the chastening awe the Greeks once knew, and the stout faith in human greatness that was part of it.

This book, then, is mostly my own remembrance of the good times in my own life when wonder was. Recollections of the urge to learn it has kept burning in me, and the heady joy of every new discovery. The exciting places where we camped on our trek in the covered wagon, the year I was seven. The excitement of the sciences, as I've seen them unfolding all the mysteries of the atom and language and mankind. The stars at night, and my first telescope, and the volcanoes of Io. The "sense of wonder" —the awe and the promise of new worlds revealed—that I've felt in science fiction and tried to write into stories of my own.

If technology is the illustrious son of pure science, science fiction is surely the prodigal sibling. Through most of a lifetime, I've watched and shared its slow growth toward what it ought to be.

The book glances, too, at the troubled history of wonder in our recent world. I like to think of wonder as one more rich gift of what Walter Prescott Webb calls the Great Frontier. It lives best on new horizons. With the frontiers closing and old horizons fading like mirages, its living space has sadly narrowed.

I remember when I, and many of us, saw science as the shining new frontier; when we watched technological progress as the magical means to make everything better. I've watched that cheerful faith decay. The shift began long before I was born, but we still had heroes in the world where I grew up. Those we most admired were scientists and engineers. Modern magicians, they were building us those better worlds, until a bad thing happened on the way to wonderland. That tragic shadow has chilled science fiction since H. G. Wells, and darkened all our lives since Hiroshima. Even my own.

Within the limits of memory, manners, and a habit of reticence, I've tried to make the book as honest as I can. The opening chapters focus briefly on my parents and their roots. What I know of my father's family comes mostly from a memoir written in 1932 by his younger sister, Hattie French, edited and published by her daughter, Irene French Braswell.

For my mother's people, there's nothing quite so formal. Besides my own recollections of talk I used to hear, and my brother's, I have fragmentary notes she left and her collection of family photographs and correspondence, some of the fading letters written in beautiful copperplate script before the Civil War.

To aid my own uncertain memories of more recent times, there are files of correspondence, magazines and manuscripts, and the diary I kept for a few months in the South Pacific. Perhaps best of all, the names and notes and photos in the book Blanche has been asking guests to sign while the candle burned every Christmas for the past forty years.

1.

MY FATHER,

1868–1964

Jim Gunn says the Williamsons are a sept of the Gunns. I rather like the notion, especially the hint that perhaps the clan first got to Scotland in dragon-headed Viking longships. The American line begins with a John Williamson who came to New Jersey about 1691 from Fife, which juts into the North Sea between the firths of Forth and Tay. His wife died at sea; he married again and left two sons, Samuel and David.

Aunt Hattie's memoir is a long look back across the American frontier. She follows generation after generation trekking west into the wilderness. Samuel's son, Joseph, was born in New Jersey in 1765; he died in Portsmouth, Ohio, in 1830. His descendants were plain, prolific people, devout Methodists by then, always headed farther west.

Joseph's wife was born Martha de Feurt; her people had come from France in the 1600s. In wilderness Ohio, they raised a family of six sons and two daughters. One of the sons, James, married a former bondservant named Christina Schaffer.

Christina's life could make a novel. She was born in Württemberg in 1807, the youngest daughter of Adam and Sabina Schaffer. The family, including three sisters and three brothers, migrated to America in 1819, partly because the brothers wanted to escape military conscription.

The leaky ship had to put in to Lisbon for repair, and the voyage to Boston took seven weeks. The brothers had agreed to enter bond service to pay for the family's passage, but the canny

4

Bostonians were afraid they'd run away. The sisters, instead, had to be sold.

Christina, twelve years old, was bought by a Philadelphia merchant named Mayer. She took care of his twin children and was grief-stricken when measles killed them. She was treated well, allowed to go to school. After her four years were over, she stayed on with the family, working for wages.

She had moved with them to Boston before her brother George came to take her out to Ohio. She found the family scattered, her mother dead and the sisters married, two of them to brothers of James Williamson, who began courting her. She was at first indignant when the sisters urged her to accept "that clodhopper," but something changed her mind.

Married in 1832, she and James went west again into Indiana, settling on the west fork of White River, 12 miles from Indianapolis. He contracted to pay for 320 acres of land with 19 months of labor. When it was his own, he cut and burned trees to clear the land, built a log house and a brick dwelling later.

A slight city girl, 84 pounds when she married, Christina must have found the Indiana forests an awesome challenge. She cooked in the beginning over an open fire and did the family wash down on Indian Creek Run. She worked flax into linen.

She sheared sheep, carded wool and spun it, wove and dyed cloth, made garments for her family, and finally pieced scraps from worn clothing into patchwork quilts; I remember the mothball reek of one that came down to my father, the cloth dark and coarse and ugly. She bore James three daughters and nine sons, three of whom died in infancy.

Most of his life, Hattie writes, James wrestled with the Lord. "His good wife Christina had accepted Jesus Christ as her Savior, and had joined the Methodist Church, but James took no stock in such things, for he thought himself a better man than the church members. . . . To lie and cheat was beneath him; he paid his debts and looked the world in the face as an upright man."

His resistance grew stronger when a wily churchman beat him in a horse trade, and he used to leave the house when Christina brought the minister home to dinner. Just in time, he found salvation. "Six months after his conversion," when he was cutting firewood, "a falling limb struck him on the head, killing him at once."

Peter, his oldest surviving son, became my father's father. Hardly rugged enough to fit the frontier, he had an early thirst for learning. He hunted coons and sold their skins to pay for his first book, a life of Daniel Boone. At age twenty-one, as if to break the pioneering tradition, he entered a school at Terre Haute, studying German and planning to become a merchant. Instead, for whatever reasons, he married Joanna Harriet Mosley and went on west by oxcart to claim a homestead in Minnesota.

According to Hattie's family history, the Mosleys had come from England to South Carolina a few generations earlier. Joanna, born in 1836, was the first white child in La Porte, Indiana, then an Indian village. One day while she was still a baby, as the family legend has it, she was kidnapped by an Indian woman grieving for a lost infant of her own. Joanna's father found her a few days later in the arms of the squaw and brought her back home.

She had a brother and two sisters. The family lived several years near La Porte in an abandoned Jesuit mission, but when the mother died the father had to scatter them into foster homes. She worked as a seamstress in an Indianapolis sweatshop before she met Peter and rode the oxcart west.

Though Hattie says she loved the Minnesota lakes and woods, times stayed hard. Peter's health was uncertain, though he found vigor enough to keep her pregnant. Once they had to retreat to Indiana for a winter. When the Indians rose against the whites, I imagine with cause enough, she lived in fear of massacree until the U.S. militia drove the survivors into Dakota.

Their Minnesota adventure ended with a fire in May of 1866 that destroyed almost everything, though they saved a Seth Thomas clock I used to see. Left barefoot in the snow, the family walked to a neighbor to beg for help. Looking for a kinder climate, they set out again one September morning in a mule-drawn wagon, bound somehow for Texas instead of Oregon.

Peter was still ailing; in Springfield, Missouri, he had to stop for two weeks under a doctor's care. It was mid-December

My father's family, about 1895. Peter and Joanna, seated, Hattie sitting by Peter and Almira by Joanna. In the back row, Jimmie, the oldest son, is bearded. Frank wears the moustache. My father stands by Jimmie, Albert by him. John stands by Frank, and George at the end.

before they got across the Indian Territory, now Oklahoma, and struck camp in Bell County, Texas. There, among Texans hostile to such Yankee invaders, they bought land and stayed, living at first in a one-room log cabin.

Peter seems to have found health and prosperity in Texas. He planted gardens and orchards, built a better home and bought more land, kept bees, took his family every summer for ten days to the Methodist camp meetings on Nolan Creek. He sired three daughters and seven sons, my father among them. A white-bearded patriarch, he died there in 1914, at age eighty-three.

I never saw him, but I knew Joanna and Frank, the bachelor son who had stayed at home. After Peter's death, they sold the Texas farm and moved to New Mexico soon after my own parents did. Through most of my childhood and youth, we were sharecroppers on land they owned, a fact I must have resented. I never loved them.

They were still sternly faithful to their primitive Methodism, though there was no church of any denomination near enough for them to attend. In their house, which always had bedbugs, we had to kneel for family prayers, which Frank intoned in the peculiar hollow voice reserved for communication with God. I always felt that devotion to the Lord and themselves left them very little love for anybody else.

Frank was always harshly critical of me and everything I did, though it strikes me now that perhaps I should have felt some compassion for him. His life must have been bleakly empty. Ignorant and prejudiced, he had very narrow interests. None, certainly, in my own science fiction, which he always sniffed at. "A pack of lies."

My father, Asa Lee, was the seventh child, dedicated to the Lord at his birth in 1868 and brought up for the ministry. After his early schooling at home, he attended Thomas Arnold High School at Salado, a nearby village.

A yellowed newspaper clipping from some later date shows the walls of the old building, half hidden in brush, looking as ancient and forlorn as a ruined Norman abbey. The good citizens of Salado had raised fifteen hundred dollars to set up the school after the failure of an earlier "college" had left the building vacant.

My father saved a copy of the first announcement, a document that fascinates me with its contrasts to the modern high school. The superintendent, S. J. Jones, was a Vanderbilt Ph.D. The course of study included four years of Latin and three of Greek. Tuition was fifteen dollars a quarter, board twelve dollars a month.

Working his way as a janitor—cutting wood, building fires, and ringing the bell—my father made good friends of Dr. Jones and his wife. He saved photos of her, and long letters filled with affectionate Christian concern and admonition.

From Salado, he went on to take more Latin and Greek at Texas University at Austin, from which he graduated in 1900. Earning his own way there, he worked as manager of a student residence club. He used to talk about a summer job he enjoyed, driving ox teams to haul water for a well-driller on Dry Devils River down near the Rio Grande.

In a newspaper column published in 1953, his college roommate speaks highly of "his scholarship, his studious habits and his high moral and ethical standards." For his place and time, his background in the classics was unusual. He used to recite Virgil and recall incidents from the perilous march of the "ten thousand" in Xenophon's *Anabasis*. He spent a summer in Mexico City he always enjoyed recalling, learning Mexican history and the Spanish language.

All this was too much for the fundamentalism he was born to. The break must have been painful, though he seldom said anything about it. I doubt that it was quite complete. Though we never went to church, I have a fond recollection of the old camp meeting hymn "Amazing Grace" as he used to sing it when he was the first one up in the morning, building a fire in the kitchen stove. In the lucid moments of his last illness, at ninety-six, he seemed to be facing the hereafter with mixed and uneasy expectations. At long last, he was about to know.

He never entirely escaped his Methodist conscience or his pioneer heritage. Never a churchman, he turned to teaching. Even that, however, was never really a career. I don't quite know why, because he had ability enough. His unorthodoxy was probably a handicap: he was too honest to profess what he no longer believed, too independent for easy conformity. His fundamentalist patrons must have mistrusted his theology.

He used to enjoy taking jobs in problem schools where bullies had run less militant teachers off the job, and once I saw his collection of confiscated clubs and knives, trophies of his confrontations. His love of the open and growing things was always stronger, I think, than his devotion to books.

I see him as a frontiersman at heart, born too late. He met my mother when she came to teach at the small school at Benjamin, Texas, where he was principal. In partnership with his brother Albert, he had bought a farm there. Married, he quit the job and sold his interest in the farm.

Following tradition, he and my mother went west again to join her brother Stewart in a ranching venture in northern Mexico, pioneering against a mountain wilderness no better tamed than Indiana had been a hundred years before.

2

MY MOTHER,

1874–1960

Walter Prescott Webb saw modern history shaped by what he called the Great Frontier, his phrase for all the new lands opened to Europe since Vasco da Gama and Columbus. The frontiers were escapeways into freedom. Out of tyranny, out of serfdom, out from under the Roman Church. Escapeways into democracy, private capitalism, and religious liberty. The best things of our civilization, he saw them all in growing danger now since the frontiers were gone.

I once found a novel in that notion, and I like the light it casts into the lives of my parents and their pioneering forebears. The frontier had called my father's people across the Atlantic and on into the continent. His own life can be seen as a doomed search for its vanishing gifts, south into Mexico and west of the Pecos, finally north again to the arid Llano Estacado, the "staked plain" of Eastern New Mexico where I grew up.

The frontier shaped the lives of my mother's people too, though they found it farther south and coped in different ways. One way was slavery. I've tried to understand how they felt about it. The institution had come with the territory; they rationalized it well, with no sense of guilt.

In the family myths I used to hear, slavery was something benign, emancipation a tragic disaster for black as well as white. A kinsman of my mother's father, ruined by the war, was taken in by his former slaves and cared for till he died. So the story went.

I've marveled at the tough hardihood of my father's people, eager every generation to leave all they had known to pit themselves against another wilderness farther west. Their sturdiness came partly, of course, from their simple Protestant faith in God. More of it came from their faith in themselves, their axes and plows. Maybe most of all, from greed for all the new wealth of the new lands waiting to be seized.

The Great Frontier made them what they were, new apostles of the old idea of progress, driven by the faith that they could make tomorrow better than today. Living the Puritan ethic, taking private wealth as the surest sign of God's grace, they made hard work an act of worship.

In my mother's South, most work was for slaves, but the frontier had shaped everything else. The Southerners were Protestants too, if not Puritans. They were democratic, at least in defense of states' rights, and willing, when the war came, to die for their own sort of capitalism.

They lost the war, lost their whole social system. Slavery had ingrained them with the same contempt for physical toilers and physical toil that the old Greeks had felt in another slave-based culture. Left penniless and slaveless, they were often ill-prepared for peace, as unfit for change as my father was.

In the war's aftermath, frontier America slipped into history, with small room left for the sort of self-reliant pioneer my father's folk had been. While the South lay paralyzed, cities were rising and factories building everywhere else, old lifestyles transformed by new ways of work and thought.

In the old theology, man had been safe in the great chain of being, sure of his own central place between his world and his God, but science had begun to undermine such comforting certainties. Old dogmas were unraveling. Lyell's geology had challenged Genesis. Darwin found man claiming the image of God and exposed him as only another evolving animal.

New technologies—most of them Yankee technologies—were saving labor and reshaping lifestyles. Before the war, Samuel Colt had invented the revolver and the assembly line to mass-produce it. Charles Goodyear had vulcanized rubber. Elias Howe had invented the sewing machine, Samuel Morse the tele-

graph, Cyrus McCormick the reaper—except for McCormick, a
Virginian, they were all New Englanders. Even the cotton gin
was a Yankee invention.

The typewriter and the telephone opened wider lives for
women, for Northern women first, ways out of the home and
into business. The war over, new railways raced across the continent, carrying millions of settlers into the last American frontiers. The buffalo were exterminated; the last of the Indians
were driven into shrinking reservations. In only two or three
decades after 1865, the Wild West faded out of history into
myth. The horseman gone, the 1890s became the bicycle age;
my father used to talk of riding 60 miles a day on unpaved
country roads.

That was the world where he grew up, the intellectual climate
that turned him away from the ministry. A world, I think, where
he never felt quite at home. Born for the Great Frontier, born
a generation late, he had nowhere to go.

My mother, Lucy Betty Hunt, was born in 1874. Born Southern and dispossessed. All through my childhood I heard nostal-
gic talk about her lost world, the wistful recollections of her own
mother and various elderly aunts. Later I rediscovered it in
William Faulkner's fiction, amazingly intact: the Old South,
longingly recalled by refugees still clinging to it in sad imagination. A world where family and status had been as important as
the lonely partnership with a primitive God had been to my
father's people.

After the war, my mother's people came west again in pursuit
of their own retreating frontier. I never heard much about those
left behind, but these were pioneers again. Ruined by the war,
slaves and fortunes lost, they were more civilized than my father's family, and better educated. If slavery had been a crippling thing, some of them recovered fast. Stewart Hunt, my
mother's elder brother, lived an epic of his own along that last
frontier my father never found.

Hunt is not an uncommon name, and I don't know when my
mother's first forebears got to America. At least a dozen John
Hunts migrated from England to Virginia in the 1600s, and the

Census of 1790 lists more than six hundred Hunts as heads of families.

My mother's mother, Mary Elizabeth Stewart, was born in South Carolina in 1844. If the Williamsons had been Scots, so were the Stewarts. Family legend links them proudly to the royal Stuarts. Part of what I know about them comes from a letter written in 1920 by my mother's uncle, Phillip Hunt.

Other records seem incomplete and confusing to me. They begin with the Hunts and the Dandridges, the Bedfords and Ruffins and Stewarts, apparently already well established in the old Southern aristocracy. Henry Clay was a connection. One bride is said to have been a cousin of Martha Washington, who was born a Dandridge.

John Thomas Hunt, my mother's father, was born in Tennessee in 1840. He attended a military school, served in the Civil War as "an officer without rank," and after the war was graduated in engineering from Washington University while Robert E. Lee was still its president. He married Lizzie Stewart in Como, Mississippi, in 1870. Never an actual engineer, he seems to have been a luckless misfit for postwar life.

The couple lived in Mississippi until the birth of Stewart, their first child. They came west to the Texas farm where my mother was born, returned to Mississippi for a few years on the malarial banks of the Yazoo Pass, and moved back to central Texas while my mother was still a child.

She grew up there. She seems to have loved and admired her father, though Stewart had a low opinion of him. The record is silent about his later life except to say that it ended in 1902, I believe in an asylum.

His widow, my Grandma Hunt, was made of tougher stuff. She survived until 1930. I knew and loved her through my own childhood, when she used to spend the summers with us. Always kind, she brought us small gifts. She talked to us, recalling all those plangent family myths. She helped with the housework; once when I killed a young jackrabbit, throwing a hammer at it, she fried it for me.

I was named for Stewart, as well as for my father's brother John; and Uncle Stewart was a hero figure in my childhood. His life could have made a whole series of Western novels. Twelve years old—after a quarrel, I imagine, with his father—he left home to stay. Like any Western hero, he went up the trail to Dodge City as horse wrangler with a herd of longhorns. The names and brands of the ranches where he worked and those he later owned echo through Southwestern history.

He learned Spanish. He used to venture deep into Mexico to buy half-wild cattle that he drove across mountains and desert to American markets. He leased ranches, bought them and sold them, on both sides of the border. He made fortunes in good times and survived hopefully through bad ones and became, before he died, a sort of feudal baron surrounded by assorted retainers.

Dave, the younger brother, I never knew so well, but I recall him as a quiet but likable loner, lean and blue-eyed, with a wry sense of humor but little of Stewart's optimistic enterprise.

I don't know much about my mother's girlhood. She grew up wrapped in that close-knit system of family connections I used to hear so much about, the Hunts and Stewarts and Bedfords, another disinherited heir to all their longing legends of a better past.

Preparing to teach, she attended a normal school at Denton, Texas, and a Chautauqua at Boulder, Colorado, where she saw electric lights—and called the maid one night when she caught an odd odor, to report that the electricity was escaping.

"Humph," the maid said, "'lectricity don't 'scape!"

She saw her first automobile there, and came away uncertain about whether it had to have tracks. She was a student nurse for a time at a Catholic hospital in El Paso. She went into Mexico to cook for Stewart when he was setting up a stage line, and again with another relative, Clay Bedford, who was building a Mexican railway. She was a teacher with my father for three years at Benjamin, Texas, before their marriage.

Her romantic mythology of the lost South came down from her to me, wistful legends not much different from those Faulkner fictionized. I've always known the canebrakes, the faithful and beloved darkies, the plantation mansions, the Yankee invaders and the buried family silver and the bleak survival on corn pone and pot liquor, the lost fortunes and spoiled lives and all the tragic dramas and disasters of the war, in the same way I know Barsoom. With no basis whatever in actual experience—I don't recall even seeing a black until after I was grown—that wrecked and beaten world was a fact of my childhood environment.

3.

EL RANCHO LA LOBA,

1908–1911

Webb's date for the closing of the Great Frontier is 1890, about the time my father came of age. The new worlds had been used up in stages, the best of the free land claimed, the richest mines worked out, the virgin forests cut. In the constricting aftermath, individual liberties were slowly overwhelmed, old controls restored.

Though such people as Uncle Stewart and my father clung stubbornly to the old dream of progress, it was already under intellectual attack. H. G. Wells used science fiction for his own telling assault. A little book of my own, *H. G. Wells: Critic of Progress*, glances at that aspect of Wells' early stories, the works that made his name.

In *The Time Machine* and *The War of the Worlds*, he explores the cosmic limits to human progress. Since Darwin, we're no longer the chosen darlings of God, but only one more evolving species, striving in competition with other evolving creatures for survival in a universe that doesn't care who wins.

In *The Island of Dr. Moreau* and *The Invisible Man*, he looks at our own inborn limits. Our own evolution has made us merely Beast-Folk, better adapted for the jungle than utopia.

In *When the Sleeper Wakes* and *The First Men in the Moon*, he sees progress as simply better fitness for survival, never as a divinely guided climb toward any utopian perfection. Ostrog prefigures Big Brother in Orwell's *1984*, Hitler and Stalin in reality. Evolutionary advance has turned his moon folk into things like insects, specialized for efficiency yet monstrously inhuman.

16

*My parents at the time of their
marriage, 1907.*

In the actual world, however, as the new century began, progress still looked real to nearly everybody. With the free lands
gone, science was becoming the alluring new frontier. Its revelations looked like universal truth. Applied as technology, it could
solve all problems, make the whole world wonderful.

The Wright brothers were taking off from Kitty Hawk by
1903. Finlay, Reed, and Gorgas were conquering yellow fever;
Panama was freed of it by 1905. Albert Einstein, that same year,
published his now-famous equation linking energy and matter.
A bright new key to the mysterious cosmic box, its awesome
consequences were not yet suspected.

My parents were married in Mineral Wells, Texas, June 21,
1907, a date that now seems long ago. Streetcar fares in Cleveland were cut that year to only three cents. The *Lusitania*, the
world's largest ship, set a speed record on her maiden Atlantic
crossing. Guglielmo Marconi spanned the ocean in an even
more dramatic way, talking from Nova Scotia to Ireland by wireless telegraph.

The 1907 Sears Roebuck catalog still lists sixty-seven pages of buggies and accessories, but the motorcar is coming. Mr. and Mrs. Charles M. Glidden have completed an "epoch-making" tour of the world. On the road since 1901, they had to return their Napier car to its makers only twice for repair. The first taxicabs have reached the streets of New York.

I was born April 29, 1908, in Bisbee, Arizona. When we were back there in 1940, my father pointed out my birthplace, a little iron-roofed building in Lowell Canyon. While my mother waited for me to arrive, he had been working as a "mucker," shoveling ore deep underground in the Copper Queen.

The doctors said babies were like puppies, best moved young, and I was only six weeks old when we followed my Uncle Stewart into Mexico, to *El Rancho la Loba*. The Bitch-Wolf Ranch. It lay on the headwaters of the Yaqui River, high in the Sierra Madre between Chihuahua and Sonora.

The liberating power that Webb discovered in the Great Frontier had failed to free Latin America. That looks ironic, because it offered open space and natural wealth enough. Michael Novak blames the failure on the Catholic Church and its habit of allying with heavy-handed governments.

Whatever the causes, Latin revolutions have never freed the

 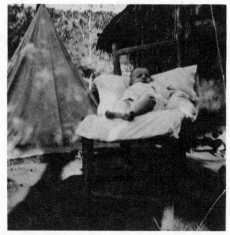

My first home, on El Rancho La Loba.

The author on El Rancho La Loba *in Sonora, Mexico, 1908.*

people. Homegrown oligarchs and juntas always became as oppressive as the old Spanish tyranny. The end of slavery brought peonage. Mexico's strong man, Porfirio Díaz, had tried to foster progress, at least for his own upper crust, but by 1908 he was near the end of his sway.

Mexico today is full of people, spilling over the border in hungry millions to do the work that is too hard or too dirty or otherwise too demanding for Anglos, but things were different in 1908. Chihuahua and Sonora were only thinly settled, the frontier regions still wild enough to tempt such hardy souls as Stewart. There were villages in the river valleys, scattered mining towns, a few Mormon colonies, but the rugged summits of the Sierra Madre Occidental had hardly been touched.

The journey there took us almost back to the Stone Age. It must have been high adventure to my father, but I think my mother found it a hard and sometimes frightening ordeal.

We crossed the border at Agua Prieta and went on south, by rail and stage and finally by horseback. The ranch was a long day's ride beyond the last stage station, as my mother used to put it. I rode on a pillow in front of my father. The luggage was on packmules. There was no road for wheels.

That was my own first world. We left it before I was three. I'm not certain that I really recall it at all, yet it existed in my mind all through childhood, kept alive in my dreams by talk about it as the old South was, a sort of primitive paradise lost—a realm of strange romance, maybe dangerous, yet exotic and alluring. I wonder sometimes if it set the pattern for the dream worlds of science fiction that have always captivated me.

In that high mountain valley, the two-room house had walls laid up from unshaped stone, with earth floors and a grass roof. The furniture was improvised there, the tables split from logs, the beds made of sapling frames laced with rawhide strips. The doors were only canvas curtains, and there were no yard fences. I remember my mother telling of a time when two bulls terrified her, fighting around the house. She was afraid they would charge inside.

She spoke very little Spanish, and she used to say she saw only two white women during her years in Mexico. She was afraid of many things, less for herself than for me. The land itself was

Stewart Hunt, my mother's elder brother and my favorite uncle. The picture was probably taken on El Rancho la Loba, c 1908.

violent: the dry lower slopes scattered with spiny desert growth; the high ridges often naked stone, boulder-piled and scarred with earthquake cracks; the rocky canyons subject to sudden floods.

Mountain lions were killing cattle on the range, and once a bear broke into a shed below the house. There were scorpions whose sting was said to kill a baby. Most of the Anglos were fugitives from the law or things they didn't like across the line, but she was more afraid of Indians.

Though the Yaquis were peaceful, survivors of Geronimo's Apache band were hiding on the ranch. They were discovered when they began killing saddle horses and packmules, animals tame enough to be caught and led to the high caves, where they were hidden and slaughtered for food. When Stewart and my father complained, the *rurales* gave them field glasses and permission to kill the renegades.

I don't think that authority was ever used—but once, when the lion hunters with their hounds bayed an old Apache woman, they brought her into camp. She seemed sick and helpless; they fed her. Her kinfolk must have followed, because she vanished one day when she was left alone, the camp stripped of such treasures as oilcans and blankets.

As late as 1924, Apaches were blamed for the death of Jack Fisher, a man working for Stewart. Riding alone, he was shot through the mouth, maybe by marauders who wanted the supplies on a packhorse he was leading. He outran the attackers, but when he had to dismount to open a pasture gate, he was too weak from loss of blood to mount again. He died there.

Such challenges seem nearly as severe as those my father's people had met generations earlier on their own frontier. Yet, even for my mother, there were rich compensations. In her talk about them later, those three years became a tale of exotic romance. That was not her first Mexican adventure, and I think she shared my father's joy in resourceful coping.

He enjoyed roughing it, camping in the open, making new trails. He had wistful recollections of his hunting trips and long rides across new country to buy supplies in Mexican villages where he had never been. Once he killed a bear. He shot deer to feed the hounds, and he liked to recall the day he got five with six shots. One of my own fondest almost-memories is of standing among the hounds out in the yard with El Tío, who was grinding pieces of jerked venison on an Indian *metate* to feed the dogs, giving choice morsels to me.

By 1911, gringos were no longer quite so welcome. Francisco Madero and Pancho Villa were in revolt against the Díaz dictatorship, and Mexico was toppling into turmoil. On March 7, twenty thousand American troops were ordered to the Texas line. Already, by then, my father had brought us out.

Stewart, however, stayed the rest of his life in Mexico or just across the border from it. His Spanish was fluent, and he learned to cope with the unfriendly intricacies of Mexican law and the *morditas* of petty officials. He raised a son, Pepe. Late in life he married Lucia, a Spanish-speaking matron who was a gracious hostess when we saw her now and then at their home in Agua Prieta.

In my twenties, I got back to Mexico on several summer visits to other ranches of Stewart's. The last one he owned, El Tapila, was north of La Loba but high in the same rugged mountain range, itself almost an empire.

In one Depression year when cattle were worthless, I found

him living in another grass-roofed hut, growing on the ranch everything his people needed except for sugar and coffee and horseshoe nails, dreaming up expansive projects for the better days he expected.

Never in vain. He became for a while the largest exporter of cattle from Mexico. One summer he had a crew of men cutting and roasting the maguey plants in the lower valleys, to be fermented and distilled into mescal. Later I saw new roads bulldozed up the canyons, and trucks hauling huge logs from timber stands on the higher slopes.

Pepe was four or five years old when I first met him. His mother had been the widow of Jack Fisher, the ranch hand who was murdered. She herself was Indian, and Stewart used to call Pepe "a little Apache." A wild little brown-skinned urchin, already at home on a horse, he had ridden with his father across the mountains from Chihuahua, seventy miles in one day.

When Stewart died, old and nearly blind but still a *patrón*, surrounded with dependent relatives and retainers, Pepe was the heir. It's many years now since I saw him last, and Mexico has changed. I'd like to know what his life has been.

Mexico. Perhaps I was too young for any clear recollection, and my parents had brought out only a few mementos—I remember the bright-striped serape my mother kept in her trunk and the little book of photos my Uncle John had taken on a summer visit there—but their talk kept it alive for them and for me, a dimension of magic reality, a place of escape from the dull familiarity I knew too well.

My first world of wonder. A dreamlike image, shining in my imagination, Mexico must have shared in shaping the haunting discontents with everything I knew and all the yearnings for something more rewarding that turned me later toward science fiction.

4.

WEST OF THE PECOS,

1911–1915

Outside that Mexico wilderness, technology had been running on. In 1909, Lee De Forest spoke by wireless telephone from the Eiffel Tower to Marseilles; Louis Blériot flew his airplane across the English Channel; Wilbur Wright set a new flight record, staying aloft over an hour.

Mark Twain died in 1910, and I'm told that I saw Halley's comet. Glenn Curtiss made a takeoff from water in 1911, and Albert Berry jumped to a safe parachute landing. Taft was president by then; Woodrow Wilson governor of New Jersey. A landmark Supreme Court decision dissolved the Standard Oil Company. In Paris, the Mona Lisa was found missing from its frame.

Refugees from the Mexican Revolution, we spent a few months back in Arizona while my father was looking for another home. He went to Eastern New Mexico and rented a horse in Elida to ride the thirty-odd miles to Milnesand where two of his brothers, Albert and John, had gone into ranching. Deciding not to join them, he bought a farm near Pecos, Texas.

I almost died there in Arizona from something then called *cholera infantum*. A deadly diarrhea. Recovering at last, I had to learn everything over again. One of my first actual memories is crawling across a floor of splintery pine boards before I was strong enough to walk, following two big glass marbles. I kept the marbles a long time, worn and scarred but dear to me.

My father had accumulated some five thousand dollars. Not much today, it used to sound like a fortune to me, and it was certainly more than he owned again for a good many years. With that and what he borrowed, he bought a farm near Pecos, Texas, and put part of it under irrigation.

I'm not sure the rest was fit to farm; there were catclaw thickets and an alkali flat around a playa lake that we called the *laguna*. That became a place of wonder when I had grown old enough to venture there, hearing wild things rustling in the small jungle around it and smelling its queer mud-scents and discovering the tadpoles swimming in it when there had been rain.

We had a centrifugal pump at the bottom of a mysterious dark pit where spiders lived. A huge engine powered it, the flywheels as tall as a man. The water ran to the fields in a ditch that seemed immense to me. In proud imitation, I learned from my father to lie on my stomach and drink out of the ditch.

The investment turned out badly, I'm not sure why. My father was a competent farmer who loved the land; he worked hard and displayed no expensive vices. I remember his talk of the knockers and pushers he knew in town, the pessimists and the evangelists of progress.

Perhaps he should have listened more skeptically to the land agents and sooner to the knockers. I suppose he was too much given to optimistic planning, with too little of Stewart's shrewd ability to make the visions real. Though maybe I'm unfair. Farming, like writing science fiction, has always been a risky enterprise. Certainly, he was unlucky.

The land was productive enough, at least till alkali from the irrigation water began collecting in the soil, but the market for what it produced was nearly always disappointing. One year we put most of the farm in cantaloupes. They grew to fragrant golden perfection, but a carload shipped to Chicago couldn't be sold because of a market glut. We had to send money to pay the freight.

My remembrances of our five years there are only fragmentary, but mostly happy enough. My sister Jo was born the first spring, just before I was three, my brother Jim a year and a half later. Neighbors who lived on the road into Pecos had two young daughters I saw now and then, and there was a Mexican girl about my age whose father worked on the farm; but most of the time I played alone.

I remember a farm of my own beside the irrigation ditch, with one stalk of something I called "an oat." I had a doll named Felix Eaton who was killed in a tragic accident. Working with me, standing on the tower of a toy well drill I had built, he fell off and shattered his china head. I cried for him.

I learned the alphabet from a picture book brightly printed on tough linen pages; the first page read, "A is for Archer, who shot at a frog." I remember insisting, for no reason I can recall, that it should be "an frog."

My mother used to read stories to us; when she was writing a letter, she could be stopped to draw a picture of the three crosses where Jesus and the two thieves had been hanged. I was taught the child's prayer beginning "Now I lay me down to sleep," but I refused to say the rest of it, or even to think of dying.

That's about all the religious instruction I recall. We never went to church, maybe because we were too far from town. My father must have been reluctant to share his own uneasy skepticism. My mother used to call herself a Campbellite; she seldom spoke of her own beliefs, but I think she felt happy with them.

I recall going along with my father when he took the Jersey milk cow to be served by a neighbor's bull. Horrified, I found the courage to ask if human beings began the same way. My father said they did. That's all the sex instruction I remember.

I rarely got into Pecos, but I recall a long hot day at the county fair. Jim and my mother were triumphant winners in the well-baby contest, and we all had our pictures taken. For years I kept a trophy of the day: a cheap saltshaker that came with candy inside. It had the shape of a toy lantern with a red glass globe.

One summer afternoon we saw an ugly black thundercloud in the distance, and next day my father took me with him in the hack to see rows of big trees the wind had uprooted. I remember staying alone with him during our last summer on the farm while my mother and the two younger children were away. We were busy mixing Black Leaf 40, which was an odious nicotine concentrate, to spray the aphids infesting the cantaloupe leaves. Every day he made fried potatoes, which I loved.

Machines were fascinating. The immense irrigation engine always awed me. It was sometimes hard to start and sometimes

had to be repaired. I watched what my father did and he told me
how it worked. I saw an automobile. A black Ford touring car,
it belonged to a neighbor farmer who cranked it up and turned
on the magneto headlamps to astonish me. He didn't take us
riding.

I remember being sick with what must have been rheumatic
fever, though it was called "growing pains." I remember staying
in a chair that people dragged around the house, because moving hurt so much. The only treatment I recall is drinking water
out of a glass jug filled with rusty nails. The iron was supposed
to do me good.

Years later, while I was still in my teens, a doctor said he heard
a murmur in my heart and asked about rheumatic fever. I imagined then that my time was going to be short, but later tests have
shown no damage.

I never knew much about our financial difficulties, but they
evidently grew. My father owed money at the Pecos Mercantile,
where he bought supplies. For I think two winters, he taught at
a school in Pecos where most or all of his students were Mexican
kids. He used to talk about them fondly, but what he earned
didn't save the farm.

Finally, in the fall of 1915 he went back to New Mexico and
filed on a homestead adjoining the ranch his brothers were
operating. He built a shack on it and came back to salvage what
he could and take us there. For him and my mother, the move
must have been a painful retreat. For me, it was pure adventure.

By 1915 the covered wagon was vanishing into history, but my
father had more pioneer know-how than funds for shipment by
rail. He built an overjet on our wagon, with bows to hold the
white canvas cover. The chickens rode in a coop on the old hack,
which trailed behind the wagon. We had a few cattle, the milk
cows and their calves; and my father rode the old roan mare to
herd them while my mother drove the wagon.

When we came to the Pecos, the first day out, the cattle were
afraid of the bridge, I suppose because of the hollow rumble of
the floorboards under their feet. My father rode the old mare to
a lather and shouted himself hoarse before he got them across.

I had never seen the river, though we had lived so near, and
it seemed equally strange and dangerous to me, a mysterious

and frightening slash through the safe and walkable land, steep clay cliffs walling salt cedar jungles and wastes of bare red mud and the boiling, mud-colored water.

Beyond the river, we were seventeen days on the road. Though the distance was only a couple of hundred miles, the cattle and the hobbled horses needed time to graze. The fall weather was fine. I think we kids slept on pallets spread over household goods in the wagon, our parents on the ground outside.

We cooked over campfires, baking bread in a cast-iron Dutch oven. The fare must have been monotonous, because I recall very vividly a big bucket of clabbered milk given us by a Good Samaritan ranch woman when we passed her place. Our situa-

The author, seven years old, at Pecos, Texas. It is a blazing summer day, but the overcoat had just come in a gift package from some relative, and I was proud of it.

tion must have looked pretty desperate; I was never fully aware of that, but I've seldom tasted anything more delicious than that clabber.

We lived through drama enough that I did know about. Once when we were camped and my father was away—perhaps to find water and grass for the livestock—my mother missed Jim, who was just three years old. Searching, she caught sight of him far down the road, running back the way we had come, crying too hard to hear her calling. In desperate pursuit, she was almost exhausted before she overtook him.

On another day, my father put me on the roan mare to follow the cattle. That was my first ride, and the mare wasn't used to kids. Things went well enough at first, but then she got frightened and ran with me. She wasn't bucking, but soon I saw the wagon falling too far behind. Hanging with both hands to the saddle horn, I waited for a clear space in the catclaw thickets and gave up my grip. I fell on bare gravel, able to get up and walk crying back to the wagon. My mother was almost hysterical, my father distressingly calm.

Most of the trip, at least for me, was better fun. We were explorers, camping each night at places we had never seen before. I remember one camp in strange sand dunes, and another near a vacant house abandoned by homesteaders no more fortunate than we were. Venturing into the house, I found a worn deck of playing cards, relics of unknown people and their strange ways of life, as exciting to me as a new tomb to an archaeologist.

I remember feeling let down when the wagon stopped beside the tiny pine shack that stood all alone on bare grassy flatness and I knew the adventure was over.

5.

SANDHILL CLAIM,

1915–1918

Though in 1912 I wasn't yet awake to history, I remember seeing a newspaper drawing of the *Titanic* going down. Alexis Carrel won a Nobel Prize that year for his work with tissue cultures and tissue transplants, and the *New York Sun* carried ads for the Disco Self-Starter.

In 1913 the income tax amendment was adopted. At the South Pole, Scott and his party found that Amundsen had got there first; on the way back, they died on the ice. Motion pictures had become a billion-dollar industry, Mary Pickford its queen, and ranchers had a labor problem because so many star-struck cowboys had gone to Hollywood.

In 1914, the Wanamaker stores made the first radio broadcasts. Henry Ford startled industry by raising the minimum wage in his plants to five dollars a day.

In June of that year, the Sarajevo assassinations touched off World War I, though I don't recall hearing about it then. A shattering blow to the hope that high technology might mean utopia, yet the dream died stubbornly. No longer the critic of progress, H. G. Wells had become an eloquent evangelist. Not out of any rosy faith in brighter futures coming, but from his fear of world collapse. The atom was already haunting him. In *The World Set Free*, published in 1913, he had foreseen war fought with uranium fission bombs.

The first battle in the air was fought in 1914, when a French aviator dived his plane into a German Zeppelin. Here in America, technology still seemed more benign. The Panama Canal was opened. In 1915 the telephone system joined New York and San Francisco, and Ford built his millionth car.

It was early November, 1915, when we reached the shack in New Mexico. Built of raw pine, measuring only 10 by 12 feet, it still exists, sheathed now in sheet iron and used as a tackroom on my brother's ranch. It was kitchen, living room, and bedroom for our parents; we kids slept in the body of the covered wagon, set off the wheels outside the east window, which we used for a door.

I remember being sick with flu that winter, lying on my pallet and staring up at the translucent canvas stretched across the bows. My mother was the physician when we were ill. Though she had been a student nurse, she depended largely on medical traditions handed down from family members who had practiced on their slaves.

In diagnosis, she inspected the tongue. When it was "coated," the patient was bilious. Her standard remedy was a "course of calomel"—which is mercurous chloride—followed by a dose of a villainously bitter patent medicine called Black Draught. She was tenderly kind, and we survived.

I remember a fire one night that had somehow spread into the kitchen end of the shack from the cookstove to a pile of the cow chips we used for fuel. When my father smelled the smoke, he shoveled them out in time to save us and the house. My gift that Christmas was a toy train, a cast iron engine with cars. It had no track.

We had come too late to get good land. Too many settlers had begun homesteading the open range that such ranchers as my father's brothers had been using, and I remember bitter talk of nesters and squatters and gun-toting claim-jumpers and ninety-mile wagon trips to file lawsuits at Roswell.

Albert, the youngest brother, survived such troubles to hold the ranch. He lived there until one summer day of 1933. During a thunderstorm, he was sitting under a mulberry tree in the yard when lightning struck. He was killed. Ted, his oldest son, still owns the ranch.

John, named John Wesley for the founder of Methodism, was my father's favorite. Like my father, he had earned his degree from the University of Texas and taught for a few years. He seemed bright and warmly friendly when I first knew him, full of interesting things to say. Once he gave me a pocketknife. He never married, and his later life was a long slide into failure.

I'm not quite sure what went wrong. He left the ranch, served a few years as county superintendent of schools, and farmed unsuccessfully. For several years he lived with or near us, half dependent on my father. Misfortune changed him. My mother came to resent him as a sponger, and my affection faded.

Our own early years were hard. My father moved the shack that first spring off the flat land where he had built it, to a homestead in a range of sandhills unfit for farming and with no water beneath them that well-drillers ever found.

We lived there three years, "proving up" to get legal title. My father built another little room beside the first. For shelter against the summer sun, he cut yucca—we called it beargrass— to cover chicken wire stretched over posts between the shacks. My mother planted a few flowers and a balsam vine beside the door, saving dishwater and bathwater to keep them alive.

Water was always a problem. My father dug a cistern, a pit a dozen feet deep, enlarged to a sphere at the bottom and plastered inside with thin concrete. He let me help with the digging; I remember the hollow boom when we spoke inside it, and the reek of beetles that fell in and died there. To fill it, we hauled water in a wagon tank.

I remember wash days, weekly ordeals that took place out near the cistern. The well water was hard. We heated it with an open fire under a big cast-iron pot, softened it with borax, skimmed off a thick brown scum, made suds with vile-odored homemade lye soap, punched the soiled clothes through the yellow suds with a broom handle and scrubbed them on a rub board, rinsed them through tubs of precious water, twisting them by hand to wring them, finally hanging them on the barbed-wire fence to dry. When the rare rains came, we set every available pot and pan in the drip under the eaves to catch the sweet-tasting rainwater for washing and cooking.

We lived close to nature. Though I never knew many botanical names, I recall the look and feel and smell and taste of whatever grew in the sand: the wonder of sleek green acorns swelling in their ornamental cups on the low-growing oak brush we called shinnery; the magic promise of a tiny, tender watermelon growing out of its dying bloom; the mystery of the sensitive plants that shut their leaves when you touched them. There was sweet nectar to be sucked from one white, deep-necked bloom. Grassburrs and goatheads had to be avoided in the summers, when we were happily barefoot.

I remember running from the narrow shadow of one little bush to the cooler shadow of another on blazing summer days when the sand burned my feet. I envied the darting grace of dragonflies, and squatted to puzzle over the ants, each blindly frantic in its mindless-seeming motion, yet all of them together somehow building roads and digging their underground homes.

I watched dung beetles rolling and burying their neat brown balls. I remember the quick little lizards shining like green gems when they stopped on hot days to pant, and the butcherbirds that caught and impaled them on barbed wire to dry. I recall the awesome splendor of a thunderstorm and the feel of distant lightning when it hit the fence wires and the slashing savagery of hail.

I can still see every twist of the road that ran through the dunes to the claim. Most vivid, perhaps, is a night when I was walking home, or running when I had breath enough, carrying a gallon of milk in a tin syrup bucket. I was all alone, the dusk getting thicker and coyotes howling all around me. I had been told they were harmless, but I couldn't help thinking they might like milk.

One of our first neighbors was "Big Jack" Ralston, a tall, laconic Scot who had been a windmill repairman on the old DZ ranch when it still covered most of the county. Now and then he talked, and I heard talk about him. A veteran of a more exciting age, he became a sort of Paul Bunyan in my mind, an almost superhuman hero.

The nesters had won their range wars by then, but I remember stories about the drunken cowboys who threw empty bottles at the dugouts on their way back to the job after a binge in Portales, and sometimes I found their bottles in the sandhills, turned a beautiful opalescent blue by years under the sun, fascinating relics of more romantic times.

Our claim was on a narrow climatic line between the regions east of us that had rain enough to make farming possible and the semi-desert not far west where one cow must graze many acres to survive. That line shifted unpredictably, bringing sudden summer floods or, more often, ruinous drought.

In a few wet years before we arrived, hopeful settlers had taken up all the better land in 160-acre homesteads. Dry times came and the rain stopped falling. Year by year, more and more defeated settlers gave up and left. We hung on, perhaps because we had nowhere else to go.

Our own homestead was a section, 640 acres. My brother has improved it now, piping stock water to it, spraying the brush with herbicides, and stringing electric fences to set up a new grazing system, but it was nearly worthless to us then.

Always optimistic, my father plowed a level flat between the dunes. For a year or two, until the grass roots rotted, it was productive, but then the spring winds began piling the loosened soil into new dunes. I recall too many heartbreaks when the wind came up to cover a fine young crop with drifting sand.

With cattle, too, we had cruel disasters. In the early springs before rain came for grass, the shinnery put out tender leaves that were slow poison for grazing cattle. A painful recollection, because I had cattle once.

That sad venture began at Pecos, with a bicycle my father gave me when he won it at a raffle. He sold it when we moved, and later gave me a half-Holstein heifer to replace it. Named Easter, for the day she was born. Her offspring and theirs were mine, at least to claim, until I owned half a dozen head. One dry spring, the shinnery killed them all except a single dogie yearling. Even he died that summer, standing against a barbed-wire fence when lightning struck it. If science fiction is a way of escape, such losses left me looking for it.

My father had misadventures of his own on a somewhat larger scale. He borrowed money to buy Hereford cattle. They might have done better, but in 1918, as he always recalled, there was no rain even to sprout tumbleweeds until August 8. Uncle Frank had cattle, also starving. In search of pasture, he and my father herded them south and east into Texas. I went with them to drive the chuck wagon, following the herd.

That fall there was still no grass. My father shipped the hungry herd to Kansas City. I remember the lump in my throat when I stood waving to him on the caboose as the train took him away. Too lean for good beef, the cattle sold cheap, graded as "canners and cutters." The bank got all the money.

With nothing left even for rail fare, my father worked on Kansas farms to earn money to pay his way to Bisbee, where he went back underground in the copper mines, working through the winter in a "bonus" drift for extra pay. I think he enjoyed himself. He liked hard labor—after he was ninety, I found him once at work with pick and shovel deepening a not-very-necessary ditch to drain his orchard.

He spent a lot of spare time that winter with books and magazines in the public library and came home full of new interests and enthusiasms for literature and world affairs; I recall his talk about "Marse Henry" Watterson's newspaper columns.

We were soon subscribing to good magazines—*Harper's* and *Scribner's* at various times; *World's Work* and *Review of Reviews*; always the *Saturday Evening Post*. We kids used to ride six or eight miles to get the mail at the Richland post office—or later at a box just as far away—on those red-letter days when the *Post* would be coming with new installments of serials by Ben Ames Williams and P. G. Wodehouse and George Barr McCutcheon.

That hard year can't have been so pleasant for my mother. The winter of '18 was always recalled in local legend as a bitter one, with snow on the ground week after week. My younger sister, Katie Lee, had just turned two, and my mother had four of us to care for.

When Frank built a new house for Grandma Williamson and himself, we moved off the claim into the old two-room house they vacated—burning sulfur in it first to kill the bedbugs. In nicer weather, we picked up cow chips for fuel to keep us warm.

We got through the winter, but that spring disaster struck again. The house burned. I'm not sure whether my father was still in Arizona, but that day he wasn't at home. When we discovered fire in the attic, Jo and I ran to call Uncle Frank. He helped carry a few things out, but most of what we had was lost.

I remember picking sadly through the ashes for the black and twisted metal remnants. The skeleton of the clock, my mother's wedding silver melted into shapeless lumps, my marbles turned to blobs of dirty glass. Uncle Stewart, generous as ever, sent my mother five hundred dollars. I recall telling Frank about how happy we were with the gift and being sternly reprimanded for my indiscretion.

Nobody had told me not to talk.

6.
AWAKENING,
1919–1920

In 1916, Pancho Villa had raided Columbus, New Mexico, vanishing into the Mexican mountains when Pershing was sent to catch him. Dimly, I recall the talk about that, but history had hardly begun to touch me. I must have heard about the German U-boat sinking ships in sight of the American coast, but that has left no recollection.

In April, 1917, the United States declared war on the Imperial German Government. Influenza crippled the country in late 1918. In the Army camps, it killed half as many men as fell in battle. In November, the Armistice was signed. Airmail service had opened between New York and Washington. John and Ethel Barrymore were starring on the New York stage.

Nine years old when war was declared, I recall talk of high prices and a twenty-five-cent War Savings Stamp my father bought for me and the tough brown bread my mother baked out of no-wheat flour. Not much else. We were far from everything, our only link to the world outside that twisting road though the dunes, too sandy for cars and difficult even for wagons.

Now and then I went along in the farm wagon to Richland. A tiny place, gone and forgotten now, it was eight miles from the homestead, two hours and more by wagon. Wednesdays were "cream days," when farmers brought cream and eggs to market.

The cream, kept since the last cream day without refrigeration, had acquired an overpowering sour reek. The merchant candled the eggs to reject those too near hatching. We kids had gathered the eggs and helped milk the cows and turn the cream separator, but we never saw any of the money. Necessities were bought for us, but I longed for money of my own and grew up parsimonious.

The eggs and cream went for clothing and a few essential staples: overalls, shoes for winter, flour and sugar and coffee. My mother made undergarments out of flour sacks. We lived on what we grew: meal ground from our own corn; home-smoked pork—pig-killing time was a murderous ordeal. The victim was a friend we had known all his life. We had to watch him shot and bled and rolled into a barrel to be scalded, his hair scraped off, his spilled guts reeking.

Beef commonly came from a milk-pen calf, even more beloved. Its sacrificed flesh was hard to keep, but in winter a quarter could be chilled at night, hanging on the windmill tower, and wrapped by day to keep it cold. In summers we jerked meat, hanging salted slices on the barbed-wire fence to cure in the sun. Later we bought a sealer and learned to can meat in tin.

We drank a lot of milk; we churned butter; sometimes we made cheese—the Mormons in Mexico had taught my father how. In the springs, before garden vegetables came in, we gathered pigweed and even young Russian thistles for greens. Fall turnips could be saved through the winter. Fresh fruit was scarce; late spring freezes commonly killed the buds on the fruit trees my father put out. An orange was a rare Christmas treat.

Prices were high at Richland, and my father went to Portales for most buying. A few times he took me with him on the three-day expedition. Portales was the county seat, thirty-five miles from home, a long day's drive each way on the unimproved roads. We stayed two nights at the wagon yard, which had a camphouse for people, feed and water for the team. The camphouse had bedbugs; our own bedding had to be shaken out carefully and hung a long time in the sun before we took it back in the house.

Other things about those trips were more exciting. The electric light hanging in the camphouse—I took the bulb out and stuck my thumb in the socket to feel the wonderful current, not just once but several times. The great Fairbanks-Morse engines

in the town powerhouse, and the tall steel water tower, which I
once climbed to get a look from the top—high places always
drew me. Motion pictures, though I must have been fifteen
before I got to see one. The first was *The Golden Bed*; the wonder
of it haunted me for weeks. Doing dull farm chores, I began to
dream of writing for the screen.

I grew up in a social gulf, cut off by more than merely distance.
My parents had little in common with our neighbors, mostly
people of little education and narrowly fundamentalist religion,
when they professed any faith at all. The earlier comers, too, had
claimed better land and made more money. My mother felt our
poverty keenly, but I had known nothing else. We had few close
friends—I had none at all that I remember, and not much
chance to learn to make them.

My father did find fellow spirits among the merchants he met
in Portales, and sometimes he attended the Odd Fellows Lodge
at Richland. My mother seldom left the place. I think she felt
pretty bitterly that misfortune had exiled her from her own
social class; I know she envied the townsfolk when she read or
heard about their social activities.

Struggling all my life in that paralyzing web of isolation, I have
never broken entirely free. Yet, turning eleven years old in 1919,
I was at least stirring in the trap, awakening to worlds outside.
My mother used to read aloud with a good deal of oral skill.
Treasure Island. David Copperfield. A couple of novels by Jean
Stratton Porter. The stories in the *Saturday Evening Post.*

I recall the thrill of learning how to find my own vicarious
adventure in the pages of a book. Grandma Hunt used to give
me subscriptions to *Youth's Companion*, and later to *Boy's Life* and
American Boy, which had better stories—even now and then a bit
of early science fiction. I was awed by a monster that must have
been a surviving dinosaur in "The Thunder Beast," by J. Alan
Dunn.

Once I saw an exciting meteor. I don't know the date, but I
was the right age to feel its wonder. I was out in the cowpen just
at dusk, closing a barbed-wire gate, when I happened to look up
and see it sliding silently down out of the south across the dark
eastern sky. A large, jagged rock. Not knowing whether it was
yards or many miles away, I still can't guess how big it was.

Its velocity must have been relatively slow, because only the sharp projections were glowing from air friction, all the hollows dark. It broke up as I watched, jagged black cracks spreading through it. Bright sparks rained out of them. The fragments dimmed quickly, and soon the whole thing was gone. There was no sound. Though I wondered if pieces had struck the ground, I had no notion where to search. I heard nothing about it from anybody else, yet it was something I've never forgotten. An early hint of the reality and the strangeness of space.

We were too far from school for me to attend. Even when my father taught one year at a one-room school called Tartop, he didn't take me. He and my mother gave me lessons at home, but never in any very systematic way. I had magazines at hand, if not many books, and encouragement to read them, but I got a slow start in arithmetic.

Actual schooling began the year my father taught at Center, a two-room school four miles from where we lived. Jo and I rode to school behind him on that old roan mare. I started in the fourth grade except in arithmetic, where I was put in the third. Even there, when we were doing addition on the blackboard, I once felt driven to copy answers from the student next to me—and I still feel grateful to Miss Leona Forbes, my teacher, for reproving me so gently.

All she said was, "One person cheated." I tried once more, trusting that her eyes were on somebody else. When she said it again, I gave up the effort. That feeling of mathematical inadequacy is something I've never entirely outgrown; when I returned to college in the 1950s, I was surprised to find myself earning A's in analytical geometry and calculus.

I dreaded recesses, because I was hazed pretty roughly. I was the teacher's son, defenseless because I had never learned to cope with people. A gang of boys used to take me down, open my pants, and show their knives, threatening to castrate me. I never tattled. No physical harm was ever done me, but the mental scars took a long time healing, and even now I find a certain pleasure in reflecting that I've outlived most or maybe all of those early enemies.

Reluctant to awake in such a world, I still lived half in dreamland. We invented worlds, my sisters and my brother and I.

Worlds real enough to us, though not as literary or exotic as
those of the young Brontës. We had governments, currencies,
cities and nations mapped out on the ground, staging campaigns
to conquer or defend them.

There were other dreamworlds, too, all my own. Summers
and harvest times were filled with monotonous work, herding
cattle, riding a cultivator behind a team of mules, hoeing out
weeds, pulling broomcorn and heading maize, picking cotton.
From such mind-killing toil, I always retreated into imagination.
Into endless cycles of adventure in which a more fortunate self
was the hero; sometimes, as I grew older, into fantasies of sex.
At last, still later, into dreaming stories that I dreamed of selling.

I don't know when that began. We used to get circulars with
pictures of Mark Twain, advertising his books. Somebody said
he got a dollar a word. I remember asking if that included even
the easy words like *the*. Told that it did, I thought writing would
make a fine life.

7

SCHOOLBOY,

1921–1926

In the history of progress, Henry Ford stands out as an odd contradiction. Few men have done more to cause technological change; he revolutionized industry with his assembly lines for the Model T, the cheap universal car that reshaped American life. Yet he refused to improve that simple black machine until General Motors was leaving him behind, and he came to long wistfully for the world as it had been before he touched it.

Warren G. Harding was elected president in 1920. The Ku Klux Klan was being revived. The woman's suffrage amendment was adopted. National prohibition made bootlegging a major industry, creating the American criminal underworld. E. M. Hull published *The Sheik* in 1921, and Charlie Chaplin was featured in *The Kid.*

Thirteen years old in 1921, I went back to Center after two years at home for my second year of school. Consolidations had begun, and there were four or five teachers. Kids from other districts came in buses, but I rode five miles on a little blue-gray pony named Loki. I was in the seventh grade. The sixth graders sat on the other side of the room; one of them was an attractive, athletic girl named Blanche Slaten.

Girls had begun to interest me by then, but I had none of the social know-how it took to do anything about them, nor any athletic skills. At bat, I always shut my eyes and missed the ball. At recess, Blanche was always out with the boys playing basketball, our school sport. Unless the teacher ordered me out to the playground, I sat reading at my desk.

One dusty book I found in the school library, Bulwer-Lytton's *Coming Race*, lost me in an underground wonderland. Somebody loaned me a battered copy of *Tarzan of the Apes* that took me to an equally unlikely Africa.

That year went much better than the first. I don't recall being picked on. In the spring I took and passed the state eighth-grade examinations, which let me into high school. The teacher I recall most fondly there was named Nieves. Among other courses, he taught manual training. In the shop through the fall term, I learned a good deal about working wood. We spent most of the spring term digging twelve-foot toilet pits for new four-holers, one for boys and one for girls. Maybe not very educational, but we got paid for it. Money I could keep.

Perhaps the best thing he did was to give me an old two-volume encyclopedia, a treasure house where I found more science than ever came up in the general science class. Another fine thing was loaning me his set of Mark Twain, volume by volume. The one I loved best was *A Connecticut Yankee in King Arthur's Court*. Most of the satire went over my head, but the romantic derring-do he meant to ridicule enthralled me as much as the dazzling notion of travel through time.

One year the schoolhouse was moved from Center to Richland, several miles farther from us. The local schools had been community centers and symbols of community pride, and our nearest neighbors fought the move bitterly, some of them I suppose from the sheer joy of feuding. It left the community divided into hostile factions, with all my few friends and the girls I admired in the enemy camp, Blanche among them.

I remember petitions and expensive lawsuits and claims of perjured testimony. My father got himself elected to the school board, hoping to make peace. Such efforts failed, and warfare went on until the school was burned the year after I finished. I heard years later that the arsonist got twenty-five dollars for touching it off.

In spite of all that, I was learning—doing better with books than with people. I took Latin when my father found a teacher for it. Blanche was in the class, though we seldom speak it now. I went on to read part of Caesar's *Gallic Wars* at home the next summer.

I took Spanish and fell in love with the teacher, La Von Brown, a pretty girl hardly older than I was. I doubt that she ever knew how infatuated I was; certainly I never told her. On the school stage one spring I played Mark Fields, a victim of the demon rum in a temperance drama, *Broken Promises*. Never having seen anybody drunk, I had to be instructed in how to stagger.

Unexpectedly, I learned to drive—at the wheel of a school bus filled with passengers. No license was then required, and one afternoon when the regular driver was going off with the basketball team I found myself assigned to take the bus home.

It was built on a Model T Ford truck, and I knew how it ran from watching the driver. With no instruction, I set out. We veered wildly back and forth across the road at first, but I soon got the hang of the steering wheel and managed to complete the run without disaster. The next year, when my father got a bus contract and put a covered body on the Model T he had bought, I became a regular driver.

We had moved off the claim by then, to a series of farms outside the sandhills where there was water for windmills and slightly better land, though the original owners had all given up and gone. We raised crops on the shares. Corn, grain sorghums, cotton, broomcorn, none very profitable. The weather was often disastrous; when it wasn't, prices unexpectedly fell. The year we didn't plant broomcorn, it sold for four hundred dollars a ton; the year we did, we got twenty-five.

Other projects were usually no more successful. When we tried raising turkeys, the coyotes got most of them. We grew watermelons, but they were hard to sell. I drove the Ford truck to haul them to towns as far as a hundred miles away, offering them to merchants who rarely wanted them or trying to peddle them off the truck or house to house to people who seldom bought. I hated asking anyone to buy, hated being rebuffed, hated the whole enterprise.

Sometimes, though, the trips were educational. In Roswell once, I found a circus in town. When I asked to work my way in, the management did give me a job. It soon turned out that I'd been hired as a shill for what was called a game of chance—not that I knew the word then. I must have looked the hayseed I was.

The game looked simple. The players drew penny matchboxes out of a revolving drum, and the operator opened them to show numbers stenciled on the bottoms of the boxes. I soon discovered that all the winning numbers were in the teens, the losing numbers in the forties.

Actually, all the boxes were losers, but the operator could make any look like a winner by sliding the box only partway out of the cover. The winners were tossed quickly back into the basket. To convince the victims that they had honestly lost, the operator opened the losing boxes all the way and sometimes passed them around to be inspected. He was jittery and sweating, no doubt in terror of exposure.

I stood beside him at the table, "winning" money to be held for just an instant, until he grasped for it under the table. On the melon truck next day, when some of the losers spoke of my remarkable luck, I felt heartily ashamed. But, for a farm kid as naive as I must have looked, that was a memorable lesson in the way people were and what not to believe.

Out of high school by then, I was still living at home and working on the farm, without much prospect for anything better. I thought I wanted to be a scientist, though I knew nearly nothing of what scientists actually did. I was learning what science I could from magazines and that old encyclopedia.

I used to improvise experiments, often from materials so hopelessly wrong they had to fail. I made batteries and motors that didn't work. A water-drop microscope that did. A model airplane with a whittled prop and pasted newspaper wings and a rubber-band motor, which made one thrilling flight before it crashed. An adding machine carved out of pine sticks. A little steam engine—the boiler was a lye can, which soon exploded. Luckily injuring nobody.

Later, when radio came in, I found money to buy parts for a simple crystal set and then for a one-tube regenerative receiver that really worked—I think such sets are illegal today because of the squeals they broadcast while you're tuning them, but mine was magical then, picking up stations far away. I listened to the New Year coming in—it must have been 1927—as it got to station after station all across the continent.

One winter when money was even scarcer than common, Jim

and I went with our father to work on farms down in the Pecos Valley below Roswell. We spent three months there, out of school, living in a tent, picking cotton when we could find a job. We cooked on a gasoline camp stove. I remember a near disaster when somebody set a can of gasoline on the stove, thinking it was water. We got it off before it exploded.

A bucket of sugared honey erupted while we were heating it to liquify it; boiling honey sprayed the tent, but once more we weren't hurt. I wasn't nimble-fingered enough to pick much cotton, but I was hired for a time to weigh what others picked and I made a little money freighting with the truck—money for the family, never for myself. Though hard times, we did stay alive, and my mind kept growing.

Blanche had slipped out of my world. In 1925, only sixteen and still in high school, she married a local baseball pitcher named Elmer Harp. Part Cherokee, the Harps had come from Oklahoma. Elmer was a happy-go-lucky individual who never made much money or even wanted to. Blanche says he had a good curveball, good enough to be paid five or ten dollars for pitching a game. They lived with Blanche's family the first year. She spent the next year finishing high school in Portales, a star on the girl's basketball team.

It might seem romantic now to say Blanche and I had been childhood sweethearts, but that wouldn't be entirely true. There were other girls I admired, though always at a distance. I don't recall that she and I even talked very much. Though we liked each other, I knew very little to say to any girl.

I'd have been seventeen the year she married. Just out of our country high school, with no visible future. Efforts were made to find something for me to do. When Uncle John was elected country school superintendent, he and my father tried to get me a job as courthouse janitor. I don't remember being really sorry when somebody else was hired. Still living in dreamland, by now I was dreaming of dreams for sale. My mother had always wanted to write, and she got several small things into print. Perhaps I caught the virus from her.

She had bought a mail-order course in writing short stories and film plays from something called the Palmer School of Authorship. I studied the little booklets, which were not altogether useless; I still recall some of the classic dicta quoted from Edgar Allan Poe.

I asked the editors of *Triple X Western* for a free sample copy and worked for weeks on a story I meant to submit, scrawling it with a stub pencil on scraps of paper bags and old wallpaper. Though I had seen very few actual films, I sent things I thought were scripts to a Hollywood producer. Though he did dignify them with a courteous return, a less likely candidate for author-ship would have been hard to find.

Something else happened, however, in the spring of 1926, the first year I was out of high school. Something that changed my life. Hugo Gernsback launched a new pulp magazine, filled with reprinted stories by Jules Verne and H. G. Wells and A. Merritt and Edgar Rice Burroughs, stories he called "scientifiction."

The magazine was *Amazing Stories*.

8.

AMAZING STORY,

1926–1928

In the world outside, the world I didn't know, history had been moving, technology advancing, lifestyles changing. In 1922 the "nightclub" was invented. Henry Ford announced that he would fire any man caught with "the odor of beer, wine, or liquor on his breath."

Daily radio news broadcasts began. King Tut's tomb was unsealed. Alexis Carrel discovered that leukocytes, white blood corpuscles, fight infection. The marathon dance was the new fad of 1923. Ford built his ten-millionth automobile in 1924.

The craze of 1925 was the crossword puzzle. A Tennessee jury found John Thomas Scopes guilty of teaching evolution. Edwin Hubble published proof that many of the hazy astronomical objects called "nebulas" were in fact galaxies outside our own.

I sometimes saw such items in the county weekly or in a farm paper my father took or in copies of the old *Literary Digest* that Uncle Frank passed on to us. They were never quite so real as the events of my own imagination, yet the universe around me had begun to take a clearer shape.

I was reading with a widened appetite. Books were scarce, though I found a precious hoard in a heavy wooden box Uncle John had brought from Texas, unopened for years. Besides outdated textbooks, there was a handsome set of Shakespeare and the second volume of Victor Hugo's *Les Misérables*. I've never read the first volume, but the tragedy of Jean Valjean

47

at the conclusion left me as sad as any actual event I recall.

There was a physics book that fascinated me, though it closed with only a few tantalizing pages about atoms and radioactivity. Science was becoming more and more alluring to me, but I had no visible road toward any sort of scientific education. Launching *Amazing*, Hugo Gernsback opened dimensions of science that I had never even dreamed of.

In my imagination, science had always been magic made real, the promise of unlimited wisdom and power that even I might hope to learn and use—distinctions between wisdom and knowledge had not begun to trouble me then. And "scientifiction," far from being the trash most people took it for, was present science transformed into future prophecy. That was Gernsback's message. He used it to push his magazines, but I think he really believed it. To such kids as I was, it was dazing revelation.

The masthead of the old *Amazing* shows the tomb of Jules Verne at Amiens, the immortal writer rising beneath the lifted stone. The myth it embodied captured me. To show its hold, here's a quote from the first thing I wrote for Gernsback, a guest editorial published in the fall issue of *Amazing Stories Quarterly* for 1928. Looked at now, it seems to claim a bit too much, but it's what I felt then.

"Science goes on, with scientifiction as the searchlight. Here is the picture, if we can but see it. A universe ruled by the human mind. A new Golden Age of fair cities, of new laws and new machines, of human capabilities undreamed of, of a civilization that has conquered matter and Nature, distance and time, disease and death.

"A glorious picture of an empire that lies away past a million flaming suns until it reaches the black infinity of unknown space, and extends beyond. . . . The idea of the final product of evolution is beyond us. But a sublime picture it is that scientifiction may build through the ages, and that science may realize for the ultimate advancement of man."

That wasn't just my own credo. Nor only Hugo's. To nearly everybody except a few disillusioned intellectuals I had never even heard about, science was still a great good thing. Year by year, it revealed exciting new secrets, opened new doors into more enchanting futures. Year by model year, technology was improving everything. Cars ran faster, aircraft flew higher, new inventions bloomed. Progress could keep on climbing forever. To me, to a lot of such wonder-struck kids as I was, that was almost a religious vision.

Nobody now can feel the thrill of finding science fiction the way we did then, because then it was new, its wonder not yet ·:·orn thin with repetition or tarnished with mistrust in the whole human enterprise. My own trust in science and progress didn't seem so wildly overstated then.

Gernsback had grown up in Luxembourg. He came to America the year he was twenty, with two hundred dollars and a new battery of his own invention. His battery project failed, but he went into business importing technical equipment. By 1908, the year I was born, his mail-order catalog had become a radio magazine, *Modern Electrics*, later retitled *Electrical Experimenter* and then *Science and Invention*. He had been testing his own gadgeteering future fiction there for several years before he launched *Amazing Stories* with the issue for May, 1926. His associate editor was Edison's aging son-in-law, T. O'Conor Sloane.

As founder of *Amazing*, Hugo has become a hallowed figure in science fiction fandom. Our prestigious annual awards, the Hugos, are named in his honor. I knew him too well for such idolatry, yet I do owe him a certain gratitude for putting me into print, and a certain respect for what he did for science fiction. He knew it well, genuinely liked it. He invented the name we call it by. He used it to preach the gospel of universal progress, cannily enough yet more or less sincerely. I can't help feeling that the world was gravely wounded when so much of it lost the shining dream we shared with him.

I first heard about *Amazing* from a friend of mine, Edlie Walker, a radio ham confined to a wheelchair. The magazine was only a few months old when he loaned me the issue with the opening installment of "The Second Deluge," by Garrett P. Serviss. That was an epic of cosmic disaster that Hollywood might have welcomed later. I was excited over it, but not yet completely captured.

That winter I saw sample copies advertised in a little farm journal, the *Pathfinder*. The free copy I got was the one for March, 1927. It hit me harder. Everything in it seemed blazingly new. Though most of the stories were reprints, I had never seen them before or even guessed that such breathtaking marvels existed.

I had read and reread the short stories of Edgar Allan Poe, and that old Bulwer-Lytton romance, but I had never even heard of Wells' great early work. *Argosy* and a few other all-fiction pulps had been running Burroughs and Merritt and other fabulous stuff, but such pulp fiction had been outside my narrow world—my father felt that it was "unhealthy for the mind." I remember the stir of eager curiosity once when I saw a copy of *Weird Tales* on a newsstand. It was already running wonderful stuff, but I had no money for a copy and no actual inkling of what it might contain.

Frank R. Paul had done the cover picture on that free issue of *Amazing* to illustrate a reprint of "The Green Splotches," a novelette by T. S. Stribling. Perhaps forgotten since, but mind-widening to me then. The cover showed the hyper-civilized green-blooded plant people of Jupiter taking off from that strange Andean valley in a spectacular spacecraft driven by the pressure of light. Paul's people are wooden dummies when I look back at them today, but people didn't matter to me then. He had a great gift for starships and monsters and future cities and not-yet-invented machines.

Stribling's story wasn't all. Maybe not even the best. The magazine was crammed with heart-stopping wonder. Wells' "Under the Knife" was a convincing tour of the whole stellar universe. Burroughs carried me into fantastic adventure with the second part of "The Land That Time Forgot."

Perhaps the greatest impact came from Merritt's "The People of the Pit." With its exotic style and Arctic settings and dimly glimpsed Aliens, it cast a spell I've never forgotten. The following year, it gave me a pattern for the first story I sold.

My sister Jo helped me raise two dollars for a subscription. It began with the May issue. The Paul cover, lurid and crude as it may look now, was sheer magic then. Illustrating the second installment of Merritt's first novel, *The Moon Pool*, it carried me into a fantastic world of strange beings and terrifying powers and desperate adventures under the Pacific. My own enchantment was complete.

Merritt was a newspaperman who in time became the highly paid editor of the Hearst Sunday supplement, *The American Weekly*. His fiction was only an avocation, and critics ignore it now. I've been afraid in these recent years to look back at it because I don't want to spoil the wonder I recall, but it captured me totally then, any literary faults invisible. Merritt was my first model.

I borrowed a typewriter from Uncle John and spent my spare time for the next year writing things to try on Gernsback. The machine was an ancient basket-model Remington in which the keys struck the bottom of the platen so that you had to lift the carriage to see what you had written; the purple ribbon, never changed, had gone a little pale.

Out of a good many starts, only a handful of stories were finished. I mailed them in and dreamed of wealth and literary fame until they came back with printed rejection slips. Not surprisingly. I misspelled *vacuum* even in the title of "Via the Vacuum Tubeway"—though the story idea has a certain appeal, even today.

Updating Verne's *Around the World in Eighty Days*, I had my hero winning his race around the earth on a railway running inside an evacuated tube, in only eighty minutes. Done with a bit more skill, the yarn might have sold. I still had too much to learn. I was trying too hard to be funny—in his haste to be first, my hero loses his pants. I soon decided that my stories ought to be told with the straightest possible face, no humor visible.

My beginning in *Amazing* was modest indeed: a letter printed in the back of the book. A stilted, self-conscious missive, not much different from a good many others. It praised the magazine and begged for colored illustrations. Those letter columns must have been the beginning of science fiction fandom. They carried names and addresses, and we wrote to one another.

Dr. Miles J. Breuer was another beginning writer I met through those letters. Jerry Siegel gave me Ed Hamilton's address and sent me a story of his own for comment. His characters were all geometric solids, not terribly exciting, but I think their world was an earlier vision of Krypton, from which Superman came.

My first actual checks from Gernsback were only a dollar each, for two gags I invented for *French Humor*, another of his magazines—an inveterate innovator, he was always testing some new publication. The most successful must have been *Sexology*, which was on newsstands for many years.

Actual pay for authorship!

Cheered, I kept on trying. Gernsback had offered fifty-dollar prizes for guest editorials. In the summer of 1918, I wrote, or maybe overwrote, the rave about scientifiction I've quoted above, and then a new short story, "The Metal Man."

Working about the farm, I composed them in my head, keeping paragraphs in mind until I could put them on paper, a habit that left me sometimes pretty inattentive to what I should have been doing. (I still work the same way, even on this book, and I'm afraid I'm still too often inattentive.) Hopefully, I mailed the story and the editorial to *Amazing*. Months passed, with no response.

That summer my father got an unexpected windfall from the sandhill homestead, a thousand dollars for royalty rights to any minerals underneath it. (Though the seismograph crews still come, no actual oil has ever been discovered.) Generously, he used part of the money to send me and my sister Jo away to school at Canyon, Texas.

I kept haunting newsstands there, in spite of all the odds, until one big day when I found my editorial in print in the fall number of *Amazing Stories Quarterly*. A week or two later, on an even bigger day, I recognized my metal man being carried aloft by the crystal creature in Frank Paul's cover illustration for the December *Amazing*.

Incredibly, the blurb compared me to Merritt. "Not since we published 'The Moon Pool' has such a story been published by us. 'The Metal Man' contains an abundant matter of mystery, adventure, and for a short story, a surprising amount of true science. Unless we are very much mistaken, this story will be hailed with delight by every scientifiction fan. We hope Mr. Williamson can be induced to write a number of stories in a similar vein."

Could I!

9.

APPRENTICE IN PROPHECY,

1928–1930

Progress was happening. In science, anyhow. Sir Alexander Fleming discovered penicillin in 1928, and Vladimir Zworykin patented the television tube. The automobile was transforming American lifestyles in everything from work to sex. People with wheels could live where and how they pleased.

Suburbs and vacation spots boomed, most feverishly in Florida. Land speculators made paper fortunes there, saw them swiftly doubled and redoubled. Till 1926, when the Florida bubble burst. Paper millionaires went abruptly bankrupt. Driving through the state a few years later, Ed Hamilton and I saw dead subdivisions still buried under palmetto jungle.

In a nation beginning to need heroes, Charles A. Lindbergh became an instant celebrity when he flew nonstop from New York to Paris. I don't recall being much concerned with any of that. All I really cared about was writing scientifiction.

We drove to Canyon in the old farm truck over roads not yet paved. West Texas State was still small then, not yet a university. The president, Joe Hill, was a boyhood friend of my father's, and he made us warmly welcome. We rented a little two-room house, and Jo entered high school.

Since the Richland high school was never accredited, I had to take tests for admission to college. When I was safely in, my father took me on to Amarillo to buy a second hand Remington portable typewriter that I used for many years.

Setting out as a chemistry major, I spent two good years at Canyon, enjoying nearly everything. The English courses showed me a wider range of literature. I joined the literary society and the press club, took history and math and science. The physics classes were dryly formal and remote from most of what I wanted to know. We studied motion and light and heat and magnetism and electricity, but Mr. Carter didn't seem to know or care that atoms came apart.

The chemistry man, Dr. Pierle, had more excitement to share. The child of missionaries, he had lived in China. Science to him was part of life; his computation of the tiny commercial value of the chemicals in the human body had been widely reprinted.

I found him inspiring, and we got on well. At the end of the second year, he offered to make me a student lab assistant. Though the appointment paid only a hundred dollars a year, it could have been a decisive step toward a career in science.

If I had taken it—

The year can't have been so rewarding for Jo. Without much money or clothing or social experience, she must have felt lonely and neglected, but I don't recall any awareness of that. Absorbed in my own unequal battle to succeed in science fiction, I can't have been a very understanding companion for her.

My own social life was no richer. I fell in love with Anna Throckmorton, the editor of the school paper, but all I ever did about it was to salvage a picture of her from the dead copy that came back after the annual was printed. Without a car, without money, without much knowledge of the social rules, I remained a solitary oddball with little to do but write. Now and then Jo and I went to a movie. We went to church until I was asked to teach a Sunday school class.

Alarmed at that, I stopped attending and stuck to science fiction, pounding it out at a rate that amazes me now, trying to ape the great pulp writers I'd read in *Argosy*. Max Brand (Frederick Faust) was the one I envied most. He was said to turn out four thousand words every day and sell every word, unrevised, under a whole score of pen names. A record I never came near.

Thinking up stories, I used to take long walks up the railroad track. Trains were still wonderful. I loved the sad music of a far whistle, loved standing close to the track when the trains went by, fascinated by the speed and pounding power of the locomotive, the Doppler drop in the scream of the whistle, even the hot wet breath of coal-smoke and steam.

Wildly optimistic, I'd calculated that if Gernsback paid ten cents a word for the editorial, my story at the same rate ought to bring five hundred dollars. I wrote timid inquiries. At last, sometime in January, I got two checks, fifty for the editorial, only twenty-five for "The Metal Man."

A dash of cold water, but not cold enough to stop me. By that time I had another story done, finished during the Christmas break. It was a novelette, 25,000 words, that I called "The Silver Sea"—I thought titles ought to be alliterative. I mailed it to Gernsback.

His response was a letter saying he was leaving *Amazing*. His publishing and radio enterprises had gone bankrupt, but he was planning a new magazine, *Science Wonder Stories*, which would feature "science fiction" instead of "scientifiction." He was accepting the story for that, and he would pay on publication at "regular space rates." Too naive to ask what those rates would be, I agreed.

He ran the novelette, retitled "The Alien Intelligence," as a two-part serial in the new magazine. I was delighted that he called it "certainly THE story since 'The Moon Pool,'" but when I got his check it was for only seventy-five dollars—not much over a quarter-cent a word.

Looking back at Gernsback, I've always felt more resentment than admiration. He was never a helpful or creative editor, nor even very ethical. He shouldn't have carried off those manuscripts submitted to *Amazing*. He and his brother Sidney are said to have each been drawing a thousand dollars a week when they paid H. P. Lovecraft only twenty-five dollars for his classic novelette "The Color out of Space."

Even Edgar Rice Burroughs got pretty shabby treatment, as Irwin Porges writes. Promised $1,250, which would have been about two cents a word, for *The Master Mind of Mars*, the novel featured in the first *Amazing Stories Annual*, he had to wait for his pay like the rest of us; after "heated correspondence" he had to settle for trade acceptances instead of cash.

Maybe, however, I ought to be grateful even for Gernsback's faults. Paying too little to interest established professionals, he gave such beginners as I was the heady delight of actual print while we were learning the game. Rarely tinkering with anything, he left me free to reach his readers and learn what I could from my own mistakes.

Merritt was still my literary idol. I felt overwhelmed when I got a fan letter from him saying he had liked my first stories. When Ed Hamilton heard about that, he offered the invidious but maybe plausible suggestion that Merritt was afraid I would plagiarize him, but there was never any such hint from Merritt himself. Somehow I found nerve enough to suggest that we collaborate on the sequel to his own novelette "The Face in the Abyss," a story his own readers had been begging for.

He answered that he had just finished the sequel himself, but he soon agreed, unbelievably, to work with me on a new novel based on the notion that intelligence might evolve in the mineral structures of a desert mountain—a good many of my early stories began with life imagined in some new guise. He wrote that my idea for "The Purple Mountain" was "a corking good one," adding a flattering comment on a new serial of my own, "The Green Girl," that just begun in *Amazing*.

He said it was very well done, and showed "a marked advance in my style." He asked for a carbon copy so that he wouldn't have to wait for the next issue of the magazine. If *Argosy* published "The Purple Mountain" as a five-part serial, he wrote, it "would probably be worth about $2,500 to $3,000." He suggested that I write a quarter of the story, with an outline of the rest, and send the material to him for revision, "of course only after consultation."

Inspired by dreams of such a fabulous check almost as much as by the magic of all the Merritt I had read, I spent the Thanksgiving weekend of 1930 writing a 20,000-word beginning. I sent it to him, keeping no carbon, and I don't recall ever hearing any more about it. The manuscript is no doubt lost by now, a fact I can't regret. It was written too fast. I had never been to the Gobi. Trusting too much to the magic I expected Merritt to add, I had too little to say about anything at all.

Yet I kept other projects going. In October of 1928, even before "The Metal Man" got into print, I had finished my first collaboration with Miles J. Breuer, a 6,000-word story we called

"The Egg from the Lost Planet." Gernsback received it on the eve of his bankruptcy and took it with him to his network of new corporations. He published it as "The Girl from Mars" in a little booklet he gave as a premium for new subscriptions and paid us a whole penny a word for it, $30 each.

My first book in print!

Gernsback's money problems had followed him. After only a year, *Science Wonder* and *Air Wonder* were combined as *Wonder Stories*, and I soon had to beg for money due me. He wrote in January of 1933 that Stellar Publishing Corporation had been hurt when their distributors failed. "This naturally raised the deuce with our finances, and it will be a little while before we can catch up." He begged me to be patient.

I tried to be, but no checks came. In 1934, with $334 due for four more stories, I asked help from J. J. Wildberg, attorney for the American Fiction Guild. For a well-earned 20 percent, he got Gernsback to sign notes and pay off in monthly installments.

Small checks, slow checks, or no checks, I was doing what I wanted. I had moments of bitter envy for fellow students who had money and cars and affairs with women, and I kept cultivating unrealistic dreams that fiction might win such things for me, but my endless hours at the typewriter were still more escape than goal-directed.

I was a solitary misfit—as science fiction fans in those days often were. I kept in touch with the folks at home; I remember keeping a "log," a daily journal that I mailed home every week or so, but I had made no real friends of either sex anywhere.

All I really needed was money enough to let me go on writing. Some stories sold, some didn't. Often I didn't know why; I used to shed tears of baffled rage at the failures. I hadn't learned the skills, or learned that skills alone aren't enough. My funds of emotion and experience were simply too limited. The real wonder, I suppose, is that any stories sold.

Back to 1929 and the fiction that filled my life. With "The Alien Intelligence" mailed to Gernsback in January, I wrote a short, "The Flaming Fear," which *Weird Tales* rejected. I wrote another short with Breuer that nobody bought. In March I finished two stories. *Weird Tales* rejected "The Purple Crystal."

"Red Wings" was another novelette, 15,000 words. *Argosy* rejected it.

That long roll of failed stories looks dismally insignificant now, but each one sprang from urgent hope. Each was an effort at creation. Each took days or weeks or sometimes months of toil. Each was another battle in a hard war for survival, every rejection a stab to the heart.

You try to learn to take it gracefully. The editor means no malice. Not really. So you tell yourself. A worthless story doesn't mean you are worthless. Not necessarily. The thing to do is to see what went wrong and make a better effort. If you can. Yet no matter how you try to grin and shrug it off, a failure is a failure.

Gernsback did buy "Red Wings," or anyhow 10,000 words of it, to run in *Air Wonder Stories* as "The Second Shell." The next one went even better. "The Green Girl," at 40,000 words, was almost a novel. Still a college freshman and keeping up with my classwork, I began the story in April of 1929, the month I turned twenty-one, and mailed it to *Amazing* on May 26.

The new editors were in charge by then. They ran it as a two-part serial in 1930, with my name on a fine cover by Leo Morey that showed my people in their "omnimobile" diving through the ocean roof into my imagined new world beneath it. The story had science from my chemistry classes and nearly too much Merritt. Perhaps that's why he liked it. So did the readers —most of them were still as naive as I was. It was even reprinted decades later in paperback.

Uncle Stewart took me with him back to Mexico when he came to bring Grandma for the summer. We drove down through Columbus and Palomas into Chihuahua, and I spent most of the summer on his ranch there. The Santa Maria. A vast half-desert range, it ran for many miles along the east slope of the rugged Sierra.

It was scattered with mysterious mounds, all scarred with pits where vandals had dug for treasure. I picked up an unbroken pot on one of them. The foreman shrugged when I showed it to him. *"Corriente."* Worthless. Yet the mounds haunted me. Who had the builders been? What had taken them away? That must have been the kindling spark of my interest in archaeology.

The author, the year he turned twenty-one.
The original must have been lost. Gernsback used to run this picture with my
stories. (One of the ego-pleasing rewards of authorship!)

The foreman had an adobe house, but Stewart and I unrolled
our beds under a grass roof outside. I spent the summer riding
with the *vaqueros* and absorbing the actual Mexico. It had been
a fabulous land, existing in imagination more than any actual
recollections of those years on El Rancho La Loba. Here it was
legend grown real, most of it enthralling.

Not quite all. One incident is almost too painful to record, but
I suppose it should be set down here, if only to show how little
I knew about my fellowmen. Too trustfully, I had left forty
dollars in an unlocked suitcase. When it was gone, I jumped to
the stupid conclusion that it had been taken by another guest of
Stewart's, a refugee from Texas law. Therefore a criminal,
therefore the thief. With a rifle in my hand, I demanded my
money.

Stunned at first but soon talking fast, he was able to convince
me that he didn't have it. Luckily, nothing worse happened. Like

the circus incident, it was another useful lesson in the human world, and perhaps it left me a little readier to question my own first conclusions.

On the way home, I spent several days in El Paso. I found the public library and stared at the treasures in pawnshop windows and paid two dollars and a half for a little brass telescope. Tarnished and battered, it could have been a relic of Ahab's whaling ship, but the lenses were good enough to reveal Jupiter's moons and Saturn's rings.

I rode the streetcars across the river to Juárez and walked the odorous Mexican streets, fascinated by all that was outside my own small experience. The people and their culture and the mud walls that hid so much, the street vendors and the bars and the prostitutes. A wary explorer, I kept them at a very cautious distance.

On the El Paso side, I found the airport and airplanes on the ground. The pilots let me wind up the inertia starters on the craft that had them and pull props through to start those that didn't. They yelled "Contact!" when the ignition was on, as a warning that the prop could kick back. I paid three dollars for a short flight over the two cities.

At home again, I wasted August and September on another story that failed—and left me painfully baffled because I didn't know why. "The Moon Bird," a 20,000-word novelette, it was rejected by everybody. The fantastic elements were vividly real to me. What it lacked, as I see now, was human emotion—which can't be turned on at will or by formula. Feelings have to grow.

Back at Canyon, I was a sophomore that fall. Jo didn't return. A cousin, Ted Williamson, shared the little house with me until he went home to stay when his sister died that spring. Writing at the same desperate pace, I hadn't been close to him, or to anybody.

A couple of short stories failed, but in December I wrote two that finally appeared in *Amazing*. "In the Scarlet Star" was the first of a never-finished prehistoric series planned to dramatize the evolution of civilization. A fumbling, early *Quest for Fire.*

The other story, "The Cosmic Express" was shorter and nearly too comic, but Breuer approved its attempt at theme, and it is still sometimes reprinted. Taking Merritt for a model and following Poe's dictum that fiction existed to create strong emotional effects, I hadn't cared much what a story said about anything outside itself.

The classics I loved best had been first of all vehicles of escape, taking me away from realities I hadn't learned how to face, into strange new worlds that seemed at their best so totally real and complete that nothing outside them could matter much—at least to me, there and then. For Breuer, however, that wasn't enough.

Miles J. Breuer. He had fans then, and his name on magazine covers. With little time for writing, he made it a very serious hobby. The long decades since then have almost erased his reputation, but he was among the first and best of the amateurs whose work Gernsback began to print for next to nothing when his supply of classic reprints ran low. By today's standards, his work is scarcely outstanding. John Clute calls him "an intelligent though somewhat crude writer" who was "particularly strong on the articulation of fresh ideas."

A fair enough appraisal now, but his work impressed me then. He had written friendly answers to my letters. When I suggested later that we might do something together, he said his medical practice kept him too busy for a full-time collaboration, but he did agree to take me on as a sort of student apprentice. In our joint efforts, I did most of the actual writing, guided by his comments.

Our second collaboration was a novel, *The Birth of a New Republic*. The idea came from him. If history does repeat itself, the colonization of the moon and its war for independence could recapitulate early American history. A fruitful idea, as proven by all the later versions of it, the best of them Heinlein's *The Moon Is a Harsh Mistress*—for which Bob has given us credit.

Besides pounding out several other stories and working with Anna Throckmorton on the college paper and keeping up my grade-point, I wrote the novel in the months from October, 1929, to February, 1930. In Breuer's hands by mid-March, it was sold through his agent, Charles Roy Cox. Harry Bates rejected it for *Astounding*, because it "got off too slowly" and "read too much like history."

The new editors of *Amazing* reluctantly agreed to buy it at three-quarters of a cent a word instead of their usual half cent —a raise that meant very little to Breuer and me, because Cox kept an exorbitant 25 percent commission. It was published in the winter issue of *Amazing Stories Quarterly*.

Looking back now, I see that Bates was right. As a work of fiction, it's far from perfect. Yet we had good things in it, and doing it had been good for me. My own fictional failures had generally been pure fantasies, too wild for belief. Breuer drilled me in the values of character and theme and believability, people the reader can know and love or hate or both, plots that somehow reflect the reader's actual hopes and fears. Writing the novel was a useful exercise in how to relate imagination and reality.

That was our last work together, but Breuer was a cordial and generous host when I stopped in Lincoln once to visit him. He died in California in 1947. I owe him a considerable debt for sympathetic and intelligent help when I needed it, and I'm sorry to see him so completely forgotten. He was one of our pioneers, his vision nobler than anything he did.

From a minimal beginning, my writing income had been climbing nicely. Only $235 in 1929, $878 in 1930. Easily enough, in those pre-inflation days, to have kept me in college. Yet in spite of my fondness for Dr. Pierle and the temptation of the lab job he offered me, I knew by then that I meant to be a writer instead of a chemist. Reading the old *Argosy*, I'd discovered that the pulp masters I admired had done nearly everything except learn to write in college.

That spring I left Canyon.

10

WOODPULP AND WONDER,

1930–1931

The Graf Zeppelin circled the world in 1929, and the Empire State Building was equipped with a mooring mast for such aircraft. Admiral Byrd flew from Little America to the South Pole and safely back. Edwin P. Hubble was interpreting the red shift to show that far-off galaxies are running away from us, those farther fleeing faster, the whole universe mysteriously expanding.

Economic progress had risen to a peak. Time was hailing Walter P. Chrysler as Man of the Year. In honor of Edison, Henry Ford sponsored a "Golden Jubilee" to celebrate the fiftieth anniversary of the electric light. The stock market was booming—at least until that October and the infamous Black Tuesday.

Those were the times in which I was coming of age and testing my luck as a wood-pulp fictioneer. People still read for information and amusement in those days before TV, and magazines still mattered. We had pulps and slicks and the highbrow quality group. The slicks were printed on slick paper that could carry tempting ads.

I used to envy their writers, who got up to a dollar a word for bright stories about happy people winning the rich rewards of progress, but the slicks ran no science fiction. Neither did the quality books, which were slanted for readers who claimed culture and brains. Except for an occasional critical sneer, they ignored our little ghetto.

The pulps, printed on cheap gray wood-pulp paper, were for

smaller, special-interest readerships, generally people without much education or affluence. A few at the top, however—*Black Mask* and *Adventure* and *Blue Book* and *Short Stories*, along with *Argosy*—were ably edited and written by gifted professionals. Luckily for me, most of those neither knew the science Gernsback wanted nor cared to work for what he paid.

The pulps were schools in craftsmanship, where I studied hard. At Canyon, I had taken "Narrative Writing" and "Descriptive Writing" with a Mr. Osgood who was rumored to be a secret writer for the love pulps. Our assignments for his classes were to analyze and imitate selected passages from classic fiction, and I did most of mine to be worked into the novel I did with Breuer.

I subscribed to *Author and Journalist*, and to *Writer's Digest*, which was full of how-to-do-it inspiration and ads for vanity presses and reading-fee agents. I read library books on the short story and bought books to study on my own. Thomas Uzzell's *Narrative Technique* and the books of John Gallishaw were the best; I almost memorized them.

Though Merritt had been my first model, he soon gave way to others. To Wells, the real creator of the genre; to the great pulp writers of the time, Max Brand and H. Bedford-Jones; to Dashiell Hammett when I discovered him.

When I came to look at literary theory, it struck me that Max Brand had a lot in common with Homer: the same poetic rhythms and repeated epithets, the same vast backgrounds and giant-size characters and themes of history being made. Brand's rapid typing, unrevised, wasn't all that different from oral composition. I did my best to ape his epic devices. I loved adventure movies, too, and I used to visualize a novel as a film in which I had an unlimited budget for special effects.

The Depression had begun before I left Canyon. Having so little to lose, I wasn't hurt at first. Neither were most of the pulps, perhaps because unemployed people could still pay for cheap entertainment. When the pulps died, through the next two or three decades, it was chiefly technology that killed them —radio and TV, abetted by comic books and paperbacks and schools that failed to teach the joys of reading. Even in hard 1930, luck was running with me. I broke into *Astounding*, the first real science fiction pulp.

Harry Bates, in his introduction to Alva Rogers' *Requiem for Astounding,* tells how the magazine came to be. He was an editor for William Clayton, who published an assorted string of action pulps. In 1929, a few months before the Wall Street crash, Clayton called him into the office to plan a new magazine. Pulp covers weren't pulp paper. They were printed on costly coated stock in blazing color, a major expense of production. Clayton's chain included thirteen magazines, the covers all run through the press at once in a four-by-four block, which left three spots blank and wasted. Adding three more would cost little more than the ink, and he wanted proposals.

Bates says he had once bought a copy of *Amazing.* "Awful stuff," but he thought it would be easier to get stories for a "science-monster" magazine than for the historical adventure book Clayton had suggested. He considered titles and went back to Clayton to propose *Astounding Stories of Super-Science.* Clayton approved it at once.

The first issue was dated January, 1930. The cover caught the tone Bates wanted: it was a lurid water color by "Wesso"— H. W. Wessolowski—on which a more-than-man-sized beetle is battling the handsome hero, the frightened girl cowering behind him.

Luckily for me, Bates found most of his regular contributors "woefully ignorant of science and technology." Used to selling every word they could hammer out, they were alienated by rejections or even by requests for revisions, and Bates says he did a lot of rewriting himself. However cynical, he knew his calling, and I've always felt that he made a solid contribution to what science fiction became.

Most of the stories he published look pretty crude now, but they were stories. Concise, clearly written, about people solving problems. In *Amazing,* the action could always stop for a page or two while the scientist explained the magical machines. Though Bates wanted believable science, it had to be brief. The hero had to be sympathetic, pitted against ugly evil. The conflict had to keep moving, rising steadily from a quick beginning to an exciting climax and then a triumphant resolution brought about by the hero himself.

Though such rules aren't enough to make a story great, they

do reflect fundamentals the writer has to master before he can ignore them. They are ways to win and hold interest. If the reader isn't interested, early and firmly, all else is lost.

Bates rejected about as many of my offerings as he bought. His critical comments were always laconic; the only rewriting I recall was in incidental bits to make a better fit between the story and the cover—the Wesso cover for my "Salvage in Space" had actually been done for Doc Smith's "Triplanetary." Without much personal comment, I learned useful things from him and his magazine; I think the basic discipline we got from the pulps was good for many of us then.

Bates turned out several well-remembered stories of his own before he vanished from the field. He died in 1981, almost forgotten by the new generations of critics and historians, and I think destitute; I was touched when I learned that he had spoken in his last interview about wanting to get back in touch with me.

Home from Canyon in 1930, I spent part of June writing three stories to try on him: "The Meteor Girl," "The Lake of Light," and "The Crystal Castle." In our physics classes, Mr. Carter never got to the mysteries of relativity, but I had eagerly absorbed the article about it in the *Britannica*. "The Meteor Girl" came from that, based on the notion that space and time are interchangeably akin. I rather like the story even now, simplistic as it is.

All I recall about "The Lake of Light" is a battle with giant crabs—written before I had ever seen an actual crab. "The Crystal Castle" was more ambitious, an effort to recapture the magic of Merritt's *The Ship of Ishtar*. He had sent me an autographed copy of that, a set of the unbound sheets, which I still treasure. Trying to vary the pattern, I set my own adventure in a toy-sized magic castle instead of aboard a toy-sized magic ship.

I mailed all three manuscripts to Bates on June 20. By July 10 I had his check for $360—$160 for "Meteor Girl" and $200 for "The Lake of Light." Payment on acceptance, at two cents a word! A fabulous sum in those hard times, when a farm laborer might earn a dollar a day if he could find a job.

My joy was only a little clouded when Bates turned down "The Crystal Castle." I'd thought it the best of the three, but my little castle somehow failed to equal Merritt's wonderful ship. The story never sold anywhere.

In July I finished "The Prince of Space," a 28,000-word novelette. By August 15, Bates had rejected it with only brief comment: "Well stocked with longs. Did not make the grade." *Amazing* published it in the January issue, 1932.

Looking back at it now, I'm rather proud of the future science. There are space suits, solar-powered sunships, nuclear weapons. There's a City of Space that anticipates the plans of the L-5 people: a huge hollow cylinder built of meteoric iron, spinning to create the equivalent of gravity for people inside it. But the story does lack the tension and drama Bates required.

Later in the summer, with money to spend and hungry for everything, I took the bus to California. I saw some of Los Angeles on free bus tours offered by real estate agents. The trips always ended with a pork-and-beans lunch and a determined hard sell that I learned to soften by telling the salesman how little money I had.

I got up Mount Wilson to see the big telescope. Squandering twenty-four dollars on what was then high adventure, I flew from Los Angeles to San Francisco aboard a "gigantic, four-motored Fokker passenger plane," and tried to enter the university at Berkeley to study astronomy.

An academic adviser kept me out when I wouldn't take a Shakespeare class. That seems odd to me now, because only a few years later I was recruiting Sir John Falstaff for *The Legion of Space*; later still, I took a good many hours of Shakespeare for academic credit, all with a vast and growing appreciation. I own a facsimile of the First Folio. But to me, then, Shakespeare was irrelevant to writing science fiction. Hungry as I was for knowledge, I hadn't learned what to learn.

I did stay in Berkeley most of the fall, auditing an astronomy course and exploring San Francisco. For only a nickel, I could take the Oakland auto ferry for a magical voyage across the bay to the old Ferry Building, often meeting blue walls of fog rolling in through Golden Gate—there was no bridge then. With its history and its hills and the fish market and Seal Rocks and the cable cars and Chinatown, the city was an enchanting wonderland.

I even went to the opera, I regret to say without appreciation
—I'd heard no music of any sort when I was young, and I've
never learned to find much pleasure in it. Hoping to get past
that blind spot, I later studied the physics of music and once
bought a pawned violin and taught myself to scrape out one or
two simple melodies, but there must be magic in music that I've
never learned to hear.

Most of the trip was marvelous. When funds ran low, I paid
six dollars for steerage passage on a freighter back to Los Angeles. The sea was even more enthralling than I had always
imagined it, and the sensations of that overnight voyage are still
vivid to me. The white water curling from the bow and the
breathtaking glimpse of a flying fish. The smells of the ship and
the sea, and my surmises at the lives seamen must live, and all
the nautical unknowns of the seawall and the harbor at San
Pedro when we docked. Even the big red Pacific Electric train
was another adventure when I rode it back up to Los Angeles
to take the bus home to New Mexico.

Back there in late November, I spent two days writing "The
Island of Mars." It was 8,000 words—the standard length for the
acceptable short story has shrunk woefully since, to about half
that. I mailed it to Harry Bates on November 24. By January 22,
I had his check for $160.

He ran the story that summer, with a few words added to
support the storm clouds on Wesso's stunning cover and a more
pulpish title, "The Doom from Planet 4." I'm still rather proud
of the plot: Martians in radio contact with Earth send instruc-
tions about how to build wonderful machines. The machines, it
turns out, have been designed to conquer Earth for Mars.

From that I turned to a novel-length serial, *The Stone from the
Green Star,* which I dreamed of selling to *Argosy.* The inspiration
for it came mostly from E. E. Smith's *Skylark of Space,* which had
fascinated me when Gernsback ran it in *Amazing*—I remember
getting my mother to read it aloud to the family. Expressing
credit due, I named my hero Dick Smith, for Richard Seaton,
Doc's hero, and Doc himself.

At *Argosy,* Don Moore rejected it: "Plot not strong enough to
interest us." In January, I mailed it to *Amazing.* Responding with
her usual glacial deliberation, Miriam Bourne wrote in May that

"it stands an excellent chance." About August 1, she accepted it. In September, she paid $350 for it, to be published in October and November.

It was all first draft, except that I did redo the first few pages. Actually, I doubt that I could have improved it by more revision. It was dictated not so much by any conscious craft that I understood and controlled as it was by its own upwelling of unconscious emotion. Stuff too naive for today, but many of us were younger then and not so hard to please.

Sprinkled well with Merritt's exotic adjectives, the story was written mostly in short, rhythmic sentences, many of them fragments. The editors called it "lyrical prose." It used to bring its own spell back when I reread it, but it had nothing new to say. Its picture of the future looks pretty childish now. Asked now and then to revise it for reprint, I never found enough substance for that.

Yet the editors featured both installments in cover illustrations, and Fred Pohl told me once that he was moved enough by a stray copy of the opening installment to buy the next, the first time he had ever spent money of his own for a new magazine.

In January I got a story out of that flight to San Francisco by the expedient of crashing the plane into another universe. A good dramatic situation, but what I did with it was too hasty and simplistic. Harry Bates rejected it promptly. "Have two of yours already, but read it anyhow. It failed to make the grade." Gernsback published it in the May issue of *Wonder Stories,* with a cover picture of the airliner falling through the purple-glowing dimensional door into the crimson-lit parallel world. The payment, delayed until September, was $40.

I don't know what happened to February, but the file cards show two stories completed in March. "Twelve Hours to Live!" was another first-draft effort, written March 10. Searching hard for writing secrets, I had found Frank R. Stockton's famous story "The Lady or the Tiger?" I was trying to fit a story of my own to the same pattern.

A badly fumbled effort. Overlooking the psychological dilemma that concludes the original, I ended with my baffled hero awakened from a dream. Surprisingly, *Wonder Stories* took it, for

$25. Cutting my own trite finish, the editors ran a prize contest for a new conclusion.

The other story was "The Lord of Fate." Harry Bates wrote that he wanted to buy it, but "Clayton turned thumbs down"—though Clayton read very little of the other pulp stuff he published, he seems to have become a science fiction fan. *Wonder* rejected it too, as "weak and unconvincing." A few years later, expanded into a not-very-stunning novelette, it sold to *Weird Tales*.

Weird Tales, "the unique magazine"!

It really was unique. Along with the ghost stories and werewolf stories and vampire stories, it ran science fiction, tagged "weird-scientific." Though printed on pulp paper, it was a far call from any other pulp—even from *Strange Tales*, which Clayton brought out in imitation of it. Farnsworth Wright, the man who made and kept it unique, was another great editor.

Weird Tales, when I broke in, was one more new world, infused with its own alluring witchery, its writers a memorable clan.

11.

WORLD OF WEIRD,

1931–1932

In September of 1929, at the crest of the boom, optimistic investors owed their brokers eight billion dollars. October came, and Black Tuesday, when the long wave of faith in an always-brighter future broke against unsuspected economic rocks. The stock market crash erased thirty billion paper dollars in just a few weeks. A thousand banks failed in 1930. One man in four was out of work by 1932. Darkest in the early thirties, the Great Depression hung on until World War II.

Yet even in the face of social failure, science and technology kept on climbing. Clyde Tombaugh discovered Pluto in 1930. The Institute for Advanced Studies was founded at Princeton. Dry ice and frozen foods appeared that year, and photoelectric cells began opening doors by invisible magic.

I don't remember hearing much of Blanche through those first Depression years, but they must have been hard enough for her. Married on Christmas Eve of 1925, she had finished high school in 1927, while I was still on the farm. Her first child, Adele, was born in 1928. She and Elmer lived for a time in West Texas camps with a pipeline crew. They moved to Miami, Arizona, where he worked in a copper mine. Keigm was born there in 1930.

By 1931 they were back in Portales, clerking in a dry-goods store. Blanche kept her job there after they separated. Though I saw her now and then when I was in Portales, I don't remember knowing anything about her situation. Writing science fiction still mattered more than any actual human being, except perhaps those fascinating few who produced and edited and published it.

The Depression hardly touched me for another year or two, even though the file cards show long strings of dismal defeats in the fight to stay alive. "The Crimson Cross" was rejected by *Weird Tales* and *Ghost Stories*. "The Ozark Horror" had too much of H. P. Lovecraft. "Tarantula!" and "The Black Pearl" I've totally forgotten. Every rejection another cruel blow, yet I kept on trying.

Breuer's agent, Charles Roy Cox, couldn't sell "When the World Ran Wild" and "The River of Terror" even when I paid him to read them. Years later, with vast revision, they both got into print. The first one emerged as a novelette in a 1935 *Astounding* as "The Galactic Circle." The second became another novelette, which Bob Erisman retitled "The Mistress of Machine-Age Madness" when he ran it in *Marvel* after I had tried to add the sex interest he asked for. I made him by line it Nils O. Sonderlund—it looks more insipid than daring now, but I didn't want my name on it then. For most of us in those days science fiction had to be pure as snow.

At last my luck began to turn. Harry Bates was still paying a quick two cents a word at Clayton, and I spent most of April on "Wolves of Darkness," a first-draft novelette aimed at him. His check for $500 reached me on May 27, with a three-word note, "God is love."

Five hundred dollars!

A small fortune in my world then, with the dollar worth perhaps ten times what it is today. It ran in *Strange Tales*, with a cover I loved. A nearly nude girl is kneeling in the snow, her bare arms around two snarling, green-eyed wolves.

I was proud of the story then. Recently, looking at it again, I found it well-plotted, fast-moving, and pretty effective on its own basic level. What strikes me hardest now, however, is the contrast with Stephen King's powerful shocker "The Mist," which gets so much more from a very similar story idea. In 1931, I still had a lot to learn.

I had finished two more stories before that check came. "The Lady of Light" was another novelette, far less successful. In

"Wolves of Darkness," the light-fearing aliens invade the world I knew; I recall taking long walks at night while I was plotting it, tramping over the moonlit prairie with hard-crusted snow crunching underfoot and coyotes howling far away.

"The Lady of Light" had no such effective links to reality. Bates rejected it; *Argosy* found it "not our type"; Farnsworth Wright called it unconvincing. Sold finally to *Amazing* for $125, it did get a cover, one no more intriguing than the story.

"The Pygmy Planet" was 9,000 words. Harry Bates paid $192 for it and ran it in *Astounding* with a fine Wesso cover that showed the tiny planet hanging in the laboratory. The idea was new, at least to me—the basketball-sized artificial world whose swift-spinning days equal seconds of our time—but I did too little with it. All I knew enough to care about was the sale, the lovely cover, and the letters from readers happy with the story just as it was.

Rich again, with those two checks, I agreed to meet Edmond Hamilton in Minneapolis for a trip down the Mississippi. He was four years older than I and two years ahead into print, his first fiction sale made in 1926. Though we had been writing since I got his address from Jerry Siegel, we had never met. Mark Twain had filled us both with the history and romance of the river, but I don't think either of us had ever rowed a boat.

We had a good deal in common. First of all, our dedication to science fiction. We both had worshiped A. Merritt. Ed's first story, "The Monster-God of Mamurth," like my own "The Metal Man," had been modeled after Merritt's "The People of the Pit." *Weird Tales* had been Ed's first market. His stories there had been mostly science fiction; Wright called them "weird-scientific."

Ed had broken into *Amazing* in 1928, the same year I did, with "The Comet Doom," and his popular serial, "The World Wreckers," had run there in 1930. We were near enough the same age, both college dropouts living on what we could earn from science fiction, with neither plans nor clear desires to do anything else.

Ed had more confidence and polish than I, but I think we were equally ignorant and apprehensive of sex. We seldom talked about women, but he saw them as predators, marriage as a trap into some dull job that would threaten his chosen lifestyle—he hadn't yet met Leigh Brackett. His great love was books; he read and remembered everything, history and biography and travel, even obscure poetry, as well as fantastic fiction, discussing them all with a critical discrimination that his early fiction never suggests.

He was almost the perfect pulpster. The stories he wrote then were strongly plotted and action-packed, hammered out at white heat and never revised. Typing with two vigorous fingers and sharing all the tensions his heroes felt, he was jabbing the keys so hard when he came to a climax that o's cut holes in the paper.

His readers caught that excitement. He was already one of the most popular and prolific writers in the field, and I think his work deserves more attention than the new critics give it. His ideas were often original, sometimes epic. His stories of the Interstellar Patrol were the pioneer space operas, in print well ahead of Doc Smith and John Campbell and Olaf Stapledon.

Such pulp stuff wasn't literature, nor was it meant to be. In those days it wasn't reprinted. Pulp paper itself was nearly as ephemeral as a strolling minstrel's chant. Written for the audience and the moment, Ed's early stories were crudely melodramatic, careless of style and fact and character, nearly all fitted to the same save-the-world formula. Sad faults now, but editors and most readers wanted no more then.

Wright bought forty of his stories before there was ever a rejection or even a request for revision—though Ed kept enclosing return postage with each new submission. His pulp-honed craftsmanship served him well, even after most of the pulps themselves were fading into comic books. For a good many years, in spite of all his talk of quitting, Mort Weisinger and Julie Schwartz kept him busy grinding out fast-action formula-fitted scripts for *Superman* and *Batman*.

The man was far more complex and interesting than most of his output. Now and then, even in the early thirties, he turned from the pulp formula to more sensitive and more serious work —which was often harder to sell. I think he learned a great deal from Leigh Brackett after their marriage. His later fiction shows far more care with mood and style and character.

"He That Hath Wings" and "What's It Like out There?" are memorable stories, and such novels as *Star Kings* and his final "Starwolf" series are done with impressive craftsmanship. He has been called a hack; from the viewpoint of a literary critic, much of his always hurried work may justify that label, but few of his readers were critical. As John Clute says, he took space opera seriously enough to do it well.

For many years, in spite of occasional tensions, he was my nearest friend. "Thin, dark, and wiry"—in his own words—pounding "all day on the typewriter, setting down the feverish visions that filled his head—visions of wonders to come, of great dooms sweeping down on the hapless Earth." He balanced his romanticism with a sardonic sense of humor often directed at stupidities, sometimes my own. A great talker, best of all about the books he knew. I learned a lot by listening.

We met that summer in a Minneapolis hotel room. We had planned to buy a houseboat and drift down the river. An impractical dream. We soon gave it up, settling instead for a fourteen-foot skiff with an outboard motor and rather too much camping gear. Ed insisted that we wear golf knickers; I agreed, though they looked ridiculous to me and I think to the river folk. We soon gave them up.

Equipped with a navigation guide and a whistle for the locks, happily unaware of all we didn't know, we set out to follow the channel markers down to the sea. We steered too close to the first boat we met, gawking up at it till the bow wave bounced us high. We nearly went under the slanting bow of a barge. Aground in shallow water, we broke shear pins. Our first motor failed. But we learned a little of the river and kept on going.

On the scenic upper river, we camped on the banks. Farther down, with the levies grown higher than the land and nothing to see except the willow fringes, camping lost its charm. We shipped the gear home and put up at YMCAs in the river towns. The days on the water grew long; Ed used to fill them with summaries of the books he had read and talk of his life and the *Weird Tales* people he had met.

At Fort Madison, we looked up Ted Sloat, a fellow science fictioneer who tended bar at the Elks Club. He introduced us to his patrons, mostly retired railroad men, and took us to tour the

The author in our camp in the Mississippi bank in 1931.

state penitentiary. We spent several days at Hannibal, recalling
Mark Twain and rediscovering Huck Finn's cave. Out of Vicks-
burg, our second motor failed.

We were ten days there, absorbing the historic South and
waiting for repairs to come from New Orleans. We met a bootlegging riverman who kept his stock in trade in jugs hung on
bailing wire, sunk under the two-holer at the end of his
shantyboat. One day we rode a mail-and-trading boat up the
Yazoo, with a final stop at an illicit still in the river jungle.

The spare parts never came. We sold the boat and took passage on the *Tennessee Belle,* back upriver to Arkansas and then
down again to New Orleans. A rich treat for both of us. The
pilots were veterans of the river, full of its history. They let us
roam the boat and lounge with them in the texas, listening to
tales that might have come from Twain himself.

E. Hoffmann Price, a phenomenon!

Ed had met him at the *Weird Tales* office in Chicago, and we
looked him up in New Orleans. Born in 1898, Price was older
than we and already a seasoned pulpster, with "The Rajah's
Gift" sold to *Weird* in 1924. In those days he could work or drive
all day, with life enough left to drink and talk all night; even now,

well into his eighties, he still makes automobile safaris across the continent and writes fine fantasy novels.

Married, working for Union Carbide to support his wife and child, he impressed me in spite of his domestic ties as the first real live soldier of fortune I had known. A West Pointer, he had served in the Philippines and on the Mexican border and in France with the A.E.F.

Exuding romance, Price was a swordsman, an astrologer, a connoisseur of exotic food and drink, a collector of Oriental rugs, a student of Arabic, a friend of colorful Turks and Chinese. We stayed in town a week or longer, sleeping while he worked, exploring the city with him, regaled every night with his adventures and his liquor.

The Orient still possessed a mystique in those receding times, an aura of enchantment lost forever now, since too many tourists and newsfolk and service people have seen its gritty underside. Cultivated and exploited by generations of imaginative writers from John Mandeville down to M. P. Shiel and Sax Roh-

*Edmond Hamilton in our boat on
the Mississippi in 1931.*

mer, that necromancy made the East a fabulous realm of sinister wisdom and exotic adventure.

It was always a *Weird Tales* staple, even after Wright gave it a home of its own in *Oriental Tales*. Price was deep into it then. Never fully recovered, he has good friends now in San Francisco's Chinatown and autographs his books with a Chinese chop. I caught enough of it then to color such stories as *Golden Blood*.

Homeward bound from New Orleans, I saw the rest of the river from a freighter that finally steamed up across the Texas prairie through the ship channel to Houston. There I found Kirk Mashburn, another writer-friend of Price's, an unhappy individual haunted with the same romanticism but without Price's unquenchable vitality.

Trapped at some monotonous job in a railway office, Mashburn was drinking too much and writing well-polished vampire tales for *Weird*. We kept in touch for a time; in letters I saved, he is chiding me gently for the stylistic sloppiness of my first-draft fiction and lamenting his own failure to make *Strange Tales* —Harry Bates said he "wrote too well."

I don't remember when I got home to New Mexico, but by the end of October I had finished two more stories. Bates bought "Salvage in Space" for $160. "The Moon Era" was a first-draft novelette; I remember hammering out 27 pages of it in one day after the spell of the story had captured me. My record stint.

The story derived from S. Fowler Wright's great far-future fantasy *The World Below*, which I must have learned about from Ed Hamilton. *Astounding* was running into trouble by then, but *Wonder Stories* bought my story, to run in the February issue with a different last paragraph—in my own not-very-logical ending, the first-person narrator had died with his story not yet told to anybody.

In January I wrote "Red Slag of Mars," a novelette remotely suggested by an entry in a Gernsback contest, adding the theme of world peace achieved through a threat of alien invasion. "The Electron Flame" was an exercise in technique, an effort to translate Poe's "Purloined Letter" into science fiction. Gernsback printed it on slick paper, but his checks had quit coming.

Weird Tales was paying a full cent a word, rather more reliably.

Ted Sloat with Ed Hamilton and the author on the Mississippi bank at Fort Madison, Iowa, when we stopped there on our way down the river in 1931.

I had been reading it, or trying to, for several years, caught up sometimes in its exotic spell, sometimes bewildered by arcane supernatural rites I couldn't believe or understand, sometimes turned off by stuff that looked simply bad.

Though several stories had been rejected, meeting Ed and Price and Mashburn had brought me closer to Wright and his magazine. I tried again with "The Wand of Doom." It was a short novelette, the background drawn from our river trip. The hero builds a machine that turns mental images to solid matter. His dreams turn real. One of them is a nightmare of gigantic spiders. Wright took the story after a bit of revision, and his readers praised it.

Golden Blood was a more ambitious project, a serial I hoped to place with Argosy, which still paid several cents a word. I must have begun it soon after I got home from New Orleans, because my hero was a soldier of fortune named for Price and the story takes him to exotic Arabia.

Most of the world was stranger then, in those far days before antibiotics and easy air travel and instant photography. For all anybody really knew, some hidden remnant of a lost race might be surviving in the quarter-million square miles of the Rub'al-Khali.

I had never been there; my background had come from Lawrence's *Revolt in the Desert* and George Allan England's *Flying Legion,* with detail from a few travel books and the deserts I knew in America. I compiled a little dictionary of what I thought was Arabic, and observed my sister's cat as a model for the golden tiger.

Argosy serials were done in six installments, each ten thousand words long and building up to some breath taking cliff-hanger. I did my best to fit that pattern. I had begun to realize, too, that my quick first drafts weren't always good enough, and I remember rewriting most of the novel, working by a kerosene lamp through long winter nights in the living room after the rest of the family was in bed.

Argosy rejected it, though with a kind comment on "the nice color." Wright accepted it and ran it in 1933 with two lovely covers by J. Allan St. John, the able artist who used to illustrate Edgar Rice Burroughs. Wright's letter about the first painting was another breath of wonder.

"I've just seen the rough color-sketch . . . that colossal golden tiger looming gigantic against the sky . . . and in the foreground Price and Fouad sitting astride their white camels and looking quite Lilliputian by comparison. . . . What a gorgeous splash of color—the golden-yellow tiger, the vivid green of Vekyra's robe and the intense crimson of Malikar's garment. Allah!" He added that St. John had stayed up half the night to finish reading the story and persuaded him to order another cover for the second installment.

In Chicago with Ed Hamilton a year or two later, I called at the *Weird Tales* office—840 North Michigan Avenue, an address I'll never forget—and met Wright himself. A great editor, as remarkable as his magazine. His interests were wider than it ever suggested. A frustrated Shakespearean scholar, he once published a pulp-paper edition of *A Midsummer Night's Dream* with illustrations by Virgil Finlay and notes of his own. The first volume of *Wright's Shakespeare Library.* There was no second volume.

He was a tall man with an unexpectedly earthy wit. He was already poker-faced and trembling from the disease that finally killed him—a medical friend called it "post-encephalitic Parkinsonism" when I told him about it. I always admired the determination and the cheery courage with which he kept the magazine going in spite of that disabling handicap.

The high point of that visit was a dinner party given by Otis Adelbert Kline, another member of the *Weird Tales* clan, I suppose in honor of Ed and me. We met Bill Sprenger and others; Bill was the affable young chap who got the checks out from *Weird*. Kline was running a reading-fee literary agency and playing the sedulous ape to Edgar Rice Burroughs, selling most of his work to *Argosy*. His things in *Weird* were popular enough, though I always imagined they were *Argosy* rejects.

Another Orientalist, Kline knew Arabic enough to point out some of my misused expressions in *Golden Blood*. Revising it for reprint later, I deleted nearly all of that blundering Arabic, though it had never seemed to trouble other readers. Few of them, luckily, had been any farther east of Suez than I had. I don't remember what we ate that night, but Kline served us such exotic liqueurs as anisette, and what I recall most vividly is the fragrance of our piss when we went to the bathroom next morning at the YMCA.

12.

DEPRESSION,

1932–1933

In 1929, Robert Van de Graaff had built his first electrostatic generator, one more key to the unfolding secrets of the atom. By the early 1930s, he was famous for creating "artificial lighting." Radio astronomy began in 1932, when Karl Jansky picked up a mysterious "cosmic hiss" and discovered that it was coming from toward the center of the galaxy.

I had joined the American Astronomical Society when it was founded; David Lasser, managing editor of *Wonder Stories,* was our president. It became the American Rocket Society in 1932. Our membership doubled that year to more than a hundred, and our bulletin reports that Robert Goddard has patented a new device for braking fast-moving aircraft. Newspaper ridicule had forced him to move his rocket research from Massachusetts to New Mexico and taught him not to talk about spacecraft.

The Great Depression was overtaking me. *Strange Tales* lasted only seven issues. *Astounding* quit buying in the middle of 1932, and Bates wrote me in October that "the worst has happened." Clayton had discontinued the magazine. He was returning "The Plutonian Terror" and "Dead Star Station," which he really liked, "and which would, of course, eventually have been bought and used."

Clayton was soon bankrupt—his magazine chain was still making money, Alva Rogers says, but he had gone too far into debt when he bought out his partner. The last Clayton *Astounding* featured my "Salvage in Space." Though *Weird Tales* stayed alive, it was teetering on the brink. Wright and Sprenger had to delay payment for *Golden Blood*. Their Indianapolis bank had closed.

My income for 1931 had been $1,427, but it shrank in 1932 to only $305. The only check through the first half of the year was from Gernsback, fifty dollars on "The Moon Era"—a partial payment, and the last he made till I got a lawyer.

I could live at home on nothing at all, doing a few farm chores in return for my keep, but I was hungry for experience. With forty dollars left, I bought a small backpack and tried hitch-hiking. All the cars passed me by. Feeling illogically bitter at all the fat cats in cars that didn't stop, I learned to ride the freights.

I wasn't alone: by the end of the year a million jobless people were drifting around the country, most of them younger than I was. Though the seasoned hoboes told horror tales about such sadistic railroad bulls as Denver Bob, the trainmen were surprisingly friendly. One kind conductor opened freight cars for a hundred or so of us waiting by the tracks at Trinidad.

I spent a little time in the hobo jungles, learning the lingo, but never tried panhandling. My few dollars went a long way. I could get a hotel room for fifty cents, and I lived mostly on staples I could eat in the room: peanut butter, raisins, cheese, and day-old bread.

At Pueblo, I toured the nearly idle steel mill. One day I set out to hike up Pikes Peak, but turned back short of the summit when my nose began to bleed. The friendly matron who operated the half-dollar hotel there might have initiated me into sex if my inhibitions had let me understand what I later decided she had in mind.

I stopped again to explore the edge of the Rockies above Colorado Springs, and stayed two or three weeks in Denver, visiting the capitol and the mint, reading what science fiction I could find in the public library, and trying my luck with the army of desperate optimists rewashing the sands of Cherry Creek for very little gold.

The burlesque shows at the old Empire State Theatre were a

more rewarding discovery. I had seen very little nudity, and I was delighted with the strippers. When my forty dollars ran out, I caught the D&RGW down to Amarillo. One blustery night that nearly blinded me with cinders in the steamy coal smoke, I got back to New Mexico on a Santa Fe oil tank car, tied to the frame with a rope in case I couldn't stay awake.

Back at home, I tried to put one of those drifting kids into a short story, "We Ain't Beggars." It was rejected without comment by *Harper's* and *Atlantic*, but finally published for no pay in *New Mexico Quarterly*. The editor asked me at first to delete such rude phrases as "son of a bitch," but decided in the end to let them stand.

That story is one of very few attempts I've ever made to write realistic fiction. Most such efforts became so dull and grim that I abandoned them unfinished. Non-fan friends who look down on science fiction still sometimes ask what else I've written, but science fiction has nearly always been a comfortable vehicle for whatever I wanted to say.

Two more checks came in that fall, $125 from *Amazing* and $130 from *Weird*. In funds again, I rode the freights back to Albuquerque to attend the university. Bitterly discouraged, feeling I'd failed as a writer, I had nothing else in view. I remember sending *Writer's Digest* a little piece called "A Freelance Retires" —unconscious of any irony. Far from the inspirational stuff they wanted, it earned yet another rejection.

Searching for another possible career, I thought of psychiatry. Perhaps it could help me understand others and myself, perhaps even make me a more successful writer. I wrote my medical friends in science fiction, Breuer and David H. Keller, to ask for advice. Their replies convinced me that I could never find funds for psychiatric training, but I did change my chemistry major to psychology.

Though money was awkwardly short, I recall that as a fine year. Besides the psychology, I took other courses that I hoped might help me understand mankind and myself. Freshman biology. One semester of economics; I refused to take the second because I couldn't believe in the totally rational "economic man." A couple of courses in literature, the best of them a lecture series on "The Great Books" by a really great teacher, Dr. George St. Claire. Philosophy and aesthetics, taught by Dean Knode, both absorbing.

I plunged into philosophy looking for some sort of absolute truth; when I read Pareto's wittily devastating demolition of all systems except his own, it struck me that his must be equally vulnerable. I came to feel that philosophies are all simply works of art, responses to experience organized to express the emotions of their creators, really not much different from paintings or novels or music.

I worked on the college paper and the student magazine. Better than the courses, I made new friends, the closest of them men. Langdon Backus, a civilized and idealistic Easterner, devoted to an utterly impractical liberalism. We've kept in occasional touch. I saw him again a few years ago, remarkably unchanged; the owner of a Civil War bookstore in Harpers Ferry, preserving the old family home like a museum, he was still happily devoted to the relics and history and values of a lost American past.

Gordon Greaves was another, a freshmen from Portales. He came back to edit the hometown paper his family owned, and he remained one of my closest friends until his recent death. I used to feel that he should have gone on to bigger papers and a wider career, but his life here was useful and fulfilling.

At our table in the dining hall, I got to know a circle of anthropology students absorbed in their own dedicated study of mankind. I listened to the talk about their researches and sometimes joined them in expeditions to Indian ceremonials at the nearby pueblos. At first I was astonished at their worship of everything Indian, but I soon caught a little of their eager interest, and began for the first time to get some sense of what culture is and a new respect for cultures not my own.

Women were still as alien to me as the old Anasazi. I could look at them, even dream about them, but I hadn't learned their language. I met and admired a few in my classes, but never even asked for a date. After all, I lacked the money and the car that I thought were necessary.

One afternoon, trying to learn a little more, I went downtown to a whorehouse with a couple of venturesome companions. My first actual attempt at sex. There were two women: a heavy, cold-eyed white with whiskey breath and a younger, more attractive black. I chose the black. Though she did her amiable best, I was impotent.

I got home from college with six dollars in cash and forty due the university for my last month's board. Hungry enough to write again, I bought paper and typewriter ribbons and plunged into a serial aimed at *Argosy*.

The Legion of Space. The idea came from Dr. St. Claire's lecture on Henryk Sienkiewicz and his three epic novels of Polish history. For characters, he had borrowed Dumas' Three Musketeers and Shakespeare's Sir John Falstaff. It struck me that the same literary tricks ought to work in science fiction.

I had nearly memorized Dumas years before. Still skittish of Shakespeare, I skimmed through the Henry IV plays, reading little except the words of Falstaff—which were enough to give me the ways of talk and thought that brought Giles Habibula to life in my mind.

Working through long summer days, writing one 2,000-word chapter in the morning and the other in the afternoon, I finished the novel in three weeks. Grown a little more critical of my first drafts by then, I spent three more weeks on a second, and mailed it off to *Argosy*.

The delayed checks from *Weird Tales* had begun coming in. With money again, if not much of it, I set out with my brother Jim on another economy vacation. We had an old Model T touring car I had bought for a hundred dollars. Jim stripped that down, leaving little except the windshield and front seat and a box he built for our camping gear.

Our first night out was nearly the end of the trip. We had stopped outside a junkyard to tighten the brakebands on the fantastic device Ford called a planetary transmission. Jim dropped a nut inside. Hoping it would lie there, harmless, we cranked the engine. Not quite harmless, it demolished the magneto.

Rain that night caught us sleeping on the ground. Leaks in the tarp wet our bedroll. Jim recalls that I wanted to abandon the car and get on a freight train. Instead, he borrowed a hoist from the friendly junk dealer, bought used V-magnets for very little money, and rebuilt the transmission.

In the Sacramento Mountains, we stopped to visit friends who had moved from our home community, an Irish family hard-pinched by hard times. Most of what they had to eat came out of the garden. They were poaching for meat.

When Jim and I went out with the sons to look for a deer, the father told them to wave the game warden away if we met him, kill him if he tried to come close. They seemed very serious. Jim and I were secretly appalled; we could only hope the wardens understood the rules. I suppose they did. We got our deer and nobody had to be killed.

We joined the father and the sons on a wagon expedition to pick and can wild raspberries growing where the higher mountains had been logged off and burned. On the way up we stole new potatoes and green corn from fields we passed. When they were gone, we lived for several days on cornbread cooked without grease, eaten with gravy made of cornmeal and water.

And, of course, wild raspberries. They gave us diarrhea. Cold rain fell on us while we picked them, and came through the leaky roof of the abandoned house where we slept and canned them. We came out chilled and hungry.

Back at their home, we shared a little of the jerked beef we had brought in our own supplies and drove on again, down toward the White Sands. I remember the welcome warmth of the desert sun when we camped there and spread our soggy bedroll to dry.

We stopped outside of El Paso to attend a rodeo and crossed the river to see a bullfight in Juárez, a comic opera event where one desperate bull jumped out of the ring and ran around it, jumping all the picadors and matadors back inside and earning more *olés* than they did.

Our next stop was with our mother's rancher relatives near my Arizona birthplace. They received us warmly. Uncle Stewart happened in from the Tapila, the Mexican ranch where he had retreated to weather the Depression. He invited us there and sent one of his retainers to meet us at the border and guide us in. A colorful cowman, the *vaquero* not only rolled his own smokes but lit them with flint and steel.

He had brought horses. We left the car and bypassed the authorities to ride illegally south with him to the ranch. Here, high in wild mountain country, Stewart was nearly independent of everything outside. With the cattle markets dead, he had very little money, but his people raised their own corn and beans and wheat—of course their own beef—and ground meal in their own primitive mill.

That high ranch was a frontier kingdom where Stewart still dreamed of progress, no environmental assessments required. When he could buy cement, his men were packing it in on burros and building a masonry dam across a narrow canyon. Later, when the cattle market came back, he bought an airplane to carry fresh beef to the West Coast; overloaded for the altitude, it cracked up on the first takeoff. Never daunted by such setbacks, he always had some bright new dream.

We spent nearly six weeks there, living on beef and tortillas and beans. One of the *vaqueros* had a guitar, and at night they sang sad Mexican love songs. Jim hunted deer he didn't really want to kill. I rode with the foreman and dreamed up new science fiction.

Back in Arizona, we drove across the state toward the Grand Canyon, camping anywhere, building our tiny cookfires with dry, hot-burning sagebrush and spreading our bedroll under the stars. There were voracious mosquitoes that found us under the tarp, but what I remember best is the stars—there's no better way to discover them.

The canyon was a splendid lesson in geology. With no money for the mule-back trip, we hiked down Bright Angel Trail to the Colorado, walking back through all the ages of evolution and on down into the dark granite of the steep inner gorge, beyond the last trace of life beginning. We drank at the river and hiked back to the top that same day—we were younger then.

Next day we climbed down into Meteor Crater, another fascinating record of our planetary past. Jim says I saved his life there. He was leaning to look down into one of the shafts dug during the search for fragments of the impacting object, holding himself by a rope wound on a windlass, when the windlass suddenly spun. He says I grabbed his arm and pulled him safely back.

I had forgotten the incident—and many other things—but he has been a good brother; I'm happy that we got out of the crater and back home both alive.

13.
CENT-A-WORDER,

1933–1935

Wolfgang Pauli, in 1931, had found a basis in theory for a particle with neither mass nor charge; Enrico Fermi later named it the neutrino. In 1932, James Chadwick discovered the neutron. Two more long steps into unraveling the mystery of the atom.

In those grim times, however, few felt cheered by such triumphs of science. Most of the nation's banks had closed by March of 1933, when Franklin Delano Roosevelt took over the presidency from Hoover. Industrial production was just over half its pre-crash level, and thirteen million were unemployed.

Proclaiming that all we had to fear was "fear itself," FDR called Congress into special session, outlawed the exportation of gold, and launched the New Deal. The Century of Progress opened that summer in Chicago, Sally Rand stealing the show with her fan dance.

Blanche was living in Portales through those years, clerking in Sol Finney's department store for eleven and a half a week and caring for Keigm and Adele. I saw her now and then when I was in town to shop. She says I gave her one of my stories to read, but our worlds were still far apart.

My own outlook had begun to brighten. A handwritten note from Desmond Hall brought cheering news. Street and Smith, an older and stronger firm than Clayton's, was reviving *Astounding*. The new editor was F. Orlin Tremaine. He promised quick money for short stories, though at only one cent a word.

Before the end of 1933, he had taken the last two stories Harry Bates returned, as well as a new one, "The Flame from Mars," grown out of our hike into Meteor Crater. Wright and Sprenger were making payments when they could for *Golden Blood* and "The Plutonian Terror" and "Invaders of the Ice World." I had money to move again.

Though records are lacking and the dates uncertain, after another stint of work I was off again, by bus to Chicago. Ed Hamilton joined me there; we stayed at the Y. Price was back from New Orleans, and we met more of the *Weird Tales* brotherhood. They were an engaging group, admirers of Wright and

The Hamilton family, April 13, 1939
Standing, left to right: Ed; his father, Scott; Bill Alderdice, Betty's husband;
Porter Sherwood, Adeline's husband.
Seated, left to right: Betty; Ed's sister Adeline; his mother, and Ester.
The little girl, standing, is Adeline's daughter.

happy with one another, playing games they enjoyed with their occult and Oriental lore. Never close to many of them, I was proud to be admitted as at least a 'prentice member.

After a few days in Chicago, I went on to visit Ed in Pennsylvania. New Castle was a Depression-stricken industrial city largely populated with Eastern Europeans. A new world to me, older than my own, ethnically different, Northern instead of Southwestern, with wooded hills instead of treeless flatness, grimy urban shabbiness instead of hardscrabble farms.

Ed had found a happy-seeming and undemanding way of life, still at home with his parents in the big old family house in the outskirts of the city. His father, Scott Hamilton, was a large, relaxed, not-very-responsible man of Scottish and Indian ancestry. He had taken leave of his family to join up for the Spanish-American War, serving in Alaska.

Ed's mother, perhaps since then, had been the real head of the household. She was "Black Dutch," an active, black-eyed, shrewd little woman, full of sharp-tongued advice which her husband and her children cheerfully ignored.

Ed had three sisters: Esther, a busy columnist on the *Youngstown Telegram* and I think something of a social autocrat; Adeline, happily married to a jovial steel executive; and Betty, then still in school, lively and attractive, the one closest to Ed, though they all seemed to be on excellent terms.

I remember hiking with Ed in the woods near the house, driving through new landscapes to Youngstown and downtown at night for ice cream and the *New York Times*. Through the next few years I was there several times at different seasons, enjoying a new milieu, enjoying Ed's family, enjoying Ed himself for his sharp intelligence and his sardonic wit, his professional competence and all he knew of books I hadn't read.

Ed had a car, and sometime before Christmas we drove to Florida. Al Greco, another young friend of his and I think a better friend of Betty's, came with us as far as Miami. We went on to Key West. The Florida boom was long dead by then, and the overseas highway had not been rebuilt since the last hurricane. We crossed one long gap by ferry, almost the only outsiders aboard.

The Depression had hit hard. The big resort hotel was closed. With the sponge fishers gone to better grounds, the cigar industry dead, and the naval base abandoned, half the population was unemployed that winter. By summer, Key West was in receivership, begging for New Deal aid.

That sleepy stagnation only heightened its allure for me. It was yet another environment, new to both of us, fascinating for its history and its blending cultures. Tropical enough, too, with its palms and white beaches and the coral reefs around it, to mesh with my old escapist dreams.

Our long stay there came cheap enough. For eight dollars a month, we rented a house near Ernest Hemingway's big place on the beach—he was away that winter, hunting lions in Africa. We had our own cistern and our own tropical orchard. Ed got the use of a boat in return for equipping it with mast and sail. We spent the winter on the beach or in Ed's boat or writing science fiction.

A dream vacation, yet not quite the fun I had expected. My energies were ebbing; I didn't know why. Key West isn't really tropical, and our house had no heat. I remember shivering through the miserable chill of the northers, when the wind was too cold for the beach and we had no way to get warm.

Ed spent a lot of time fishing, but I seldom joined him. I remember the time he let the sail jib and the boom swing back across us to capsize the boat. We were in shallow water near the beach; I waded ashore, leaving him to gather up the wreckage on his own.

He was more outgoing than I; he found friends among the native "Conchs" and got to know an eccentric old German who, I think, had been a lab technician in the navy hospital. He was building an odd-looking airplane near the abandoned slaughterhouse on the beach where Ed kept his boat, and I remember his anxious way of peering out at people who came near. His plane was never meant to fly; we learned later that it held the body of a Cuban girl he had loved, stolen from her grave.

The only story I recall writing there is a novelette, "Born of the Sun." My favorite way of plotting in those days was to begin with something staggeringly impossible and look for some fictional way to show it happening. Suppose the sun were a huge living creature? Suppose our planets were eggs it had laid? Suppose the Earth were to hatch?

I remember discussing the notion with Ed. It was nonsense to him, but Tremaine had announced that *Astounding* would now feature "thought variant stories," developing far-out new ideas, and I thought my idea should be far enough out. To keep the story going until the planets began hatching, I added a cult of evil Orientals and a lovely heroine to be abducted.

All as wildly impossible as Ed had called it, but Tremaine bought it. Our readers then were mostly young and generously forgiving. Isaac Asimov, fourteen that year, recalled the story well enough to include it in *Before the Golden Age*, and Forry Ackerman has reprinted it again in his more recent *Gosh Wow! Science Fiction.*

With spring coming, we took steerage passage on a steamer to Cuba to spend ten days in and around Havana. There it was tropical enough to delight me. We rented a big, high-ceilinged room off a narrow street in the old colonial section of the city; it had noisy antique plumbing and brilliant bougainvilleas all around the window.

Drinking a very few Cuba Libres and a lot of orange juice, we went to the races and a jai alai game and made bus expeditions into the suburbs and tried our little Spanish on clerks and waitresses. I remember the ancient walls of El Morro and the magnificent harbor at night, the black water glittering with the lights of the Malecon. A little more wistfully, I recall the vivid dark charm of the Cuban women, sadly untouchable for me and I think untouched by Ed.

Back from that expedition, we drove north again to Georgia. I caught a train home from Valdosta, arriving underweight and ailing. One doctor gave me quinine for malaria, but I imagine my troubles were mostly psychosomatic: eyestrain, sinusitis, indigestion, a general malaise. My scanty records show nothing at all finished and sold in 1934. I was becoming increasingly unsatisfied with myself and my writing career.

In those first few years, I had achieved a good deal. *Argosy*, of course, had kept turning down my work, and the high-paying slicks were always out of reach, but I had begun to earn something of a name in the science fiction pulps. Though my travels were never made in luxury, I had glimpsed a little of the world. Now, with those first goals won, I found myself unhappy with them—and with nothing better in view.

Most of 1934 has dimmed in my mind; perhaps there wasn't much worth remembering. But my health got better. I began gaining two pounds a week after another doctor took my tonsils out again—they had been painfully cropped some years before.

A little later, on a diagnosis of "chronic appendicitis," I let the same old surgeon remove my appendix. Probably an ill-advised operation, it left adhesions that strangled a gut and nearly killed me in a VA hospital in 1946. Both Ed and Al Greco had appendectomies soon after mine. That seemed oddly coincidental to us, but when I happened to mention that to my analyst a few years later, he didn't seem surprised.

Trying hard to get back into production, I built a little cabin on the ranch, a place where I could work without interruption. Only one small room at first, but large enough for desk and files and bookshelves and bed. Later I added a separate bedroom, a little windmill for electric lights, and even a sort of bath—though water for it had to be carried in buckets two hundred yards, and the toilet was still anywhere about the farm where you could hide from public sight, with sagebrush or whatever for tissue.

Fiction markets were still dismal. *Weird Tales* was overstocked with serials for years to come—Wright had run *Golden Blood* ahead of several he had already accepted, including one of Ed's, something not likely to happen again. With *Wonder* and *Amazing* deep in trouble, and *Argosy* a dwindling hope, *Astounding* was my only paying market.

Groping for survival, I squandered time on ill-planned things that bogged down before I got them finished, failing for reasons I couldn't discover. Reading the letters from Ed that survive, I find us discussing collaborations that always came to nothing. My income for 1935 was only $540, down from $1,157 the year before.

Yet life went on. Coached by my sisters, I was learning to

dance. Never very well—and I never knew much to say to the woman—yet I enjoyed it. Neighbors—those to whom dancing wasn't a mortal sin—took turns as hosts on Saturday nights. We danced waltzes, two-steps, sometimes a schottische. The music was fiddle and guitar, sometimes a banjo, the musicians rewarded with whatever fell into the hat when it came around. Outside in the dark, there was a little cheap wine, cheap whiskey, sometimes moonshine. We used to drive many miles to dance most of the night and get back home at daylight, with cows needing to be milked.

Late that summer, still enamored of ships and the sea, I took a longer voyage, from Houston around to New York, a trip I enjoyed. Though I was in steerage, I had a cheap but impressive-looking Korelle Reflex camera that I could carry as a disguise on the first-class deck.

I remember dancing one night with a tall, attractive housewife from Wichita; her husband was genially tolerant—I suppose he could see how harmless I was. The ship's engineer turned out to be a fan who liked my work; we talked science fiction, and he showed me through the ship.

In New York, trying to met the editors, I found a less eager welcome. Though *Amazing* had published a lot of my work, all I saw of the venerable T. O'Conor Sloane was a momentary glimpse through his office door. Gernsback gave me a few minutes of his time and a sample copy of *Gadgets,* his newest magazine. The people at *Argosy* were so friendly on my first call that I went back again-and failed to get past the receptionist. Somewhat more warmly, Tremaine took me to lunch and reported that *The Legion of Space* had been well received.

Westward bound, I stopped in New Castle for another good visit with Ed Hamilton. In Chicago, I saw Wright and Sprenger, and spent several days at The Century of Progress. I remember walking through the exhibits with "Jack Darrow," whose frequent letters in the magazines had made Chicago famous in fandom.

The next summer Ed and his sister Betty drove out to spend a few weeks with us on the ranch. Their letters seem to show that they enjoyed the West as much I had Pennsylvania. The rest of my family and some of the neighbors helped me entertain them.

I liked Betty, but only in a very casual way; Jim took her to dances. One rancher friend, Finus Tucker, had the wit and imagination to play cowboy for her, walking with a bowlegged roll in his chaps and jingling spurs, exaggerating his Southwestern drawl, teaching her to make her own Bull Durham smokes. She seemed enormously impressed.

That year, 1935, the writing went better again. Tremaine bought two more novelettes for *Astounding*. "Islands of the Sun" grew from another fantastic notion about the origins of the planets. "The Galactic Circle" had a more striking idea, a circular flight through size—the explorers in their ship shrink into infinite smallness; still shrinking at the end of the story, they return enormous, dwindling out of cosmic immensity to reach the same world they had left.

The idea was better than its execution. I suppose I was trying too hard to make it something serious, trying too hard for realistic characters with too little skill to bring them off. Some readers praised it, but Asimov calls it "rotten" in a fan letter he wrote me in 1939—he had rated eighteen of my stories. *The Cometeers* and *The Legion of Space* were graded "super-perfect," with five stars each, and I was ranked third overall, behind E. E. Smith and John W. Campbell, but "The Galactic Circle" stood alone at the bottom of the list, with only a single star.

Weird Tales accepted "The Ruler of Fate" that year, to run as a serial in 1936. Another story that should have been better than it is. A welcome sale, even though the magazine was still in trouble, paying Ed only $25 a month on a debt of some $700. I think Sprenger and Wright were doing a little better by me, but I was happy that fall to find another market, one that reported and paid with less delay.

That was the *Thrilling* group, published by Standard Magazines. The chain was owned by Ned Pines and very efficiently edited by Leo Margulies and such junior associates as Mort Weisinger. Ed had been writing detective stories for them, and I think he helped open the way for me. By the end of 1935 I had begun selling occasional horror novelettes to *Thrilling Mystery*.

Gernsback's floundering *Wonder* became *Thrilling Wonder* when Pines bought it in 1936. I sold a few stories there, and two unmemorable novels to *Startling Stories*, the lower-paying companion magazine launched in 1939. Though checks were almost instant, at a full cent a word for *Thrilling Mystery* and *Thrilling Wonder*, Leo required every story to fit a very rigid pattern.

Mort told me once that they had no actual objection to good writing, but all that really mattered was fitting the formula. I learned the horror pattern well enough to invent a variation on it that I sold to *Author and Journalist,* but writing for Leo was never much fun.

Ed evidently enjoyed it more than I did. He and Mort became good friends. He wrote all but two or three of the *Captain Future* novels, which began appearing in 1940 in their own magazine, more juvenile than *Thrilling Wonder* and done to fit a formula of Mort's design.

In the fall of 1935, Tremaine offered me a break from such suffocating limits. Others besides Asimov had liked *The Legion of Space*—another fan a few years later tabulated the comments in the published letters and reported that my antiheroic Giles Habibula had been the most popular character of the 1930s. When Tremaine asked for a sequel, I plunged eagerly into *The Cometeers.*

With old Giles alive again, it absorbed me. The manuscript I sent Tremaine was 65,000 words. He had me cut 10,000 words, but generously paid me for them. His check for $650, received in early 1936, was the best I had received; it brought that year's income to $1,430.

A nice burst of prosperity, but not enough to content me. Wanting more out of life than I had found, I was beginning to think of psychoanalysis.

14.

UNDER ANALYSIS,

1936–1937

Ernest O. Lawrence patented the cyclotron in 1934, and the Dionne Quints were born. On July 22, John Dillinger walked out of a Chicago movie theater into a hail of gunfire from the FBI. Nylon was invented in 1935, and the *Normandie* made her maiden voyage to New York. The *Queen Mary* followed in 1936. In October, the *China Clipper* finished its first round-trip flight to Manila. Mae West earned $480,000 that year; Shirley Temple turned seven; Margaret Mitchell published *Gone with the Wind*. Hitler fortified the Rhine.

Though FDR was trying hard here in America, with the NRA and the CCC and the TVA and the AAA and the WPA, the Great Depression still dragged on. A long drought was blighting farmlands. In 1936, the Ohio Valley suffered the worst flood in history.

I remember the Okies trekking west across New Mexico, and the great clouds of dust rolling after them out of the north and east, settling over everything and turning the whole landscape a dull blue-gray. Though the searing Kansas heat wave in the summer of 1936, my analyst tried to cool his office with a fan blowing air against a block of ice.

I've sometimes wondered if I might have been happier, coming of age in better times. Probably not. I had been luckier than many, able to escape hard labor and hunger, as free to do what I wanted as my own inner limits allowed. Yet with 1936 beginning, I felt as deeply troubled as the whole world was.

There's a glimpse of my own private depression in a scrap of journal I kept that year, from February through March. The entries are rigidly inhibited, though written for "my eyes only," and bleak enough to show why I didn't carry them farther, but they do describe my unhappy situation and document my efforts to escape.

I've been reading Spengler's *Decline of the West,* a work with more weight than good cheer. I'm still a virgin, haunted with longings for sex and my old fears of it. Living at home on the ranch, and trying to work in that narrow cabin, I'm recovering from flu, limping about on painful feet after a long run in shoes not fit for it, suffering from frequent colds and eyestrain. Most of my projects are horror stories aimed at *Thrilling Mystery,* bits of hackwork designed to fit a stifling formula.

The Cometeers was more fun to do, but Tremaine has been silent about it. In mid-February he returns two installments to be condensed into one, but he's buying it. The revisions take five days; I mail them back to him on February 19. His check for $650 arrives the same afternoon, but the journal reports no elation.

Nor much more when Leo Margulies writes that he has bought *Wonder Stories* and wants novelettes at a cent a word. Instead of plunging into some new story, I'm buying a chromatic harmonica that I hope to learn to play by note—a doomed undertaking, because I've no ear at all.

Jo, my older sister, is gravely ill when the journal opens, though soon improving. A slice of Tremaine's check goes for her hospital bills, and worry over her future is one more burden.

An attractive neighbor girl has been going with me to movies and dances. I learn now that she has just married a man I'd never known about; he has been away somewhere in military service. Though I admired her, my sense of loss is soon blunted—I've always known she really wasn't for me; we have too few interests in common.

Yet I've quit going out with Jim and my sister Katie. In early March I mail "The Ice Entity" to Leo Margulies and begin a series of eye treatments with an optometrist at five dollars a visit.

As well as Freud and a bit of Jung, I've been reading Karl Menninger's *The Human Mind,* and *Facts and Theories of Psychoanalysis* by Ives Hendricks. On February 29 I write to ask about coming to Boston for analysis with him. He refers me to the Menninger Clinic in Topeka. I write Karl Menninger, who agrees to see me on April 13. The journal ends as I set out.

Topeka is the capital of Kansas, but far overshadowed by Kansas City, only 70 miles away. A few years later, some of my own impressions of it were fictionized in *Darker Than You Think.* I recall it as a quiet little city, half asleep in those hard times. Its best-known citizens were Senator Arthur Capper, publisher of the daily *Capital* and *Capper's Weekly,* and Alf Landon, governor of the state.

Out of mere curiosity, I called on Landon the morning after the 1936 Republican Convention nominated him to run for the presidency against FDR. His secretary let me in. I found him alone in his office, with time to shake hands and inquire about Republican power in New Mexico, of which I had to confess I knew nothing. When election time came, he carried only Maine and Vermont.

The Menninger Clinic then occupied a big, aging building with lawns and trees around it. I took physical tests that included a head X ray and talked to a good many psychiatrists; most of them must have been interns. One of them commented that writing science fiction was symptomatic of neurosis. His casual promise that I could be cured of that became one more mental problem, because I wanted no remedy for writing.

When the tests were over, I began analysis with Dr. Charles W. Tidd, meeting him five hours a week at five dollars an hour —a low fee, even in those times, though it was finally too much for me. I liked him at once, and I'm grateful for all he did for me.

Before I left the clinic I wrote an article about that first year. Turned down without comment by *Atlantic* and the like, the piece has never been published, but a draft still exists and bits of it may show something of what the analysis was for me. The over-labored lead paragraph is about the Kaw River, which runs through Topeka.

It must once have been deep and clear; but now it is choked with bars of mud, red-stained with the life-blood of the despoiled and dying land, turbulent with whirlpools that make it dangerous for swimmers. . . . Sometimes I have imagined myself leaping down into that murky stream. . . . There are several reasons for this fearful covert wish to die: a blind savage anger at my own failings, with the guilty need of self-punishment; a childish, irrational desire to injure the analyst by my death; the fact that the leap stands for impulsive abandonment, for the final fatal rebellion against the old false tyranny of self-control.

This year I have learned all these things, and now I shall never kill myself. . . .

It has been a lonely year. I am sitting, this quiet April afternoon, in the upstairs front room that costs me ten dollars a month—I had neither the money nor the need to live in the sanitarium. The room is furnished with two chairs, bedstead, dresser, and my typewriter on the table. It sometimes seems chill and bare, and during the winter I was driven to various ingenious expedients to keep my feet warm while I worked. Habitually I eat down at the Greek's place, where a square meal is fifteen cents. My clothing was shabby at the beginning, and becomes inevitably more so. I have made few friends, in spite of fumbling efforts, because of the intangible barriers of fear.

My profession is the writing of adventure stories for certain of those rough-paper magazines known as 'pulps.' One of them now lies on my desk, with my name in white letters across a garish cover illustration. Beside it is a note from the editor, asking me to do another yarn. Almost desperately, I need the cent a word he would pay. Hopefully, I run a sheet of clean paper into the machine and begin:

Martin Drake listened in terrible apprehension to the heavy footsteps coming up the stair. His breath stopped, at the abrupt harsh grate of the key in the lock. Cold with a sudden sweat, he crouched beside the door.

From years of practice, I have gathered many technical tricks that build simple interest and suspense. Familiar word-patterns rise mechanically. But even a 'wood-pulp' story must be the expression of genuine feeling: words are valueless without emotion. And this story has no reality for me; I care nothing for Martin Drake and the cause of his trepidation. My feelings are confused and turbid as the river.

Still I try to make myself go on. I stare at the sheet of paper, knot my hands, double up as if with cramping agony. I begin to weep, out of sheer helpless frustration.

This is all childish, I say; silly. I want to write, perhaps more than anything else I could do. There is no visible reason why I can't, and every necessity that I should. So I try again. But the machine mocks me. The few words I write are dry and empty. . . . I rip the page out. . . . Baffled, defeated, I throw myself down on the bed. But I am too tense to relax, too bitter. I get up and try to read, try to study some other man's story. But it seems as hollow as my own. And I know the tricks well enough, if I could only muster up the feeling.

Hence the little essay, an effort to record real emotions of my own that didn't fit any story I knew how to write.

Five times a week I go for the fifty-minute "hour." I always start thirty minutes early, lest I be delayed. The old fear strikes me when the girl at the desk calls my name. (She's a pretty girl, and I've learned that part of my fear is due to desire for her, and my unconscious jealous apprehension of the analyst.)

Walking lightly and hastily, a little breathless, sometimes with a pounding heart, I climb the stairs and walk across the hall and enter the office of the analyst. He has laid a paper napkin ready for me across the pillow on the couch. He stands and bows to meet me, a handsome man with an easy, friendly smile—and yet I feel confused and afraid.

Quickly, feeling a self-conscious restraint, I lie supine on the couch. It is difficult to begin speaking. I delay: my hands ball into fists; my body tenses; I make aimless striking motions.

"Just say what you feel," the analyst prompts me quietly. He is sitting relaxed in his chair behind my head. His manner is always easy, unsurprised. His low voice is sympathetic, encouraging. 'Just tell me all your thoughts.'

With a convulsive effort, I begin. I try to talk rapidly, because there is so much to say; because the time is so costly, and I do not wish to waste it; perhaps because I wish to hurry over some painful, shameful thing; also because the talk eases tensions and sometimes I become relaxed and comfortable toward the end of the hour.

My hurried voice is low—all though life I have spoken softly, as I have stooped, to make myself inconspicuous and avoid aggression and danger. Sometimes I become inaudible. The analyst asks me to repeat, and I make a brief effort to speak distinctly.

Continually, too, he must urge me to go on. For when I have come to a difficult matter, my voice checks and stops. To speak each word takes a desperate new effort. I catch a deep breath or make random body movements to delay the need to speak. I search for painless asides and diversions. Often the thoughts themselves flee away and leave my mind a blank. Hopefully, I inquire if the hour isn't already gone.

The analyst usually says little, except for his continual, sometimes tormenting pressure to "go on. . . . Yes. . . . Yes. . . . Just tell me all about it." But his rare

pointed questions, his suggestions and disarmingly
tentative explanations tear the veil from many a dis-
guised expression. Slowly I have come to understand
myself, though I know even less psychoanalytic theory
than when I came. Such words as 'libido' and 'id'
seem strange when I recall them, for I was reques-
ted at the beginning to stop reading Freud and his
followers.

There have been dramatic moments. Once in the
middle of the hour I began to cry, and talked through
my sobs about "my little black doggie." The dog, I
said, had been mine when I was a tiny child, and I had
caused its death. When the hour was over, I walked
away from the clinic into a nearby cemetery, where I
could cry like a heartbroken child. That abandonment
of grief was the most complete I have ever known, and
it became more grist for the analytic mill. Because it
seems that this little black dog never actually existed;
it was only one more disguise for things still too painful
for me to face.

A year of cramping limits, spent in what now looks like painful
poverty. At first I lived in a boarding house, where I did make
a few casual friends. One was a pretty little girl, five or six years
old, with a widowed mother who was grooming her to be another Shirley Temple. The child's affection for me was happily
uninhibited, but I hadn't learned to get on so easily with older
women.

With less money than ever, no car and no confidence, I could
only envy men who had female friends. Yet with the moral
support of my analyst, I made uneasy efforts against that old
dread of sex. Prostitution was still wide open in Topeka, and I
was lucky enough to find a friendly-seeming girl already familiar
with the quirks of Menninger patients. I've always been grateful
for her helpful therapy, but I didn't even attempt anything further among the private sector.

Back from a week at home at Christmas, I moved into
that ten-dollar room to save a little money. Stretching what I

had, I allowed myself a nickel for an ice cream cone or a candy bar when I walked out alone in the evening. Out of boredom more than talent, I took WPA courses in tap dancing and drawing; for a long time I kept my sketch of one class-mate, an attractive French-named girl I would have liked to know.

One night I paid a few precious dollars for a flight over Topeka in a Ford Trimotor that took off between two rows of lanterns across a wheat field. I used to climb to a lookout point high in the state capitol, for the pleasure I felt in seeing every-thing else shrunk to toylike size. Sometimes in the afternoon, when movies were cheap, I found a brief escape into dream-land.

I haunted the candy store, searching the racks of pulp maga-zines for clues to writing skill. I got to know the owner. Never a friend, he was a lecherous old man with designs on young Mexican girls. I met a few science-fiction readers there, and one or two would-be writers who seemed to envy my small success.

One friend I recall was an able but troubled newspaperman who drank too much, lost his job, and left Topeka before I did; he was a homeless drifter the last I knew, searching the nation for things he never found. I remember one young fan who went out with me to hear a hell-fire evangelist preaching in a tent; I had gone as an amused people-watcher, and I felt amazed and a little appalled when he found God.

A lonely year. I remember walking the river bridge many times that dry summer, when low water wandered between red mud banks, and again on bitter winter days when the river lay frozen under drifting snow, and in the spring when it ran high, choked with drifting rafts of dirty ice.

A year of little human contact, except those analytic hours. If I had made few friends, perhaps I didn't really want them. Every-thing I did, all those uncertain meetings, even my own penny-pinching, became matter for more analysis. More than any-where, I lived inside myself. With Dr. Tidd for a guide, I was discovering at least a little of myself.

A difficult year, but good for me. Somewhat to Ed Hamilton's surprise. In a letter written when I first came to Topeka, he says he's "mystified and a little alarmed." He admits that I'm introverted, but he says I need analysis "no more than a fencepost." In later letters he keeps urging me to give it up and come on to Pennsylvania for another visit with him. But I stayed on as long as I could—until my payments to the clinic were three months behind, with another fifty due my brother for money he lent me to live on.

In theory, I should have turned out fiction enough to meet the clinic's modest fees, but my writing had gone badly, with only one novelette sold to Tremaine and a couple of horror yarns to Margulies. Most of my effort had been wasted on two or three longer projects that I must have known were hopeless, because, as Dr. Tidd suggested, I wanted them to fail. Such "unconscious resistance" became part of the process.

My health was improving. On Dr. Tidd's advice, I had taken my eye problems to an ophthalmologist, who gave me a special stereoscope with which to treat myself for exophoria and fitted me with new glasses that I wore comfortably for many years. A podiatrist threw away the arch supports that had kept me limping and taught me how to care for my feet.

Better than any of that, I was escaping at least a few of my old internal conflicts, correcting my old notion that will and feeling and reason must be always at war. Slowly, uncertainly, I had begun to find a less divided inner self that I could like, and to accept parts of me that I had always tried to deny.

No analysis ever ends. As Dr. Tidd once put it, the process is like peeling an infinite onion. Everything becomes symbolic of something deeper, with no final truth ever revealed. With those old internal feuds not half resolved, I—one part of me—wanted to stay on with Dr. Tidd. I liked him. I wanted more of his sympathetic support. I needed to go on healing that division in myself. But the outlaw part, still spoiling my work, made that impossible. In April, Dr. Tidd agreed that we had reached a dead end.

When Ed Hamilton heard that we were breaking it off, he wrote that if I could raise the fare to New Castle and fifteen or twenty bucks to support me for a week in the big town, he would take me with him on a trip he was planning to New York. Then, if I would stay till June, we could drive west again together.

I accepted that generous offer.

15

OUT FROM UNDER,

1937–1938

In 1936, Hitler was on the Rhine. Mussolini was taking Addis Ababa, Franco nearing Madrid, Edward VIII giving up the British Empire for Wallace Warfield Simpson. Americans, not yet much troubled, were leaving the central cities for the suburbs and the highways. There were 160,000 trailers on the open roads.

I don't recall being much concerned with world affairs when I left the clinic that spring. What I felt strongest was joy at escape from analysis. Yet most of the restraints on my life in Topeka had been self-imposed, and I kept in touch with Dr. Tidd. With my permission, he published an article about my case. Though I've never read it, I once found a footnote reference to it in Karl Menninger's *Man Against Himself.*

Dr. Tidd bought me a drink in Pittsburgh that summer, when he was there at a medical meeting and I was in town with Ed. When he moved his practice to California a little later, he let me know.

On the way east, my first stop was Chicago. Farnsworth Wright received me warmly and took me home for dinner. To his wife's dismay, I'm afraid; his paralysis was getting visibly worse, and she was trying to protect him. He offered to give me those magnificent cover paintings St. John had done for *Golden Blood;* alas, I had nowhere to keep them.

We talked about my stay in Topeka. I felt a new affection for him and a new need of his support; in the aftermath of the analysis, I suppose some of my feelings for Dr. Tidd had trans-ferred themselves to him. Though he later bought another se-rial, that must have been the last time I saw him. A great editor, too seldom remembered.

I went with Ed up to New York. At Standard Magazines, where Ed was now a valued regular contributor, we saw Margulies and Weisinger, and also Julius Schwartz—Ed's agent then and a bridge fanatic, later a *Superman* editor. Ed wrote scripts for their comic books for many years, always muttering about their stifl-ing requirements, yet never quite rebelling.

One day he and I stopped at the Hearst *American Weekly* and asked to see A. Merritt. Amazingly, he let us come up to his office and talked science fiction with us for an hour, chewing tobacco so unobtrusively that I didn't notice till Ed remarked about it later, spitting into the city out of his high window. Though my early worship had begun to fade by then, he had been one of our giants, and that cordial reception left a bright spot in my memory.

I got to know John W. Campbell, who was already doing editorial work for *Astounding*. He replaced Tremaine there that September and stayed for the rest of his life, becoming the greatest shaper of modern science fiction. He had become an able literary craftsman, first as Doc Smith's major rival in far-out space opera, later and with growing mastery as Don A. Stuart.

Campbell knew science enough, with physics courses begun at MIT, though he failed German there and had to finish his degree at Duke. Most important, he was serious about science fiction. As much as anybody, he breathed the sense of wonder that we all felt then, back before the nukes shadowed it with terror, an exhilarating faith in science as revelation of a splendid cosmos and a limitless power to create a splendid human future in it. Nobody since Wells has equaled his influence.

As editor, he lived for the magazine and inspired a lot of us with the same contagious enthusiasm, shared through his long letters and his monthly editorials and his talk in the office or at lunch or out at his New Jersey home. He generated an unending flow of speculative ideas, always original, always creative, always meant to challenge received assumptions. Not that he was radical in politics. Too conservative, rather, for the new liberalism that was to follow the war.

So was I. He and I had grown up in the same time frame and I felt congenial with nearly everything about him then, though later I deplored his increasing weakness for unorthodox notions that I felt were nonsense. Parapsychology, the Dean drive, dianetics. Too much of his nonstop talk could overwhelm me, but I owe a great debt to him.

In June, Ed and I drove west to New Mexico. The long drought was over, and what I remember best is the wheat coming into harvest, mile after golden mile. I must have had a little money by then, because I bargained with Ed to pay for part of the gas if he would let me drive part of the time. He agreed, a little doubtfully, and gave me the only real instruction I had ever had in how to drive—he loved that little car, and he didn't want me to wreck it.

The money must have come from "Entropy Released." It was a quick novelette I had finished at Topeka in my first flush of elation over escaping from analysis; Tremaine paid me $300 for 25,000 words, but appalled me somewhat when he changed the title. Himself a gifted editor, he was no scientist. My own title had been "Entropy Reversed." I suppose his was meant to seem more dramatic, but it struck me as scientific nonsense.

Ed spent a few weeks with us on the ranch. When he had gone on, I think to California, I got back to work. My first major project was another serial for Wright, which he accepted in September. "They That Sleep" had been my title; he renamed it "Dreadful Sleep"—another change I didn't much like. A story of the whole planet in stasis. Some of the images still cling in my memory: as my heroes wander the stopped world, trying to get it moving again, they find people and animals turned to living statues and cross oceans hard as glass. Once I tried to rewrite the story, but gave up when I found too much unbelievable fantasy. Treated with more logic and conviction, it might have been better.

Wildly unlikely as it was, Wright published and paid for it in 1938. His first check was only half the unpaid bill I had left at the clinic, but I got them to accept it as payment in full. An uncomfortable compromise, but one I felt compelled to ask for.

With my 1937 income shrunk to less than a thousand dollars and new production faltering, the debt itself had come to seem a disabling handicap.

With that obligation eased, things did go better. *Thrilling Wonder* bought a short novelette, "The Infinite Enemy." I turned from it to another notion that caught my imagination to become a short novel, *The Legion of Time*. I had read "Ancestral Voice," by Nat Schachner, about objects in our present time that vanish when time travellers go back to remove their roots in the past.

It struck me that people placed in danger of such instant obliteration would fight to defend themselves. In my own story, two possible future worlds battle for survival, sending time-ships back to discover and control the critical past event that will let one exist and erase the other.

My first draft was only 12,000 words. It grew as I retyped it, to nearly 40,000. Campbell praised it, though he cut my bonus rate back to a straight cent a word, and ran it in 1938 as a three-part serial and the first of his announced "mutant" stories.

"The Crucible of Power" pleased him even more. It came from another creative accident—there was still a lot of trial and error in my writing, as I suppose there always will be. I had set out to tell a first-person story of the exploration of Mars, opening with what my intended hero wrote about his father. Unexpectedly, the father evolved into "a hero with a heart of purest brass," as Campbell put it. The novelette ran in early 1939 with a wonderful Hubert Rogers cover showing my brazen half-hero staggering away from the wreckage of his rocket where it has crashed on Mars.

"After World's End" was a longer novelette, and one I always liked for its mood and color, though it lacks any very new plot idea. I was happy with the sandbat, the alien creature in it, but Campbell and Wright weren't entirely taken. Erisman bought it at half a cent a word and ran it in *Marvel Science* with a rather lurid Wesso cover.

Another try at *Argosy* turned out more happily. Long-distance flights were still earning headlines; Howard Hughes had flown around the world that summer in less than four days. I'd read Lord Dunsany's satire on such exploits in "Distant Cousins," where Joseph Jorkens tells of his flight from Earth to Mars in an open airplane, and my own idea was simply to translate that fine tall tale into slightly more serious science fiction.

Some ten years after my first try there, *Argosy* bought "Non-Stop to Mars." Sadly, however, in an age already unkind to pulp magazines, that once great book had dropped its pay rate to only a cent and a quarter a word.

Thrilling Wonder bought a short, "Passage to Saturn," but my major project that fall was *One Against the Legion,* another book in the saga of Giles Habibula. Once again, he breathed his own wheezy life into the story. Most of the science was manufactured to fit the plot, not very valid outside it. Yet today, when I meet the 'droids in George Lucas's *Star Wars* films, I wonder if they aren't remotely descended from the androids I invented for the Legion stories, even though mine were biological, not mechanical.

I've found a sort of postscript to that brief journal, dated November 9, 1938. The tone is still pretty downbeat: "recently I have been increasingly dissatisfied with my life." I don't own a car. I still feel exiled from society. My work has been slowed by a lingering case of flu.

At home on the ranch, I'm remote from my fellow science-fictioneers, the still-small family circle where I feel best understood. I have few local friends. Though the farm and ranch neighbors around us are neighborly, we live in different worlds. Blanche is still in Portales, but I seldom see her. Gordon Greaves, home from the university, is working with his father on the family paper and writing a column of his own; he reports my travels and my stories, but our meetings are brief and casual.

I know the newsdealers who sometimes carry magazines with my stories, and I've met a few faculty members at the recently opened college, which hasn't yet dared call itself a university. Yet, to most of the people I know, science fiction writers are still puzzling freaks. With more sanity and better common sense, I might have looked for a higher-paying occupation, but the drive to write science fiction has never really wavered. I shrink from any entanglements that might get in the way.

Yet, as that brief entry reports, I'm not without cheer. Many things are better than they were before I saw Dr. Tidd. Jo has recovered from the first critical phase of her illness. I've spent the end of the summer in Santa Fe, escaping the hay fever season at home and finishing *One Against the Legion.*

Doing physical work for the past month, adding the new room and installing the Wincharger lights, I've put on five pounds and admit that I feel better. Though "the exchequer is in a precarious state," Campbell's check for *One Against the Legion* should come by December 10.

In fact it did, bringing my 1938 income to $1,452, the best year yet. Next year it fell again to only $1,186, but I kept on writing. Never quite sure the analysis had really set me free, I kept on reaching, though never very daringly, for a little more of life.

16

OLD SANTA FE,

1938–1940

The *Hindenburg* burned at Lakehurst in 1939, ending dreams that the Empire State Building might become a world air terminal. Japan began the conquest of China. On the Chase & Sanborn radio hour, Edgar Bergen and Charlie McCarthy became instant celebrities.

All that was far away. I kept writing madly, writing for survival, hoping to find that now, after analysis, I could let myself accept some richer way of life.

In January, a note from Leo Margulies called for stories for a new fantasy magazine, *Strange Stories*. Though he was paying only half a cent, I sent him a novelette I called "The Miraculous Gift." It came back with Mort Weisinger's letter telling what was wrong. Though Margulies was the nominal editor of all the whole Standard group, Mort was the actual and very able editor of *Thrilling Wonder* and its later siblings. Never creative in the way Campbell was, he was a shrewd story doctor, and he taught me a good deal about the mechanics of fiction.

When I had this story rewritten, it looked too good for half a cent. I sent it to *Argosy*. Accepted, it ran as "Star Bright." It's still a thing I like, for its blend of wonder and the commonplace and my own affection for little Mr. Peabody, who receives the cosmic gift. Mort chided me once for not sending it back to him, but not too bitterly when I pointed out the disparity in pay.

A letter from Campbell on February 6 announced another new fantasy magazine, one that promised to be far more exciting. That was *Unknown*. He wanted better-written fiction than Lovecraft had been doing for *Weird Tales*, with "no reams of phony atmosphere" or "unpleasant gods and godlings" and "nude and beauteous maidens waiting to be sacrified." The first thing I tried for him was a total failure—all I recall about it is an evil *afrit* out the Arabian Nights somehow let loose in contemporary Africa—but later I had better luck.

By early May, I was back in New York, calling on Campbell at the old red brick building at 79 Seventh Avenue which housed Street & Smith, presses as well as editors. Armed now with a better notion of what he wanted, I worked out another story. Good fantasy, like good science fiction, has to fit the pattern Wells had described long before—a single new premise logically and believably developed.

What if magic had still been alive in Minoan Crete until rising science killed it? An idea fresher then than it may seem today. I tried to learn what I could about the prehistoric Mediterranean world. For a plot, I assumed that the myth of Theseus reflects historic fact. He was my hero, a contemporary buccaneer in conflict with the ancient magicians.

Doing research, I spent two or three months in New York, living in a tiny studio apartment at the Columbia Residence Club on 114th Street just off Riverside Drive. A quiet, clean street then, with a fine view of the Palisades from the park along the river; the rent was only about twenty dollars a month.

I read Minoan archaeology at the public library and haunted museums in search of Minoan artifacts. For details of ships and weaponry, I recall picking the brains of such scholarly friends as Sprague de Camp. I had met him a few years before, high on the elation of his very first sale to Campbell, and found him generously willing to share his remarkable knowledge of nearly everything.

I rode the subway a good many times out to Long Island and the fair. The Trilon and Perisphere. The General Motors Futurama. My first glimpse of TV. For me and my science fiction friends, it was a dazzling glimpse of the dawning "World of Tomorrow," where technology promised great good things.

And I wrote another novel. Mort Weisinger wanted it for *Startling Stories*. I didn't like working for half a cent, but he promised guidance and a quick check. I think he suggested the idea—which wasn't all that inspiring—and I know we talked about the plot.

I pounded out a fast first draft, which came out so bad that it had to have still more guidance. Parts of it, Mort said, read like goofy dreams, but I was able to improve it enough to run in the November *Startling* with my name and the title, *The Fortress of Utopia,* splashed across a fine cover by Howard Brown that showed animals in pairs marching up a ramp into the Ark of Space.

I saw other old friends and found a good many new ones. In Campbell's office, I met Eric Frank Russell, here from England on his check for *Sinister Barriers,* the feature novel in the initial issue of *Unknown.* Russell was a traveling salesman when he wasn't writing his popular stories or researching Charles Fort. What I remember best is his appetite for dirty jokes—he kept retelling one of my own, distressing me with his peculiar imitation of my Southwestern drawl.

A congenial little group used to gather at Steuben's Tavern somewhere near the Standard office on West 48th. Weisinger was often there, Ed Hamilton when he was in town, Manly Wade Wellman, Jack and Otto Binder—Earl, the other half of Eando, was still in Chicago. Jack was a striving artist. Otto and I had a lot in common, striving in much the same way to build our lives on science fiction. I liked him, and we kept in touch for years.

The most appealing people I got to know were the Futurians, bright young people, passionate fans only beginning to emerge as brilliant pros, most of them living in a sort of commune. Widely famous now, since the book-length confessions of Damon Knight and Fred Pohl, they were already notorious in fandom.

Isaac Asimov and I had exchanged a few cards and letters; he phoned and called at my room, a slim and rather diffident kid with no hint that I recall of the disarmingly ironic show of self-esteem he cultivates today. I think he told me how to find the Queens Science Fiction League. I attended several meetings and met more Futurians at the First World Science Fiction Convention, which happened on Sunday, July 2, 1939.

The Futurians were at war with New Fandom—a group led by

The young Forrest J. Ackerman at the first world science fiction convention in 1939, I think standing outside the hall in which it was held. He's wearing the cape of his "Worlds to Come" outfit.

Sam Moskowitz and Will Sykora and Jim Turasi, who regarded them as dangerously Red. In control of the convention, New Fandom locked most of the Futurians out, though Asimov, recognized as an author, was allowed inside.

I spent most of the morning sitting with the exiles in an Automat across the street. Don Wollheim, Doc Lowndes, Jack Gillespie, Cyril Kornbluth, Fred Pohl when he got back from the dentist, and "Leslie Perri"—who was Doris Baumgardt, a beautiful girl and herself another reason the Futurians seemed so attractive to me; she and Fred were later married. Influenced by her as much as anything, I went back to the hall to plead the Futurian cause, but Sam stood firm. And the Futurians, of course, enjoyed the feud too much to beg for admission.

I've just discovered something long forgotten: I'm a Futurian myself!

A letter from Fred Pohl—the first of a file that has grown into volumes—says that because of my efforts on behalf of the Futurian Society at the convention, and for being "a consistently readable writer," I have been voted the very first honorary member. He also wants to know why the "lepers" were excluded from the convention, something they "have been absolutely unable to find out." So he says.

Inside the hall that afternoon, I met a good many more science-fictioneers. I must have shaken hands with Frank R. Paul, who was the main speaker. Surely with Ray Cummings, whose *Girl in the Golden Atom* I had admired. I remember Forry Ackerman and "Morojo"—Myrtle Douglas—there from California, wearing costumes out of *Things to Come* and preaching Esperanto. Most impressions of the others have faded—that was long ago! The convention made *Time*, though the story on it was a sardonic putdown.

I left New York not much later, riding back to New Castle with Ed Hamilton—a note from Mort dated July 20 is addressed to me there. It must have been on this drive that we stopped to call on David H. Keller, whose stories we both liked. Ed said later that the good doc hadn't seemed to appreciate my praise for the "admirable simplicity of his style," but he did give us signed copies of his first book, *The Sign of the Burning Hart,* which I suppose is rare by now.

From New Castle, I went on to Detroit to buy a Ford V-8 sedan, a symbol and instrument of freedom long yearned for. It cost only $640—a figure that shows what time and inflation have since done to the value of money. Driving slow to break it in, I came back west, first to Jackson, Michigan, where I stopped a couple of days to visit Doc Smith.

The Skylark of Space had enchanted me. I still respected Doc as the great pioneer of space opera, and he received me cordially enough, though his job as a doughnut chemist left him little time

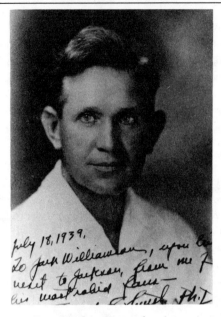

Doc Smith gave me the picture
when I stopped to see him in Jackson in 1939.

for talk. I enjoyed his family more. Jeanne, his adoring wife. Verna and Honey, two adorable daughters. A close-knit, old-fashioned family, all devoted to Doc. He worked hard enough to support them, and I think they all spoiled him in return.

I must confess that my early worship for him had begun to cool by then. We remained good friends; Doc and Jeanne drove their motor home to visit us in New Mexico after he retired, but I've never read all of his later work. His craftsmanship had failed to grow with his space-shaking ideas.

Back at home, soon sneezing and weeping from hay fever, I went back to Santa Fe. The fall before, with no car and very little money, I had kept to my furnished room and finished my novel, seeing very little of the town. Now, getting to know it better, I was enchanted.

My own Llano Estacado is flat and featureless. Coronado, crossing it in search of the Seven Cities of Cíbola, discovered nothing at all. Almost waterless, almost empty, it had no history until the gringos came. Santa Fe had more of everything.

History: the old adobe Place of the Governors, built in 1610 on the site of a prehistoric Tiwa pueblo and retaken by de Vargas in 1692 after the Pueblo rebellion, that event still recalled in the annual Fiesta. Air: dry and cool at 7,000 feet, nearly free of pollens and pollution then. Colors: yellow desert, evergreen slopes, pristine snow on the Sangre de Cristo, turquoise and silver, Navajo rugs and Pueblo pottery. People: Indian and Hispanic and Anglo, anthropologists and artists and politicians.

Old Santa Fe was already almost a religion to those few who knew it, but the faith had not yet spread to infect all the tourists now swarming in to spoil all that has drawn them. The atomic scientists were yet to come. The city was quieter and more inviting then, and cheap enough for me.

I found a basement room on Canyon Road for twelve dollars a month and set to work in mid-August, plunging into *The Reign of Wizardry*. Theseus against the magicians. The story went well. Campbell's check for $510—a penny a word—reached me in October. He ran it in *Unknown* as a three-part serial, with a cover and fine interior illustrations by Edd Cartier.

Tremaine was out of Street and Smith by then, launching *Comet*, a magazine that came and went fast enough to fit the title. He wanted me to do a serial—another *Legion of Space*, but with not just one but a whole team of beautiful girls, each guarding her own fantastic secret. The things I tried to plan never looked good enough to write, but I did get out a so-so novelette, "The Star of Dreams," that he bought.

In September, Mort Weisinger approved my plot for "The Sun Maker," a 20,000-word novelette for *Thrilling Wonder*. He sent the first draft of that back for revision, and the opening chapters back for another—along with $50 in advance to keep me at it. Accepted and paid for in January, it ran that summer. Cramped to fit his rigid requirements, it had more plot than emotion.

"Hindsight," a short that Campbell bought, suffered from the same failing. Fred Pohl took "The Girl in the Bottle" for *Super Science*, one of the new magazines he was editing for Popular almost without a budget. Another indifferent story, it must have been bounced from better-paying markets.

After that burst in the fall, my production sagged badly. Part of my problem was Santa Fe itself; I liked it too well to leave, even after the pollens had settled at home. Though still without much money, I had wheels and at least a bit more social ease. At the museums, I discovered a whole school of old friends in anthropology, fellow students when we were at the university, professionals now.

Finding new friends, I met John L. Sinclair, a moody but likable literary Scot who had come to New Mexico in his teens to be a cowboy; Jean Cady, an Eastern girl with anthropological interests and a museum job in the old palace; and Brian Boru Dunn, an old friend of H. G. Wells and once an aide to Senator Bronson Cutting, who had left him a generous legacy. An individualistic Irishman, B.B. rode a motor scooter and presided as a sort of civic host in the lobby at La Fonda.

Alfred Morang was a painter whose patient wife, Dorothy, allowed him to open their house on Saturday nights to the whole Santa Fe colony of artists and writers. Real, would-be, and make-believe, they were altogether a varied and interesting lot. Morang was full of fine-spun aesthetic theory, but cheerfully willing to accept science fiction as a sister art. He had found generous sponsors; Erskine Caldwell was a houseguest one weekend.

I explored Santa Fe, learning to relish its historic multicultural charms. I went to Morang's parties and other parties, went to Indian dances with Jean and my other anthropological friends. I bought skis and learned to use them—safely at least, if with no real skill. I'd never heard of ski lifts; we climbed the slopes, or sometimes drove to the top, to earn the fun of coming down. Skiing is one of very few athletic activities I've ever really enjoyed.

I fell far enough in love with Jean to think seriously of marriage, and always thought better of it. Partly, perhaps, because she didn't think much of science fiction, which still meant more to me than anything. A larger reason must have been my growing feeling that I had let the analysis break off too soon. As keenly as ever, I still yearned to find a better fit between my need to write and the confused directions of my life.

Later, when I was looking into the early life of H. G. Wells, it struck me that my own essential problem, like his, could be seen as the universal conflict between the individual and society. As I like to phrase it, we are all born naked screaming egomaniacs. Yet, never born alone, we can't exist alone. As the price of survival, the primal ego must accept the folkways it finds, surrendering at least a fraction of itself to the socializing pressures of the family, the school, the law, the church, the job. Life, I came to feel, is an endless series of uncertain compromises between the drives of the self and those unending social demands.

That conflict is the stuff of most fiction. I saw it in Wells, most clearly in the Invisible Man, who defies his world and dies. I think it energized all Wells's early fiction; his later work, done after he made his own successful compromises, is weaker for lack of its drama. At the most basic level, literature works to socialize us—hence all the themes of altruism and self-sacrifice and sense of duty triumphant. At another level, literature can show society killing the self when it claims too much. See Ibsen. My own favorite fictional pattern has become what critics sometimes call the bildungsroman, the story of the individual growing up to discover and establish his right social role. That's the pattern of the best juvenile fiction, and also of Joyce's *Portrait of the Artist as a Young Man.*

That old dilemma, I've come to believe, was my haunting problem then. Groping toward some compromise, I was afraid of yielding too much. If art can be called a function of the ego, it strikes me that the artist can make one of the best possible bargains, winning his place in society through the expression of himself. If science fiction can be called an art, my own precarious success with it had become too precious to risk.

Wrestling with such problems, I turned again to Dr. Tidd, who had set up his analysis in Beverly Hills. His schedule was full when I first inquired, but he wrote in May that I might come on out to talk things over.

17

THE MAÑANA LITERARY SOCIETY,

1940–1941

In Nazi Germany, Otto Hahn and Fritz Strassmann discovered nuclear fission in 1938. Lise Meitner slipped out to Sweden with the news, which was published in *Nature* in 1939. When Enrico Fermi heard it, he suggested that free neutrons from fissioning atoms might fission more atoms. The genie was out of the bottle, though few of us knew it.

In early May of 1940, when I came back to Southern California, it seemed an unspoiled paradise. I loved the lush vegetation, the mild climate, the good smell of the air and the feeling of prosperous peace. All around the point where Marineland is today, nature had scarcely been touched.

Sometimes, after I had begun to find friends, we used to park above the cliffs and climb down them to gather driftwood for a picnic fire above the breaking surf, feeling as totally alone as if we had been the first ashore on the empty beach.

I found an upstairs room in a big house at 1224 Fifth Avenue, then a wide, quiet street walled with tall palms. The rent was low, perhaps fifteen dollars a week, and I made my own economical meals on a hot plate in the room. A cheap lifestyle, but I was used to it. I had the car and at least a little money. I did find friends, and I can look back fondly now at that interlude in Eden.

Dr. Tidd was in a Beverly Hills medical building, at 415 North Camden Drive—a street now changed beyond recognition. He was able to see me twice a week, somehow able to charge me only five dollars an hour. That second year of analysis must have generated less emotion than the first; I don't recall it quite so vividly, but it was still good for me. Certainly, that year was more fun than the first.

I found more friends, most of them through science fiction. My work went better, at least sometimes. In June, Campbell is writing that he likes "Captain Planeteer," but can't take it just now because his inventory is full. *Argosy* did take it, for $140, and ran it as "Racketeers in the Sky."

Another letter from Campbell, dated August 6, requests a novel for *Unknown*. *Darker Than You Think* must have been already written, because just a week later he says it's "a darned good job," which he is accepting at the bonus rate. Five hundred dollars for 40,000 words—the later book version is twice that long. Though books are like children, too different for any fair comparison, *Darker* has always been close to my heart, perhaps because of what it let me say about myself.

Dr. Glenn, the analyst in the story, has hints of Dr. Tidd, and it strikes me now that the novel can be read as a comment on my own inner conflicts as I discovered and grappled with them under the analysis. In the story, Will Barbee is at first bewildered and horrified by the emerging strangeness in himself; at the end, he has come to accept himself as a werewolf. A conclusion I found oddly satisfying, though occasional readers have been appalled. I think it reflects my own growing willingness to accept bits of myself that I had always feared or hated.

In May, Mort Weisinger approved a plot for another *Startling* novel. It went slowly. A wire, dated November 19, asks "Where is promised novel?" On December 13, he is sending the manuscript back with a four-page list of problems—and, to keep me on the job, his promise of $100 in advance.

By January 3 I have his thanks "for a splendid revision" and the rest of the not-very-thrilling $250. It ran in the July *Startling* as *Gateway to Paradise*—the later paperback version, in an Ace double, became *Dome Around America*. It has ideas and images I like, but it's a very minor work, written more to fit Mort's fiction formula than to express my own emotion.

"The Iron God" is another novelette written sometime in 1940. A fumbling effort to do something better. Breuer read an early version and cheered the theme, but the final effect fell somehow flat, perhaps because too little came from anything I had lived. Good markets bounced it; Bob Erisman bought it, at $65 for 13,000 words, to run in *Marvel.*

If Los Angeles was Eden, then I had brought my own serpent. Analysis clarified some of my problems, but it failed to solve them all. After those two novels, my output dried up again. My total income for 1940 was a little under $800; for 1941, very little more. One barrier may have been the same old demon, "unconscious resistance"—it seemed that I was sabotaging the analytic process by not making money enough to pay even that nominal five dollars an hour.

Another difficulty, of course, was the sad fact that I hadn't been born a better writer. Yet another was the mere nature of the creative process—at least as it has always worked or failed to work for me.

Creating a story takes time. In the beginning stages, people and places and the stream of events are plastic, tentative, easy to manipulate. As I live with them through weeks or sometimes many months, meaning flows into them. They gather their own charges of emotion, rising mostly out of the unconscious; many a story problem has been solved while I slept, the answer suddenly clear next morning. As places and people gather reality, major revisions become very difficult. Errors are hard to correct, sometimes impossible for me even to see.

In those old days, writing for a living at a cent a word or less, I had no time to let stories grow. I had to keep pushing. Under less pressure now, I never try to write anything till it's ready; until I believe in the theme and care about the people. In 1982, with *Manseed* finished and sold, and the next novel still germinating, I felt free to try this nonfiction project. Though autobiography may sometimes become creative, it requires a different sort of effort.

Even with production slowing, that year was still good. Ed Hamilton came out to Los Angeles in 1940, perhaps with Mort Weisinger and Julie Schwartz—I remember seeing all three at a tourist court where they were staying. I met Leigh Brackett there. She had just begun to sell; her first story must have been "Martian Quest" in the February *Astounding.*

Maybe not beautiful, Leigh was attractive enough, athletic and bright and engaging; I got a sense of quietly stubborn conflict with her mundane family environment. She had an admirable awe of such old hands as Ed and I were, and we both enjoyed her.

Ed and I drove up to Redwood City for a mildly alcoholic weekend with Price, who still cherished the friendships of his pulp fiction career though he had turned to other means of survival. We went with him to Auburn, out in the Sacramento Valley, to see Clark Ashton Smith—Klar Kash Ton to the *Weird Tales* clan.

He was a lean, tall loner as I recall him, not so talkative as Ed and Price. I was struck with the contrast between his commonplace small-town surroundings and the exotic worlds and mannered language of his fiction. He, too, had almost quit writing by then; he was carving his imaginary monsters into grotesque little figurines. To me, he seemed defeated and pathetic.

At LASFS—the Los Angeles Science Fantasy Society, which used to meet in Clifton's Cafeteria—I encountered more science-fictioneers, fans and pros and such would-be pros as Ray Bradbury, who was still selling newspapers, publishing his own fan magazine, and writing a thousand words of still pretty dreadful fiction every day.

He showed me some of it; I tried to make useful comments, though I can't claim much credit for the gifts he came to reveal. He was still living at home; once he got his mother to make Swedish meatballs for me, and I met his brother Skip.

Walt Daugherty and Russ Hodgkins were active fans. I remember Bruce Yerke, making himself pretty obnoxious with his way of twisting General Semantics into a device for putting people down, a habit that earned his role as model for the corpse in Tony Boucher's *Rocket to the Morgue*. Forry Ackerman was already a Big-Name Fan.

Art Barnes was a pro, writing a popular series for *Thrilling Wonder*. It was the sort of thing Mort loved, the translation of some successful contemporary cliché into a future setting, this time a Frank Buck takeoff about an intrepid girl collecting alien creatures for an interplanetary zoo.

I met John Parsons. An odd enigma to me, he was a rocket engineer with unexpected leanings toward the occult. He

wanted to meet me because I'd written *Darker Than You Think*—
a good many people have taken it more seriously than I ever did;
witches now and then have taken me for a fellow Wiccan.

Parsons belonged to the OTO, an underground order
founded, I think, by the satanist Aleister Crowley. One night
Cleve Cartmill and I were allowed to climb after him into an attic
to attend a secret meeting. The ritual was disappointingly tame.
There was no nude virgin on the altar. Satan was not invoked.

Yet the priest impressed me. He was a lean, dynamic little man
with bright, light blue eyes, driven by a virulent hatred of God.
Talking to him after the ceremony, I found that he was the son
of a British clergyman who must have been the real target of that
savage animosity.

In Pasadena not long ago, walking across the grounds of the
Jet Propulsion Laboratory, I was jolted to see Parsons' name on
a memorial tablet set up to honor the first martyrs to space. He
had written me once about testing multicellular solid-fuel rockets designed after those in my story "The Crucible of Power."
When I first heard about his death I wondered if my own rockets
had killed him, but Sprague de Camp tells me that he dropped
a bottle of picric acid.

The new friend who mattered most was Bob Heinlein. He had
just begun to sell, with "Lifeline" and "Misfit" published in
1939, but he was already among the brightest stars in the
"Golden Age," the decade of exciting innovation that began
when Campbell took over the editorship of *Astounding*.

Science fiction until then had been just another pulp category,
not much different from mystery fiction or war stories or sea
stories except to such fans as I was. Campbell had dazzling
visions to share, and he kindled visions in a whole cluster of
gifted new dreamers: Asimov, Lester del Rey, Theodore Stur-
geon, A. E. van Vogt, and Heinlein himself. Discovering them
and inspiring such adaptable survivors as de Camp, L. Ron
Hubbard, and Cliff Simak, Campbell was making science fiction
something new.

Heinlein's early work was sometimes clumsy, but his ideas
were always exciting and he learned fast. By 1941, he had earned
recognition as Guest of Honor at Denvention. He had a fine
mind and he knew a lot. Alertly critical of the world around him,

he lived the futures he wrote about and he made them live for us. His style was utilitarian, deliberately unliterary but brightened with his own corn-pone humor. I used to feel he was the most truly civilized person I had ever known. Knowing him was one more good chapter in my education.

He and Leslyn, his first wife, were living on Laurel Canyon, up in the Hollywood hills, and I was vastly delighted when he invited me to the little Saturday-night gatherings he called the Mañana Literary Society.

A remarkable group. Cleve Cartmill, crippled from polio, a sardonic but likable newspaperman who knew the seamy underside of Los Angeles politics; later he made his name with "Deadfall," a story that alarmed military security with all it said about how to build a bomb. Cleve was no engineer, and most of the detail must have come from Campbell.

Tony Boucher and Phyllis. Mick and Annette McComas. Sometimes I was allowed to bring Ray Bradbury, though he was still so brash and noisy that Leslyn didn't always want him. Henry Kuttner and C. L. Moore were there now and then. Leigh Brackett. Art Barnes. Sometimes such visiting notables as Willy Ley and de Camp and Hubbard. I remember a fetching redhead named Marda Brown.

We drank a little wine—mostly cheap white sherry—and told shaggy dog stories and recited dirty limericks and talked about science fiction and life in the future and sex and nearly everything.

Legally, Tony was William Anthony Parker White—I think the "Tony Boucher" name was coined to mean "fat check." He struck me, as Heinlein did, as a citizen of a richer, wider culture where I was still a naive stranger. He was a practising Catholic, a musicologist specializing in Gregorian chant, and, as H. H. Holmes, a prolific writer and reviewer of mystery novels. He put our society into his 1942 novel *Rocket to the Morgue*. Heinlein is there as Austin Carter, a chief suspect. Hubbard is D. Vance Wimple and Campbell is Don Stewart. Ed Hamilton and I are combined into Joe Henderson.

Tony had more sophisticated literary tastes than most of us. Both he and Mick McComas became discriminating editors. After the war, Mick and Ray Healy edited the first great science fiction anthology, *Adventures in Time and Space,* a landmark project which began convincing skeptics that science fiction books could sell.

A little later, Tony and Mick persuaded Lawrence Spivak to bankroll a trial issue of *The Magazine of Fantasy.* Soon renamed *Fantasy and Science Fiction,* it had a level of craftsmanship and quality new to the field. Mick resigned in 1954. Tony stayed on as sole editor until 1958. Such later editors as Ed Ferman have held *F&SF* to the same high curve.

In May of 1941, I came to the end of that second year with Dr. Tidd. Yet another, or even several more, might have done me good. I felt half anxious to go on, yet I had managed to fall behind again even with his nominal fees. That may have been the device of a still-rebellious unconscious in search of escape. However that may be, we agreed to suspend the analysis again.

18

CAMPBELL AS COACH,

1941–1942

Hitler had devoured Austria and destroyed Czechoslovakia. On August 31, 1939, he ordered the invasion of Poland. The false peace had ended. Great Britain and France declared war on Germany. Stalin marched east into Poland to meet Hitler, and north against Finland. France fell in 1940. On Sunday morning, December 7, 1941, Japan attacked Pearl Harbor.

Through his first dozen years at the helm, John Campbell was science fiction. Not that his *Astounding* stood entirely alone. Under such able editors as Sam Merwin, *Startling Stories* burst out of its juvenile formulas to become an intelligent competitor. *Planet,* launched as an even more luridly sensational pulp, began featuring fine work by Leigh Brackett and Ray Bradbury. Others came and went, but Campbell always led the pack.

Those were exciting times. Campbell followed no formulas. Sharing his own ideas, he also welcomed ours and generally left us free to work out their fictional consequences. His suggestions were always open-ended, never restrictive. Together, we were all exploring possible human futures—most of them still seeming splendid in those years before the bomb. Though his standard rate was only a cent a word, his top writers got bonuses. Most of us wrote first of all for him, membership in his gifted crew as important as the money. The best stories in the competing magazines were often his rejects.

I hoped to stay on his team.

My father came out for a few days in Los Angeles when my

131

time with Dr. Tidd ran out, and we drove home together. My younger sister, Katie, was a teacher. That summer we took a vacation trip together. I drove her and a girl friend of hers down the new highway through Monterey to Mexico City. Though Mexico was still fascinating, the trip wasn't the fun it should have been.

Leaving Topeka, I had felt an exhilarating emotional release. A sense of escape, delightful at first, though of course it soon proved to be mostly illusion. That rebound didn't happen again, perhaps because I saw too many problems still unsolved. As always, I had too little money, and small frustrations haunted me through Mexico.

My smallpox vaccination made an ugly, slow-healing sore. Sitting in the rain through a bullfight, I got a kink in my neck that stayed with me till Bob Heinlein snapped it out that fall. When we were striking south to Acapulco, savage diarrhea turned us back.

Through the rest of the summer, I worked at home on two more stories for Campbell. "Backlash" was an undistinguished short—short stories have always been hard for me, I suppose because I need space to let people and their problems grow. Without freedom to expand, I'm apt to leave the bones of plot too naked, without flesh enough to live.

"Breakdown" was more successful. A novelette, it gave me room to build the essential illusions of reality and a chance to express things I wanted to say. Campbell featured it, with an impressive Rogers cover, in the first of the few "bed-sheet"-size issues of *Astounding*.

The story sprang from my fascination with Arnold Toynbee's notion that civilizations are super-organisms with life spans of centuries. As I adapted the idea, the life of every culture is its own historic purpose. When the purpose is realized or abandoned, the culture dies—though its individual citizens may survive.

In my story, that vitalizing purpose had been the human conquest of the solar system; with the conquest complete, its destiny fulfilled, the space empire breaks down. I felt a sense of truth in that, and enjoyed the sense of tragic drama. Encouraged by the way it went, I planned a sequel.

I called that *Star of Empire*. It was to carry the same historic theme to a larger stage, picturing the fall of a vast interstellar civilization. By early fall, with pages enough—certainly with content enough—I could see that it was going badly wrong, though the reasons baffled me. Years later Jim Gunn and I finished it together, as *Star Bridge*, but then I had to give it up.

When I confessed my dilemmas to Campbell, he came to the rescue. Of all my tutors in craftsmanship, he was perhaps the best. I saved his letters, which were inspiring instruction. In one dated October 7, 1941—which he typed himself, because Miss Tarrant was busy with make up—he begins by saying that a few of us old hands in the field—he names Ed Hamilton and Doc Smith as well as me—are better writers than we let ourselves be, most of the time.

Citing his own experience, he says his own work had too much of Doc Smith and Ray Cummings until he read some of C. E. Scoggins' Central American stories. "That man had style, he had tricks of writing that were genuine and powerful. . . . I started the Don A. Stuart name and style after realizing what could—and should—be done.

"At present, the strongest science-fiction writers are Heinlein and van Vogt—two brand-new men. Asimov is really pushing upward, too. Reason, I think, is that neither of the first two ever really liked the early scf styles—they were free to roll their own. . . . Asimov, a little later, has actually formed his stuff on theirs. . . . Anything goes, so long as it takes one reasonable premise, one reasonable future background, and expands on those in a coherent, logical manner."

Heinlein and others of the "Heinlein-trained Mañana Literary Society, are pushing out a number of old-timers because they've been trained on that basis. They haven't pushed you out simply because, despite several self-imposed handicaps, you can write. If you'd break those old habits, you'd push several of them out. You're a better writer to start with, and you've had more training."

He analyzes my handicaps. I'm known for a certain type of story, but "the whole manner of science fiction has changed radically." My work has changed, but too slowly. "You have grown from a kid to a man. . . . You are no longer the Jack

Williamson that started writing science fiction at the end of the 20's and got a hell of a kick out of seeing your name and your stuff published. Would the style and presentation of 'The Green Girl' begin to tell the story of 'Breakdown'?

"Fundamentally, I think a 'Don A. Stuart' stunt would help you a hell of a lot. . . . If you gave yourself a clean-cut break, became a wholly new personality—your own, present, fully-developed personality—your whole psychology of approach would be entirely different. Look what that change did for me! When you write as a different person, you half-consciously throw out elements of your old style, so that those super-keen fans won't be able to spot the false whiskers the first time over. You're starting now on a completely new type of material. . . . Start a new—your own present—personality to tell it."

It's Don A. Stuart, he says, who's editing *Astounding*. He needs a new story by December 1. Bob Heinlein has an idea, but hasn't written any of it because he "can't hear 'em talking." If the Japs try to take the Philippines or attack Singapore "you'd better get going full-blast, because Bob won't be writing." (Even with war in the air, his uneasy premonitions fell short of foreseeing Pearl Harbor.)

Answering, I tell him about the analysis. He agrees that it might be a paying venture, but he feels that I really shouldn't want to be helped too much. Except for the one-shot writers, those who succeed are "definitely abnormal personalities. They must be; all normal personalities are gray and uninteresting as a blank fog. They play bridge by the hour when they have get-togethers because they are afraid to think."

I write that I've absorbed a lot of Bob Heinlein's ideas in the long sessions of the Mañana Literary Society. Some of them are going into "Star of Empire." Bob has been commenting on the inadequate social and cultural backgrounds of Doc's interstellar stories, and I hope to do something better.

I write that I've shared his admiration for Scoggins. Along with J. P. Marquand and William Somerset Maugham, he's one of the commercial writers that seem most worth emulating. Maugham is probably the best of the three, but the one with the fewest discoverable tricks. The notion of a pen name is "worth thinking over."

When "Star of Empire" keeps on balking, Campbell suggests that I put it on the shelf for a time. "Forgetfulness" bounced and had to stew in its own juices ten months before he picked it up again and saw how to rework it; "Frictional Losses" took four years and a dozen plots and 100,000 words of writing before "the obvious setup clicked."

Bob Heinlein has finally got rolling on his stalled serial, and Campbell won't need another at once. Commenting that "you'll probably get more and better work done if you quit pushing when things begin to stick," he says I might make my own novel "the chronological background for a dozen or two dozen shorts and novelettes."

Looking for a new name and something entirely new to write, I come up with "Will Stewart" and the idea for a series about the planetary engineers who would "terraform" new planets to fit them for colonization—the word, I think, is my own coinage. He likes the idea and suggests the interesting problems they might meet on contraterrene worlds. "Contraterrene" was the term for antimatter then. Campbell's abbreviation was CT, and I spelled it out, "seetee."

A fine challenge for my engineers. Discovery of the positron had recently proven that seetee must actually exist. It's twin stuff to our common matter, except that signs are reversed, the atomic cores negative instead of positive, orbited by positrons instead of electrons. Remarkably tricky for any human character to touch, because negative and positive charges cancel each other. Seetee and common matter annihilate each other on contact, releasing something like a thousand times the energy of nuclear fission.

The seetee stories, bylined Will Stewart, were almost collaborations with John Campbell. On November 21, he writes a long letter about CT physics. He outlines a story idea he had offered Heinlein, who isn't going to use it because he has "more on hand than he wants to write anyway."

It's about building a CT machine shop on an airless terrene asteroid—terrene air would react with it, lethally. Parts made of

CT steel would be "anchored almost immovably by dense magnetic fields gripping special bed-plate arms that make no contact with T matter." If Heinlein doesn't want the idea, he wants me to try it.

Heinlein doesn't. On December 9, two days after Pearl Harbor, Campbell writes that "conditions have changed somewhat." Heinlein, Hubbard, and probably Malcolm Jameson will be gone to war. "That leaves de Camp, you, and van Vogt as the primary steady writers available." He needs my help, and he's air-mailing a hundred-dollar check for "Conscience Limited," a pretty mediocre short I had written for *Unknown.* Three more pages discuss my planned background for the seetee series.

A January letter comments on my problems about setting up story background. "Heinlein always starts with everything . . . already developed and in common use. He writes a story of the year 2134 as though he were writing for a magazine of 2134. . . . The one and only thing needed by way of explanation is the human reactions of the characters." About books on writing, he comments that Hubbard and Murray Leinster have done good stories deliberately breaking all the rules.

"Will Stewart" turned out three seetee stories in 1942. My only sales that year, they ran to 92,000 words and brought $1,142.50. "Collision Orbit" and "Minus Sign" were novelettes, followed by a serial, "Opposites—React." I rewrote them after the war into a book, *Seetee Ship.*

The serial balked for a time, because I had measles and then because I had begun to feel unhappy with the 4-F status Dr. Tidd had arranged for me. Though he was still doubtful about it, I volunteered for induction. That brought the stalled story back to miraculous life. Writing ten hours a day, I mailed it to Campbell on July 31.

On August 5, I reported at Fort Bliss for active service.

19.
ARMY WEATHERMAN,

1942–1944

Science and technology had been swept headlong on the torrents of war. Mussolini let Enrico Fermi leave Italy to receive the Nobel Prize. Instead of returning, he came to America. Working in that historic lab in a squash court at the University of Chicago, he created the first self-sustaining nuclear chain reaction.

That happened on December 2, 1942. Early next year, strangers from everywhere began turning up in Santa Fe, looking for some hush-hush military project out at Los Alamos. One July night of 1945, a sudden puzzling mistimed dawn burned and died in the sky above New Mexico.

I won't forget that first night in Fort Bliss in 1942, and the old soldier who introduced me to the Army. We sat up late, he and I and several other new recruits, talking in his tent. Even his casual obscenity was a dazzling linguistic revelation. A hard-drinking yardbird who seemed to know no other life, he had sometimes been a PFC or even a corporal, but had always been broken back to the guardhouse. A colorful character, though almost alarming. His world seemed as strange to me as Mars.

Some of my science-fictioneering friends had bad times in the war, but the years as an Air Forces weatherman turned out rather well for me. I enjoyed mastering meteorology, at least well enough to use it. I enjoyed the men around me—shuffled a good many times from one outfit to another, I always found myself among new and dependable friends.

Weathermen. None of us much akin to that grizzled veteran,

we had been tested and selected for certain aptitudes that included math and science. From the Bronx or Wyoming, origins didn't matter. We were all recent civilians; we had enough in common, and we found pride in what we did.

Always quartered with others who had duty at odd hours—flight controllers and communications men—we enjoyed a few precious privileges. Seldom on KP, we were allowed to eat at midnight and sleep in the daytime, when other barracks had to be ready for inspection. I learned, in fact, to sleep with a poker game in progress on the next bed, players sitting on the foot of my own.

The best thing I found in the service was simply a new sense of belonging. Outside the family and the then-small science fiction community, I had commonly felt misunderstood, ignored or excluded. Through the war years, that feeling changed. Our nation was united then, in a way it hasn't been since. Absorbed in the fight to defend it, I felt a new security.

Not, of course, altogether untroubled. The highest rank I reached was staff sergeant. I used to envy officers for all their enormous social advantages, and I felt pretty bitter at occasional second lieutenants who chose me for demonstrations of their new authority, but it was nice to find that pilots cared more about well-based weather briefings than military rank.

Weather hadn't been my first choice. Out of ignorance and folly, I had listed "glider pilot" first, cryptography second. Wiser than I, the military system sent me to Chanute Field, Illinois, to be trained as a weather observer. The course took eleven weeks. Graduated, I came back to the air base at Roswell, New Mexico.

I spent half a year there, reading weather instruments and sending hourly teletype reports and plotting weather maps. We sent coded readings of our own observations and received them from hundreds of other stations. Every six hours, all of them had to be entered in ink on a big blank map of the continent. Eyestraining labor, because the symbols had to be small enough so that all the data from each station could be covered with a dime.

The forecasters analyzed the maps, made their best guesses, and briefed the pilot-training groups. A few forecasters were officers, many just enlisted men. I was eager, of course, to get back to school to learn forecasting.

Here I must make another confession. We were given an advance look at the tests for that advanced training. Such cheating, I discovered, was the only way back to Chanute, because the officers at too many other stations were letting their own men cheat. The tests were difficult, with able and grimly motivated people taking them. A passing paper had to be very nearly perfect.

Even trying to cheat, I failed on the first time around. A student pilot crashed on the runway outside the station while we were taking the test. I could see the flaming wreck from where I sat, three or four men burning to death.

Such accidents weren't uncommon, though we never got any official news about them. I watched the alert crews rushing out too late to save anybody, but the test went on with nothing said about the accident. I was too badly shattered to write a passing paper.

On the second try—with the aid of a good friend who got an advance look at the test one night while he was on duty—I did get back to Chanute Field for twenty-two weeks, from July to November 1943. We studied under heavy pressure, threatened with reassignment back to general duty if we failed. The courses were demanding, and we were pulled out of classes every week or so for a long day of KP, with no time to make up what we missed. I remember posting the list of twenty-seven cloud-type symbols we had to learn on the mess-hall wall, where I could review them when I trotted past with a load of trays.

Yet I enjoyed those months, and I finished with a high regard for the school. Out in the field after graduation, we were able to compete on even terms with the very few men who had earned college degrees in meteorology. It was the only science I had ever learned so well, and I found it absorbing.

Late in 1944 I was back in New Mexico, assigned as a forecaster at Hobbs Army Air Field. It was a four-engine pilot-training school, flying B-17s. We operated around the clock, with a new map for analysis every six hours.

Seen from today, our weather science looks primitive. With no cloud pictures from space satellites, we had to visualize—or try to visualize—everything they reveal so vividly, from whatever clues we could see in the surface data on winds and clouds and air conditions, with occasional hints about the winds and pressure patterns aloft from radiosonde balloons.

A stimulating intellectual challenge, and often an emotional burden. The pilots were student flyers, not yet competent. Like those I had seen burning, a good many were dying in training. With their lives and their airplanes at risk from uncertain weather, I felt keenly responsible.

On each shift, the forecaster on duty carried his new map to brief the group about to fly. Facing any audience had always unstrung me, and at first those briefings were severe ordeals. Here were a hundred or so men in flying gear, all of them officers, many of them inclined to skepticism about any forecast and jittery about threatening weather. Painfully aware of how far they outranked me, I had to tell them as best I could what they could expect aloft and where they could land if they couldn't get back to Hobbs.

I learned to do the job well enough at least to keep it. The group commanders came to trust me. I remember one major who took me out in a small plane for a closer look at a coming cold front after I had advised him to cancel student flights because of it. We found the front, about where I'd said it would be. Landing in the blast of dust just as it hit the station, I got a somewhat closer look than I really wanted.

Now and then I got away from Hobbs on a training flight. Drivers were kind through the war to hitchhikers in uniform; on an overnight stop in California, I could get from Riverside into Los Angeles and safely back again in time to rejoin the flight crew.

On leave, I could hitch-hike home to the ranch without much trouble, though once, when I had stretched my twenty-mile pass too far, an unfriendly first sergeant gave me a few days of extra duty repainting the white rocks laid out to mark the paths around company headquarters.

With my sisters both married and gone by then, and my brother Jim an aircraft mechanic in England, my parents were running the ranch alone. Both in their seventies, they were well and active, proud of all they could do.

I saw Blanche again at Elida when the citizens of that little cow town staged a barbecue and dance in celebration of July 4, 1944. She was there with another man, but only casually, she said; they had come with her brother and his wife.

We danced a good bit and talked about our school days together. She told me something about her children and the shop of her own she had opened just before we got into the war. I enjoyed seeing her, but the dance was soon over and I had to hitchhike back to the base.

Life there wasn't unpleasant. Off duty, I taught a physics class for the weather observers, saw all the movies at the base theater, and drank a little beer at the noncom club. I read more philosophy and wrote a good many thousand words of notes and bits for something I meant to call "Men, Time, and War: An Essay toward a Plain Philosophy." It may have helped clarify some of my own ideas, but it also showed me more clearly than ever that I was no philosopher.

I had nothing published in 1943 or 1944. One short story,

Staff-Sergeant Williamson as a weather forecaster stationed at Hobbs, New Mexico. The picture was probably made in early 1945, not long before I went overseas.

"Cold Front Coming," ran later in *Blue Book*. I was happy to make that fine old pulp before it died, but the story has more meteorology than inspiration. "Unpredictable" was a long article on weather science as it was then; it had to be cleared by military security before Campbell could run it.

He had put me on his free list and wrote several letters full of news about science fiction people, but it was only rarely that I saw anybody in science fiction. Fred Pohl, in 1943, when he turned up as another weather student at Chanute. A few others in late 1944, when I managed to get back East on furlough. The high point of that trip was a visit to Philadelphia.

Sprague de Camp was a navy lieutenant, senior grade—one officer I never resented. Bob Heinlein and Isaac Asimov were civilian scientists at the Navy Yard. Bob was doing aeronautical research, and he showed me his lab—Sprague must have arranged the pass to get me there.

On Saturday, December 2, 1944, with reservations made by Bob, I took the Heinleins, de Camps, Asimovs, and friends of Bob's named Firn out for what Isaac remembers as "a swell steak and potatoes dinner," which he says must have set me back $25. I had forgotten paying for the dinner till I read about it in his autobiography. I don't recall what the dinner cost, but that visit was a fine interlude.

After months of hoping to get overseas, I boarded a C-54 at Hamilton Field, on April 19, 1945, with sealed orders stamped "Do not open until one hour after departure."

Opened, they confirmed the rumor that our little group of weathermen was bound for Tacloban, Leyte, to report on arrival to the Commander in Chief, Southwest Pacific Area. I know the date, because I made occasional entries in a diary while I was overseas—not that I can match Isaac in either memory or documentation.

20.

SOUTHWEST PACIFIC,

1945

Back in 1925, well before the Nazis rose, a seventeen-year-old named Willy Ley had come across a book on rocketry. Two years later he joined a few other such dreamers as I was then to form the German Rocket Society. He came to America in 1935 to campaign here for the conquest of space.

His friend Wernher von Braun stayed behind. More tolerant of Hitler, maybe more willing to take any route toward the stars, he accepted support from the German army. His group was soon testing rockets at Peenemünde on the Baltic. By 1944, their V-2 missiles were falling on London.

The first spacecraft!

The war diary recalls details I'd forgotten. Gertrude Lawrence is on the plane as far as Honolulu with a USO group, and I get her signature on a dollar bill—my initiation into the "Short Snorters." We have a day on Hickam Field, near Honolulu. Kept on alert, we can't leave the field, but I'm delighted with the glimpses of palms and hibiscus and bougainvillea. The tropics have always meant exotic romance, and I'm elated with a sense of opening adventure.

At 1800 hours we take off for Johnston Island, which the diary describes as a sort of stationary aircraft carrier, runway along one side, taxi strip on the other, and buildings down the middle. Before dawn we come to Kwajalein, where I visit the weather station and learn about a typhoon between us and Guam.

We fly around the north fringe of the storm, "through broken cumulus and occasional rain squalls." It's "a magnificent sight to the south, a ragged wall of piled-up cumulus like luminous blue mountains." Guam is hot and rainy. We get there about noon, leave at midnight.

On the morning of April 23, we land on Leyte. The airstrip is on a beach lined with wrecked aircraft that have been bulldozed into the water. We're in a city of tents in a palm grove, the side walls all rolled up for ventilation.

It was cool at dawn, but the air has begun to feel like a steam bath as I write. A Filipino in GI garments too big for him is wandering through the forest of tent poles and ropes, trying to sell a small monkey on a chain. The monkey is eating his fleas and making quick grabs at flies, which commonly get away.

Next day I'm called out for a duty detail that makes a long drive in a GI truck to pack up a WAC detachment that is moving to Manila. An easy day, I report, most of it spent lounging in the furniture we were supposed to be packing. We have chow with the WACs, and they feed us well.

Perhaps I enjoy them a little too much, because I miss our truck back to Tacloban. Luckily, I remember our replacement battalion number, and I'm able to hitchhike back before I'm officially missed. Explanations might have been sticky.

On April 29, my thirty-seventh birthday, we're still waiting for our assignments in the Fifteenth Weather Squadron. I'm discovering new friends in our group; between duty assignments we go swimming or hiking. Some of us are drafted again to load a colonel's household goods for shipment to Manila.

The colonel is sitting with his wife under the tent flap when we get there; they look anxiously on to make sure we don't damage a heavy kerosene-burning refrigerator and then go to a party next door. While we sweat in the humid heat, our lieutenant keeps dropping over for another shot. The general, we hear, has ten cases of liquor to be moved, and a hundred of quartermaster rations.

All of which makes me feel once more that enlisted men get the worst of things, but I enjoy the ride back to camp, even in the jolting GI truck. The full moon is rising in a luminous sky over the hills of Samar. Ships lie in the bay, signal lights blinking. We pass a native cart with a palm-thatched roof, pulled by a water buffalo. Most of the traffic is heavy trucks, but we meet a few GIs in jeeps with their Filipino girls and glimpse a lighted dance hall in a native town. I feel vaguely envious.

In the prison stockade, the bamboo huts look better than our own tents. We see a few nearly naked Japanese. Some 300 in the stockade, we hear, 220,000 buried on Leyte, 20,000 killed since January. Maybe 2,000 still at large, but mostly out of action.

The war here is nearly over, though signs enough are left, and recollections. I talk to our driver. His truck company was sunk —personnel, equipment, service records, and all—on an LST en route to Mindoro. A destroyer picked him up out of the water. With the shrapnel picked out of his foot, he was put ashore and back to work at once.

In an outdoor theater one night, sitting on palm logs and anointed with mosquito repellent, we see *Oklahoma!* Live! The Seventh Fleet band and, I write, "sixteen beautiful girls." I love "Poor Jud Is Dead," and the whole show touches me deeply.

Captain Anderson turns up next day to make assignments. His orders scatter our little group all across the squadron. We've traveled ten thousand miles together, and I'm sorry to be leaving one more set of good companions.

At dawn on May 3, we take off for Biak in another C-46. When I go up for a look at the instruments the pilot tells me that Berlin has fallen and Hitler is dead. We stop for fuel and "good Navy chow" on Peleliu. The pilot points out bomb-torn "Bloodynose Hill," where almost a whole division died, and the field of white crosses. A flag flies at half-mast for FDR, dead since April 12.

I spend several days at Biak, checking out equipment and waiting for transportation. "A pleasant spot, drier and cooler than Leyte. Better chow." Clean hard coral instead of sand, and water enough for showers and laundry. I start reading *Innocents at Cedros* at the service club. "About Veblen. So good I must finish it." Next day I do, but all the years since have erased it utterly. The tropic sights and scents still delight me. At night I can see the Southern Cross. The jungle trees and birds are fascinating, but nobody can tell me their names or anything about them.

I go swimming with a few of the friends still with me. The beaches are beautiful, the water perfect, warm enough and so quiet you can put your hands back of your head to adjust the center of gravity and float forever with no effort at all. Frizzy-haired men come by in outrigger canoes. One waves and says hello when we do. We walk out to a little native village built on piles over the water. A black man in GI shorts stares at us. Two women in sarongs get out of sight.

Nearly everywhere, natives are out of bounds. I guess for good enough reasons, but I'd like to know them better. I envy the officers, with all their freedoms. Even as a noncom, I might have found a tour in the European theater more educational and probably more fun. Yet, indulging that old infatuation with the sea and the tropics, I feel lucky to be here and anxious to reach my duty station.

We leave Biak before dawn on May 7 for Finschhafen in a B-47, a tough little airplane. It has plywood bucket seats for twenty-four men. Hour after hour, we fly along the north coast of New Guinea, which has been the essence of jungle mystery to me ever since I was enchanted by the opening pages of Merritt's *Moon Pool.* Later, some of my impressions went into a novel that Fred Pohl rechristened for its shape on the map. *Dragon's Island.*

"Finschhafen is a beautiful spot." The airstrip lies between the sea and a jungle that looks as thick and dark and strange as Merritt made it. Ice cream at a Red Cross canteen. "The war seems far away." We hear that the world outside is celebrating V-E Day. On May 8, I take off for Bougainville in an Australian B-47. Flying with the Diggers, "there's no nonsense about Mae Wests or safety belts."

We're sent to the casual camp on Bougainville until old friends at the weather station come to rescue us from the threat of KP. They put us up in a screened tent with electric lights and cold beer. Except for the lack of milk and fresh eggs, "the chow is as good as at Hobbs." We talk tropical meteorology, which will offer new problems for me.

Closer now to the war, we can hear big guns in the distance. The other morning a Japanese sniper picked off a pilot landing on the strip. An ominous-seeming plume of smoke drifts down-wind from the green cone of a far volcano. At last, on May 11,

I reach my station on Green Island. It's in the northern Solomons, north of Bougainville and east of New Britain.

"The most beautiful island I've seen. A coral atoll 100–200 feet high, with steep or overhanging cliffs but flat on top and covered with thick jungle. Lagoon deep and clear, some five miles long, reef a quarter to half a mile wide. I'm quartered in a screened, wood-floored tent in magnificent location in edge of forest at lip of coral cliff, some fifty feet above the lagoon."

There's no fresh water, but the rainfall is nearly twenty inches a month; we bathe in rainwater, with helmets for basins. Drinking water is distilled. The swimming is great, but we're warned against jungle rot if we get skin damage from the knife-edged coral.

My duty there begins abruptly. A few minutes after I reach the weather station, the field telephone buzzes. The Marines want weather for the target area on Bougainville. I'm the only forecaster on hand. Blood pressure rising, I look at the map and confer with an observer who has been there longer. "Fortunately the weather was good. . . . I was able to make a forecast that must have verified well enough."

A New Zealand meteorologist begins my initiation. A competent, well-tanned chap in shorts, cheerfully informal. I have to learn six new confidential or secret codes and ciphers, memorize the names and station numbers of a lot of little islands up and down the chain.

I need to know all about the radio communication network and the fighter and bomber groups we're working with, the terrain of the islands and its effect on the weather. How to work up and encode the data from pilot balloons. How to use the teletype and the field telephones. I must remember to drive on the left side of the road and remind myself to convert miles per hour into knots and even learn to speak New Zealandese.

All that looks impossible at first. I note moments of depression. Delightful at first, the tropical climate soon grows monotonous. The beauty of the islands hides a raw hostility. Seen from the air, every jungle beach reveals brutal battles for survival, the winning trees outreaching the doomed to steal light and life.

The islands are mosquito-ridden and malarial; we're all soon dyed a bright Atabrine yellow. DDT is still miraculous, issued to us in pressure bombs; I spray the air inside my mosquito net every night. I hear rumors that we'll soon be shipping out again, to somewhere worse. Life without even a glimpse of women looks pretty limited, and home seems years away. Sometimes I ask myself if giving up my 4-F status had been a blunder.

I've lost contact with Dr. Tidd, who was reporting for active duty in the Navy about the time I was inducted. (He had vanished from the phone book when I tried to look him up after the war, but recently, after a lapse of forty years, people at the Menninger Institute put us back in touch. I was happy to learn that he was still living, retired after a good career. He died late in 1983, before I was able to see him again. I feel a deep debt to him, for all he did to enable me to become whatever I am.)

In spite of such troubled moments, I'm happier and more whole on that jungle island in 1945 than I was when I met him in Topeka. The sense of exotic adventure can still lift my spirits, and even the challenges of tropical weather are themselves stimulating.

The rolling cold fronts I've known all fade out long before they get here. Really severe storms are rare; typhoons never develop so near the equator. Instead, we must watch for squalls in the shifting zone of instability where the trade winds from the two hemispheres converge. The lay of the land is even more important; clouds pile up to drench windward slopes with rain, scatter again in the sinking air to leeward. "Orographic weather."

To study the sites I'll be forecasting for, I go out one afternoon as weather observer on a big flying boat, a PBY "Black Cat." It's a Dumbo mission, covering a strike by fighter planes. We're to attempt rescue if they're forced down at sea. We fly down along the coasts of Buka and Bougainville and circle near Shortland Island, waiting. Happily, there's no hostile action.

The station is here to forecast weather for Marine air groups operating against the Japanese left behind on Bougainville and New Britain, and I ask to join more flights to see the shape of the land. On a medium-level bombing raid, our target is Kangu Hill on Bougainville.

A weather sergeant tells me that a recent mission has run into hot flak there, with two planes hit. The flight forecast is bad— I'm glad it wasn't my own—and we must turn to a secondary target, an airfield where we catch no flak. Watching the endless strings of bombs raining toward the jungle from 16,000 feet, I recall Conrad's cannon firing into empty-seeming Africa.

On another afternoon, I spend three hours in a Marine B-25 over New Britain and the Duke of York islands. Heckling the bypassed Japanese there, we drop six 500-pound bombs on "targets of opportunity" and come in low to strafe huts and fishing boats hidden in the jungle. "Didn't see a moving Jap," but the jungle is threaded with white coral roads. Smoke plumes are climbing from trash fires and we see "hundreds of beautiful gardens—neat irregular shapes in various shades of green—too many to be bombed."

Not a shot is fired at us. Though the Japanese have hundreds of heavy AA guns, they're running out of ammunition. Yet "I was frightened. Tried to keep busy observing and encoding weather, which helped." The strafing runs are thrilling, with tracers streaking into the jungle ahead of us, but the dives have "a tendency to upset my stomach." In spite of the tensions, "there is a beauty in the tropic sky seen from the air that is almost unearthly. Fantastic shapes of cloud, piled up in a blue and incandescent void."

On May 20, I work my first morning shift, which is the busiest, with two weather maps and three written forecasts to do. A nerve-racking day, because "the unforecast arrival of a squall line forced a sudden warning to Air Operations." I worry about the safety of a returning nine-plane strike and the uncertain accuracy of my route forecast for Emirau. Grateful when no disaster happens, I resolve to be tougher-minded. After all, given the state of the art, some forecasts are bound to be imperfect.

Besides work and reading and the wonderful swimming, "there isn't much to do but learn my trade." Discipline is loose enough; men around the area commonly go nearly or completely naked, though the weather officer wants me to wear stripes on duty. I'd like to see more of the natives, 1,200 of them on the other side of the reef, but they're out of bounds. I do get about the rest of the island, exploring abandoned military installations that the jungle is already overrunning.

The war here is winding down. The weather station closes on July 12. Waiting to ship out again, I've managed to visit the native mission. The priest is an alert little man who came out from Maine in 1930; he spent thirteen months behind the Japanese lines on Bougainville. He has scrounged army huts and beds for a school he runs for boys.

Though he's pained by all the GI swearwords his boys have picked up, he welcomes me to mass. We sit on logs on a grassy point that juts out into the lagoon. "Native men handsome in lap-laps. Some native women the same, but some hideous in Mother Hubbards made of parachute silk." Naked children, if they're tall enough, can slip up to nurse while their bare-breasted mothers are kneeling.

I try to follow his pidgin. "One fella good fella tree make him one fella good fella fruit. One fella bad fella tree him make him one fella bad fella fruit. All same one fella good fella make him good, one fella bad fella make him bad. . . . You hide along salt water, hide along cave, hide along bush, one fella big fella way up yonder him find him one fella soul."

The Green Island chapter comes to its close on July 23. A two-hour flight on a SCAT C-47 brings me to Emirau, which is also known as Storm Island or Squally Island. It's north of New Ireland, a little larger and higher than Green, with no lagoon and, sadly, no legal swimming—a marine colonel threatens me with five days in the brig on bread and water for diving into a tidal pool where a couple of men have drowned. I hadn't known it was forbidden.

We're still on Emirau on August 7, which the diary notes as "a day that seems likely to be remembered in history." Just past noon, a breathless weather observer comes to me with the radio news that President Truman has just announced the successful use of an atomic bomb against the Japanese.

21

THE BOMB,

1945

Along the far-off fronts of peace, science kept claiming new ground. By 1943, the nucleic acids were known to be the vehicles of heredity. In 1944, Glenn T. Seaborg and his associates discovered two new elements, 95 and 96. In 1945, while the first A-bombs were falling, Melvin Calvin began revealing the secrets of photosynthesis, a more creative process.

Flying at 31,600 feet at 9:15 A.M., August 6, 1945, the *Enola Gay* toggled Little Man out over Hiroshima. About noon on August 9, only a few hours after Stalin declared war on Japan, Fat Man fell on Nagasaki.

At the weather station on Emirau, when we get there in July of 1945, the war has all but ended. We're quartered in floored tents with electric lights and fed at the New Zealand sergeants' mess.

On August 2, 1945, I write that life here "is perhaps the most easy, simple, and regular that I have ever known. Typical white-man-in-the tropics. Chow good enough. Work not too hard, and it never interferes with movies. They're pleasant, with screen set up against background of palms and flaming sunsets over the sea. Doing some serious reading, beginning to study French, hoping to finish a story."

I've made another flight over Rabaul and Kavieng, taking off at dawn in a Marine PBJ and flying at 10,000 feet. "Pleasantly cool. Sky dark blue above, greenish above horizon. Sunrise touching piles of cloud with red and golden fire. Northern New

Ireland and New Hanover spread out like dark relief maps. Saw gardens, possibly a hulk sunk in shallow water, but no installations."

August 7, the day of the bomb. Buckley, the weatherman who tells me about it, is another science fiction fan. In times of peace, he works for the *New York Daily News*. "Assuming the story to be true," I write, "atomic power threatens to upset the old world in unpredictable ways." Yet "very little excitement created by it."

Buckley and I are perhaps the only men on the island with any notion what the atom means. After we talk it over, I comment, "The ultimate result of this greatest challenge to mankind can be good—man must increase his stature somewhat, as the alternative to self-destruction."

The next entry is dated August 21. "Los Negros, off Manus, Admiralty Islands." After Hiroshima and Nagasaki, the Japanese have quit. I'm island-hopping again, back to the Philippines. At Finschhafen, two days later, I see a woman, "a very pretty WAC." By August 27 I'm back on Biak after another long flight over New Guinea. Five days there, exploring the fringes of the jungle and swapping tales with fellow weathermen together again from all across the squadron.

On the last day of August we take off in a C-47 loaded to 6,000 pounds, twice its ATC limit. Flying all day, with stops at Morotai and Leyte, we reach Manila. Next day, to celebrate the peace, I shave off the little Hitler-type mustache I've worn since we were on bivouac at Hobbs—it has been "a temporary emergency measure."

September 2, the official end of the war, I "spent the day on my cot in the tent in a mud-hole." Half disabled with a cold and dysentery and a few spots of fungus infection, I feel more let down than victorious. I've been doing a job that seemed important. It's done. I'm only a serial number now, dispensable and powerless, lost in the vast unfeeling military machine.

Men over thirty-five may go home on application. I decide to apply unless I'm ordered to Japan, an opportunity I hope for. Waiting, I visit Manila and Corregidor. Appalling damage in Intramuros, but the people "look well-fed, happy, fairly well clothed—many in GI. Most of the younger women very pretty, with a ready smile for the GI—though in five hours nobody approached me about pom-pom. Dozens of sunk ships in the harbor, masts sticking out of the water.

"Corregidor, a depressing display of wasted human handiwork. Broken trees, bomb craters, shattered concrete dugouts. Unexploded shells. An immense gun lying in wreckage of mount. A great deal of shattered rock. Climbed over broken rock into mouth of tunnel. Bits of unburied skeleton in the rubble. Jap foot and leg still in legging and canvas shoe with separate big toe. Stench. Tunnel itself full of fallen concrete and rusting machinery. Dripping water. Turned back for want of light to clamber farther over rubble.

"Power house carved into side of mountain. Huge rooms, black from fire. Immense machines, ruined and quiet—engines, generators. Sounds of water running in dark man-made caves. Rooms where Japs had lived. Piles of seaweed. Straw baskets with rotted and unidentifiable foodstuffs. Rusting tin cans. A great malodorous litter of straw matting, paper, a few Jap shoes, refuse. Machine gun positions, small concrete rooms overlooking beach. Place must have been tough to take."

Riding with friends in a weather jeep, I see a bit of the countryside. We attend a cockfight, a colorful but cruel affair; one wrinkled little man carries his dead cock away, "miserably weeping." One day we set out for Ipo Dam. A guard turns us back because we might alarm the Japanese still hiding around it who haven't yet been coaxed to surrender; they might think we had come out "to send them on their way."

On another expedition we pick up two Filipinos, a second lieutenant and a master sergeant, who tell us they served with the guerrilla forces and as spies, employed on Japanese installations and carrying information about them out to Americans who came to the Visayan Islands. Both have been Japanese prisoners, and they tell of torture.

For seven days and nights, one said, with no food or water, he was hung by a rope around his arms, which were twisted behind his back. In the ordeal, his weight fell from 130 to 100 pounds. The other man shows us charred foundations where relatives and neighbors were lined up, machine-gunned, and burned in their homes by Japanese marines, "from the youngest to the eldest." I salute the officer when we leave him, and he shakes hands with me.

With no apparent chance for Japan, I apply for discharge. Equipment turned in, my service record is checked. I get a battle star for the landing on Leyte—for the KP and labor details there; none for the combat strikes over the Solomons and the Bismarck Archipelago. I wasn't on flying status. Before the end of September, I'm in a replacement battalion with Priority Number 11,999, sweating out shipment home.

The men in our own disintegrating military machine aren't all so admirable as those two Filipinos. Quartered in a tent with seventeen veterans from a supply outfit, I record bits of their talk. "He's got quite a racket. Sells the morphine Syrettes out of navigator's kits for a hundred pesos. Twelve Syrettes in a case." "They sold 120 cases of cigarettes for eighty pesos. That made 9,600 pesos—$4,800—to be split four ways. Just one deal, too."

"The permanent party takes all the Camels and Luckies to sell to the Flips. Distributes the rest to the casuals." "I'm in a little trouble for selling sugar." "The FBI caught a dozen of 'em, selling gasoline and tires."

I hear that the cook where I do KP sells twenty sacks of sugar on a duty night, lights cigars with twenty-peso bills. Walking out of camp one day, I find the .50-caliber machine guns out of a B-17 stacked on the riverbank. Waiting, I suppose, for somebody to pick them up. For what? I decide not to linger or inquire.

Writing again, I try to put all that into a story I call "The Rajah McCarthy and the Jungle Tomato." A somewhat taller tale than any I hear in the tent, satirizing those black marketeers. I'm pleased with it—but it isn't science fiction and it has never sold. Maybe too close to reality, or perhaps it wasn't as good as I thought.

A dreary wait, with nothing good to do. On September 29, I make sick call for the fungus infection. Long lines for bad chow.

Rain keeps falling. The tent leaks and the sticky mud gets deeper. Water is scarcer for showers and laundry.

I record an odd little Freudian lapse. Sitting on my cot in the afternoon, I look at my watch. The time is 2:10, both hands together. Forgetting that I've just come from chow, I think it's still morning, the watch gone wrong, the hands maybe tangled. I set it four hours back.

Later, finding what I've done, I try to analyze the error. I'm being discharged as "overage." I've just read in some magazine that men over thirty are past their prime in both sex and creativity. The lapse involves a pun. The watch—itself a sex symbol—said it was "two" late. Setting it back from afternoon to morning was an effort to turn back the years. But actually, I comment, "I manage a good deal of courage in the face of such ideas." I come of a long-lived clan, and perhaps my own decline will be slow.

On October 27, after a short-arm and a flu shot, we fall out with baggage to be put in "manifest order," grouped by separation center and in alphabetical order by ranks into groups to board the S.S. *Canso* for shipment home.

After an endless day of waiting in the rain, we're trucked to the docks, unloaded, formed again in manifest order, and finally go aboard in single file, answering roll call with given name and middle initial. Get chow about 1800. Exhausted, feet aching, I hit the sack in Hold 3, second bunk from the top and fourth from the bottom.

Next morning, to avoid KP, I volunteer for mess-hall guard duty from 0800 to 1200 every day. "Post No. 15. Special orders, sir, to keep order in chow line, see that men wear shirts, keep unauthorized persons from passing through hall."

Homeward bound, "I feel a little better, physically and spiritually." My guard job puts me at the head of the chow line, and the duty is "mostly nominal. Spend most of the time sitting on a box at mess hall door, reading." Salt-water showers. The hold was at first hardly endurable, overflowing with sweaty men and too hot for any clothing, but I'm getting used to it.

Later, after we're at sea, I somehow meet the first mate. "A lieutenant commander. A nice young chap." He shows me the gear on the bridge, tells me about the ship. "Troop transport. Single eighteen-foot screw, turning 85 rpm. Average around twelve knots. Could make twenty knots when new, now pretty well shot."

Until November 1, we make no knots at all. Lying at anchor in the harbor, we heard rumors about the delay. We're still loading water. A steam pipe has burst and needs repair. At sea at last, we make around 300 miles a day.

I watch the North Star, higher every night. We begin to meet cold fronts. Sea sometimes rough; I lie flat a good deal but don't get actually sick. Heat rash and fungus go away. I'm reading *Tristram Shandy* and Canby's life of Whitman. Writing a few more shorts. "A Doll's Lullaby"—all I recall is the title. "The Fly Killer," a more successful effort, was finally published as "The Cold Green Eye."

"The whole experience is rather like a long convalescence. Dull, with some discomfort and a great deal of time to kill. Time to plan things to do, with a rather sinister advantage—plans can't yet be tested. Easy to plan a good novel to do when I have a typewriter, but it won't be that easy to write. . . . Stew for supper. Chow getting stale, monotonous taste. Sea still rough, ship crashing heavily into waves. Movie tonight for officers only; I'll continue reading Whitman."

Before dawn on November 21, I'm wakened by cheers on deck. We're steaming up the Columbia River to dock at Portland. "Curious that sight of a milk wagon should bring tears to my eyes." At 0900, a band and the Red Cross arrive to welcome us. WAC truck drivers take us nine miles across the river to Vancouver Barracks. Cool air smells of pines.

"At 11:30 fell in chow line for wonderful dinner. Big steak, lettuce and tomatoes, pie and real ice cream. . . . A GI latrine seems strangely luxurious. Overheard remark, 'Gee, it's nice to be in a barracks again.' "

Two long days and nights on the coaches down to California. A civilian again, discharged at Fort McArthur, November 27, 1945. Told that 20 percent of us will reenlist within twenty days. Hoping to do better, I opt not to join the reserves.

The diary ends: "Now, outside, the competition looks a bit discouraging. Housing shortage. Strikes will make it hard to buy a car. Very hard even to get stripes and patches sewed on my uniform. The moral is that I finally did it myself."

22.

UNCERTAIN CIVILIAN,

1946–1947

Operation Crossroads, in July, 1946, was a test of two atomic bombs against a target fleet of some 70 ships anchored in Bikini lagoon. The underwater weapon lifted a million tons of water in a mile-high column, and left the whole lagoon radioactive.

Here at home, that same year, Eckert and Mauchly completed ENIAC. The first general-purpose all-electronic computer, it was a thousand times faster than anything before, yet its vacuum tubes were obsolete by 1947. Engineers in the Bell Labs had invented the transistor.

A free man again, I looked up Leigh Brackett. She seemed pleased to see me, and we went out together. Never quite in love, we were fond of each other. She had written affectionate letters now and then through the war. Now I found her life changed as much as mine. A successful film writer, she was doing scripts for Howard Hawkes, talking of Bogart and Bacall and William Faulkner.

Always good with tough guys and fast dramatic action in settings drenched with uncommon color, she had worked with Faulkner on *The Big Sleep*. A quietly courteous Southern gentleman, she said; he drank a lot and kept to himself and turned in very few pages. Leigh wrote *Rio Bravo* and other fine films, down to *The Long Goodbye*. Her last work, finished only a few weeks before her death, was the script for *The Empire Strikes Back*.

Hollywood success had moved her, professionally and financially, far beyond our old world. Or so I felt. Maybe mistakenly,

Leigh Brackett and E. Hoffmann Price, 1956.

because she kept on writing fine science fiction. Her cheering letters followed me back to New Mexico and kept on coming through those first uneasy civilian months when I needed cheer. I was jolted when she wrote, late next year, that she and Ed Hamilton were engaged.

With no firm plans for anything except to write again, I had vaguely intended to live in California. Now it no longer seemed quite so close to paradise. The war had scattered too many old friends. Too many cars were roaring too fast down streets not planned for them, and smog had begun to taint the good-smelling air.

Back in New Mexico, I stopped off at Santa Fe to see Jean Cady. She was married. The Santa Fe I had known, like prewar Los Angeles, had vanished into memory. I came on home to the ranch and found my parents well, proud of having been able to keep the ranch going. My brother Jim was soon back from England, with his own war tales to tell.

Without the diary, I don't have accurate dates or documentation, but learning to be a civilian again was slower and harder than getting used to the army. A new crisis, as I see it now, in my long search for some endurable compromise with society.

The army had been good for me, granting me a warm acceptance into group after group of my fellow weathermen and a fulfilling role in something that mattered to me and sometimes to others.

That was over. Returning to the typewriter in that lonely little cabin, I soon felt trapped again in the social isolation I had been fumbling to escape. The civilian role I needed was more demanding than the military and not offered quite so readily as the uniform had been. It struck me later that the humanoids came out of that frustration.

They're the small, human-shaped robots in the first new story I tried to write. Created by men of good will in the aftermath of a future nuclear war, they're designed to save us from our own too-savage aggressions. They are governed by a Prime Directive: "To serve and obey, and guard men from harm."

The story problem is that their controlling computer interprets that injunction with the literalness of all computers, protecting most people far too well. All freedom of action is lost, even to drive a car or sew with a needle or make unsupervised love.

True at least for my unfortunate protagonists. Frank Ironsmith, a character who seems ambiguously sinister to them, is allowed to stay free because he displays none of their too-hazardous aggressiveness.

None of that was clear to me when I wrote the story, but I've come to see that those conflicts and emotional ambiguities were metaphors for my own. The humanoids, it strikes me now, are symbols for society. My rebel heroes stand for my own rebel self, an ego that wants total freedom too much to compromise.

The resentment at frustration by a ruthless benevolence must have come in part from my own early childhood, perhaps the times on the Mexican ranch when I was kept shut up in my crib because my mother was afraid a scorpion would sting me if she let me free to crawl on the ground.

The Army had been nearly as rigidly simplistic as the humanoids. Out of it now, and no Ironsmith myself, I had to make some kind of truce with more baffling civilian complexities. I wanted to write. On that, as stubborn as my doomed heroes, I refused to compromise. Yet the writing went slowly, delayed at first by a series of surgeries—blood sacrifices, perhaps, to my own cruel gods.

In 1946 I entered a VA hospital for repair of a hernia I must have got lifting helium cylinders when we were packing weather gear to leave Emirau. Still in bed from that, I had a bowel obstruction caused by old adhesions. I'm grateful to the nurse who let me cling to her hand through an endless night of agony. Grateful too for penicillin, which finally made the difference.

That night became a sort of watershed. Until then, I had felt almost immortal. Maybe even literally; Arthur Clarke used to say —rather more than twenty years ago—that if we could live another twenty years, advancing medical science could let us live forever. Lying there, groggy with narcotics that didn't do much, I was surprised to find myself whispering the Lord's Prayer. I knew I was dying, and the awareness of mortality has been part of me since.

At last, sometime next morning, my doctor turned up. He ordered X rays, called my relatives, and did an emergency bowel resection. Which of course I did survive, though the rupture soon came unstuck, and unstuck again after a second repair, and I had surgery again "for liberation of adhesions". Which left even more adhesions as well as other persistent troubles, some of them perhaps psychosomatic, because they weren't helped by treatment for amoebic dysentery. Altogether, a darker chapter than I enjoy recalling.

Another writing handicap, I suspect, was my federal guarantee of self-employment income. Twenty dollars a week for a year, for every week I didn't earn that much. In spite of good intentions, that dole became an insidious bribe not to produce.

But the bomb, I think, was the overriding reason. The long black shadow of the mushroom cloud had fallen over all of us in science fiction. Sooner, I think, than it touched most people, because we understood it earlier. It put a dark stop to the age of wonder as I had known it. Science, before, had been revealing total truth, or seeming to, and unlocking splendid power. Suddenly now the truth had become too terrible to tell, the power too much for us to manage.

No blame exists. Not for the builders of the bomb. Nor for the men who used it. The bombs on Hiroshima and Nagasaki did unthinkable things, but conventional firebombs had already killed more civilians in Tokyo than the atom did anywhere. In fact, those two A-bombs must have saved many more Japanese lives than they took. They ended the war. With the Russians coming, they probably saved Japan from being partitioned into another Korea. Certainly they saved a lot of American lives. For all I know, my own.

I've always felt that Oppenheimer blamed himself unduly. The nuclear secrets lay waiting in nature; they might easily have fallen into worse hands than his. The means of power will always be alluring. Struggles for survival will go on, as surely in the human future as as through our evolutionary past.

Fission bombs and fusion bombs won't be the last unthinkable weapons. Toward utopia or racial death, science must keep on probing because of what it is and what we are. Good or bad, new technologies are seldom uninvented. If we're to survive, we must learn to cope with the demons we create. "Man must increase his stature somewhat, as the alternative to self-destruction."

Through those first anxious years, my own hopes were thin. In the forties, I expected nuclear holocaust perhaps in the fifties, surely in the sixties. It hasn't happened. So long as it doesn't, we can hope to grow into what we must become. Even if nuclear fireballs rise again, the germs of civilization will probably live on. Perhaps with dreadful lessons learned.

In spite of the surgeons and still on the GI dole, I limped slowly back into civilian life. Jim had kept his car. We found tires for it and went out again into the neighborhood, finding nearly all the girls we had known were already married. Though new cars were hard to come by, a friend of ours sold me his not-very-old one that summer, a bright-red Ford.

In another concession to the social machine, I joined the Masonic Lodge—which faced me with an abrupt crisis of belief. Asked, in the initiation, in whom I placed my trust, I couldn't quite answer "In God." I did find myself able to say, "In a supreme being." With no definition of that demanded, I was admitted.

Perhaps I might have answered that I put my faith in science, but that would not have been altogether true. Where science and dogma conflict, I do trust science, yet I think there is a point of no conflict. Science is illuminating a rational-seeming universe, fitting fact after fact into the most awesome wonder of all. Creation.

Year by year, more and more converging lines of evidence from field after field seem to show all existence formed by natural processes from one exploding super-atom. Or—and here the wonder grows—perhaps there was never any creation. Perhaps our cosmos simply stops expansion in its own deliberate time to fall back into another super-atom, which then explodes once more in a cycle of collapse and rebirth with neither ending nor beginning.

Full of such challenging uncertainties, science can never tell us everything. The mystery of existence is still a mystery, however far we push it back. Even conceding that the whole universe has emerged from the detonation of a single dimensionless particle, maybe in infinite repetition, the potential for all we are and all we know must somehow exist in that original unimaginable burst of fire and dust.

Wonder enough.

Rationality must have limits. Since the analysis, I try to rank emotion equally with reason. The Lord's Prayer, that night I lay dying, brought a good feeling, even with no belief. Later, when friends in the ministry assured me that the church doctrine is not impossibly demanding, I was able to join Blanche in the Methodist church.

Never a very orthodox member, I've never found convincing evidence of conscious survival after death—or of any sort of personal survival except through such words as these. I've never felt aware of any God concerned with what I do or don't. In fact, I'm always tempted to distrust organized churches as more or less parasitic.

Yet I'm no enemy of faith. Born animal, we must be made human, transformed into social beings. Our culture has to humanize us. Religion does a lot of that. Even as purely symbolic, worship is our most enduring enforcement of the claims of others, of all mankind, upon ourselves. It is also the most powerful assurance that we don't stand utterly alone.

People do need devotion to figures greater than themselves.

The need must be inborn. Though the notion might pain a creationist, religion itself must be one more fruit of natural evolution, persisting because our gregarious kind needs strong leadership in the Darwinian struggle for survival. The strength of any group, family or social, business or military, depends on its leaders, and God is the ultimate commander.

Commonly, feeling no urge to attack the beliefs of anybody else, I've kept such reservations private. For myself, I was moving when I could to become a social human being. The symbols of religion were and are a part of my inheritance, foundations of the whole social system I was growing slowly to accept, though my own interpretations would please few theologians, and fundamentalist evangelism irks or offends me—as what I've written here might offend my fundamentalist friends.

Back to writing, after perhaps too much personal philosophy. When I was able, there on the ranch in 1946, I began retyping the little ironies I had brought back from Luzon. They didn't sell. Not then. When I invented the humanoids, they baffled me again. I had taken them at first as just another story problem, antagonists for my heroes to beat. The trouble came when I found that they couldn't be beaten.

They're the "perfect machines," as my story notes define them, perfect in the sense that they do what they are designed for, which is to protect mankind from himself. To do that, they must defend themselves from human meddling. I worked a couple of months before that discovery balked me. Reviewing what I had done, I found a theme that appalled me. The best machine is the worst machine.

Depressed, I put the unfinished draft aside to try something brighter, about a really good machine. That story was "The Equalizer," a deliberately optimistic reversal of that disturbing theme to show another new technology that really does increase moral stature. The equalizer is a simple new source of free and unlimited energy, which also arms every individual with an absolute weapon. My people, liberated from all tyranny, use its power to create and defend a new and better sort of civilization. The equalized individual can defy society.

John Campbell bought the story for two cents a word, $420, my first postwar sale. It ran in 1948 in what used to be *Astounding*

—he had shrunk and dimmed the adjective on the cover and made the *Science Fiction* bolder.

Cheered, I turned back to the darker side of the technological coin. Replotting the story of the humanoids as a novelette, not a serial, I found a new point of view and a way toward better dramatic unity, with the span of action cut from years to weeks and the theme made explicit—though it still appalled me. I called the story "Folded Hands," because the perfectly efficient humanoids leave no function at all for human hands. Campbell took the story. Changing the title to "With Folded Hands . . . ," he suggested a sequel, ". . . And Searching Mind."

The bomb hadn't hit him the way it had me. Still the cannily indomitable Scot, he thought he saw how to beat the humanoids. Men forced to fold their hands might develop the mental powers Joseph Rhine was looking for in his parapsychology lab at Duke, Campbell's alma mater. No believer in ESP, then or now, I read a couple of Rhine's books and wrote the serial—later revised into *The Humanoids*, my most successful book.

The ending became a new problem. If the humanoids really were as perfect as I saw them, they couldn't be stopped. If humanity could master new powers of the mind, the humanoids could do the same thing more efficiently. The novelette had said perhaps not exactly what I wanted to say, but what its own premises demanded, a theme I felt too deeply to let it be denied in any optimistic ending.

What I tried was a new version of the old one, equally tragic to me, but seen from the viewpoint of people brainwashed by the ever-cleverer humanoids to be happy about it. The result was ambiguity; every reader and reviewer seemed to see it differently. Which may be just as well.

The conflicts are real enough—terribly real—between our inner selves and what our changing worlds require. Real, and never well resolved. Our technological crisis presents dreadful new dimensions of uncertainty with no pat solutions. I like for a story to ask some vital question. Commonly, that's enough. Fictional answers seldom seem final.

Campbell's detractors have accused him of dictating theme and content. It's true that his beliefs were strong and increasingly in conflict with the ultra-liberal attitudes of a younger generation. True, too, that I had shared a good many of his prejudices. Yet even when I didn't, his comments were never demands. The humanoid victory didn't trouble him.

After the novelette came out, he wrote that it was "getting a strong and very good reaction from the readers. It is seldom that a good story with a tragic ending appears in *Astounding*, and the futility of 'With Folded Hands . . .' seems to have affected the readers strongly. You are one of the few writers who can do that well and I suggest that you keep that in mind in doing things for us. Where you have a unique strength it's worth your while to use it."

His letters were full of creative suggestions for the serial. Rhine was claiming evidence for telekinesis. If the mind could control rolling dice, Campbell wrote, it could also control the disintegration rate of the unstable potassium-40 atoms in the human body, turning men to bombs. He came back from Boston with news from a Manhattan Project physicist about the neutrino, which was still merely fascinating theory, not actually observed for another decade.

The serial was finished in the early summer of 1947. The GI dole had run out by then, but Campbell's check was something better—$1,366, at two cents a word. Good money then, at least for me. Yet I didn't start another story. Groping toward some more fulfilling lifestyle, I left the ranch to take a newspaper job in Portales.

23

BLANCHE,

1947

At Los Alamos, Robert Oppenheimer had led the team that built the A-bomb. Haunted after the war by what he had done, he tried to get the danger contained. In 1946, at his urging, the United States proposed the international control of atomic energy through the United Nations. The wartime allies already at odds, the Soviets rejected this proposal and pushed their own nuclear research. The United States established the AEC with Oppenheimer as an adviser. When the British found themselves unable to support Greece and Turkey against Soviet pressures, American aid was offered under the Truman Doctrine. The Cold War had begun.

The editor of the *Portales News-Tribune* was Gordon Greaves, now a fellow veteran who had spent most of his own war on the Chinese end of the Burma Road. When I talked to him about some of my perplexities, he offered to hire me as wire editor. Though the beginning pay was only $35 a week, I accepted. Newspaper work had always appealed to me, and I was keen to try another way of life.

Portales has been my home since then, and Blanche's since 1931. It lies on the edge of the great Ogalala aquifer, a vast gravel bed washed down from the Rockies in the geologic past and saturated with pure water that used to flow from springs and artesian wells in times before modern pumps began to suck it dry.

A few miles north of where the town is now, one spring ran for a good many thousand years into Blackwater Draw. Giant bison used to water there, Columbian mammoths and prehistoric horses and camels, along with the dire wolves and saber-toothed tigers that preyed upon them. Flint and bone tools and weapons date the arrival of the first men some 12,000 years ago, deadlier predators who exterminated all the rest.

Slow climatic change dried up the spring. With no permanent water, there were only nomadic hunters ranging here for many thousand years, in wet seasons when rains had filled the playa lakes. Tewa Indians guided Coronado across the Llano Estacado—the "staked plain" named perhaps for stakes set to mark his route across the empty prairie, perhaps for the stake-like yucca stalks, perhaps for the palisaded cliffs below the cap-rock around the rim.

Alexander Pike came through with a group of trappers in 1832. Captain Marcy, here on a survey trip in 1849, called the Llano Estacado "the great Zahara of North America . . . where no man, either savage or civilized, permanently resides." By 1864, government supply wagons were coming up the old Fort Sumner Trail from Colorado City.

"Los Portales," a watering place on the trail, appears on a map of Texas published in 1876. The Spanish name seems to have come from the gate-like or porch-like limestone ledges above the spring and the cave that was once the hideout of Billy the Kid. The Indians killed a buffalo hunter as late as 1877, but such men as John and George Causey kept up the slaughter till the great herds were gone, along with the nomadic Comanches whose subsistence they had been.

The buffalo gone and the grass grown tall, the Causeys turned to drilling wells. The windmill opened the plains to year-round settlement. Ranchers strung barbed wire and fought for water with their buffalo guns. Jim Newman, crowded out of Texas in 1893 by the XIT, drove three thousand head of cattle to Portales Spring to establish the great DZ ranch.

The railway, built north from Pecos, reached Los Portales in 1898, fourteen years before statehood. The town was wildly Western for its first few years, saloon keepers serving mounted men, with only ridicule for pedestrian Eastern drummers who didn't like being jostled by the horses.

The nesters followed fast with their Bible Belt morality, their schools and churches replacing the whorehouses and saloons. The town went dry. It stayed dry, legally at least, until a few years ago, though I can recall only two or three people I really knew to be total abstainers. Old notions still die hard; most of the hostesses I know still require unwed couples to steal from room to room in the dead of night if they want to sleep together.

Portales is still small: some ten thousand townsfolk and four thousand students at Eastern New Mexico University. Its future looks uncertain. Though it's a trading center for a wide ranch area, most of its commercial life has come from irrigation. Cheap shallow water has fed abundant crops of yams and peanuts, milk and beef, alfalfa and cotton and grain, too often grown only for storage at taxpayer expense under government loan. But wells are already failing, and the water in the aquifer will take geologic ages to replace. Assigning water rights, the state engineer looks only forty years ahead. After that, the new Zahara.

Happily, not quite yet. Though new students from the East used to call it "stickville," Blanche and I find Portales a good place to live. We are well rooted here. I've known it since those rare boyhood visits when we used to stay in the wagon yard. Though the pioneers are gone, the old frontier neighborliness is still alive. I like knowing the people I see every day at the post office and the bank and the grocery store.

The university brings stimulating people and more cultural events than we have time for. I enjoy the semi-desert climate and the air still good to breathe. Though drunken drivers sometimes run amok and Hispanic youths are prone to knife one another in the cultural rituals of machismo, other crime is still relatively rare. Until recently, when an arsonist alarmed the neighborhood, we didn't lock the house.

Blanche's family got here in 1906, well ahead of my own. She's a native New Mexican, born in 1909. Her father, Willis Slaten, came from Tennessee. Her mother, Janet Bell, was a Kansas-born Scot. They met in Texas. Married in 1904, they moved farther west in 1906 to settle on a New Mexico homestead some ten miles from the one my father claimed a few years later.

They had known hard times. Willis was twelve when his father died. With six sisters and his mother surviving, he quit school to head the family. Here in New Mexico, even on better land than ours, survival took determination. In the dry years of 1918–1919, he went away to work in the Arizona copper mines, as my own father did, while Janet and the kids ran the farm.

They came into Portales in the late twenties, I think because they wanted no more of the schoolhouse feuds, and by 1947 the Slaten family was solidly established here. Willis had his own seed and coal business, and Janet had become a respected matriarch in the town society. Blanche's three brothers were prospering businessmen, all in Portales. Her younger sister, Berwyn, had recently married Harvey Forbes, an air forces navigator retraining for dentistry.

Blanche owned her shop by then, retailing clothing for infants and children. She lived in a little house behind her parents' dwelling, built partly with her own hands. Keigm was still at home, a high school junior and a star athlete. Adele was recently married and happily pregnant.

I came into town on the last day of June, 1947, rented a room from Gordon's mother, and went to work for him on July 1. The very next week, I fell into a trap. A lively little woman named Leona Mehrens had a beauty shop in a back room at Blanche's shop. As I heard the story later, Leona had been trying to match Blanche with a man she didn't care for. When Gordon announced that I was on his staff, Blanche asked Leona to invite me sometime when she was having a party.

At that point, while Blanche was waiting on a customer, Leona called me at the news office to invite me to a picnic planned on the instant for that same night. Unaware of any plot, I accepted. The date was July 8—I kept the scrap of teletype paper on which I noted the address. I arrived in a suit and tie. Not quite the right garb for a picnic, but that didn't derail the scheme.

When we had eaten, Leona suggested we play some poker. The chips belonged to Blanche, and I drove her to pick them up. Keigm was playing softball that night, and she suggested that we come back by the diamond to watch the game for a while. Which we did. Before the evening ended, I was captured.

A willing victim, held not by any sudden blaze of passion but by old friendship and new affection. Outside of science fiction, Blanche and I had a great deal in common, and she was tolerant enough of my addiction to that. After the picnic we were together almost every evening. She insisted on a little delay, but we were married on August 15, in her parent's home.

New as my job was, Gordon cheerfully gave me a week off for the honeymoon. We drove into the Colorado Rockies and stopped in Denver to see Berwyn and Harvey. When we got back, I gave up my rented apartment and moved in with Blanche and Keigm.

My life was changed in ways too sweeping to be easily described. I had been a sometimes cynical spectator at the human drama, groping now and then out of isolation toward a role of my own to play. More than anything else, the marriage made me a participant, sometimes clumsy—sometimes uneasy, but at least a bit player. From the time I arrived overdressed for that picnic, Blanche became my social coach and mentor. I still depend on her.

We had both been too independent too long to expect any mystic fusion of souls, and I suppose there are parts of ourselves we can never share. I've heard Blanche say she will never let anybody hurt her again, I imagine because she has been hurt too cruelly.

My own habits of solitude were too old and strong to be completely broken. Writing is a solitary occupation. A few such couples as Catherine Moore and Henry Kuttner have merged their work into something better than either had been doing alone, but that seldom happens. Blanche works with me now in many useful ways besides keeping house: she reads proof and answers the phone and keeps the calendar of what I am to do. I never expected her to become a literary collaborator.

Though of course there are tensions between us, they have seldom been painful. We can always talk about them. I try not to be entirely selfish, try to understand and compromise. So does she. She has been patient and forgiving. We have have always been in love, with a great deal to share.

She has been a good companion, and I've never had regrets. Though her own life had sometimes been difficult, I've found her generally happy, stoic enough through occasional adversity, and reasonably tolerant of my habit of absence to other worlds and times. She's a practical, down-to-earth person, full of sympathetic generosity and fine common sense, facing problems with cheerful good humor. Devoted to Keigm and Adele, she had raised them well.

Adele soon made me a grandfather. A wonderful person; we've always loved each other. Her husband is Melvin "Lefty" Lovorn. He has been a bread salesman, a builder, a realtor. They live near us now, and we enjoy them. Their children are Neil and Karla. Neil went through college on athletic scholarships and became a Texas highway patrolman. He's still playing the same hard game now against car thieves and speeding truck drivers. Karla, our first granddaughter, is a lovely person, private, sensitive, and independent; for the past few years she has been teaching English to young Navajos.

Keigm never seemed to resent another man in the house. In spite of my old bias against athletics, we were always good friends. When he called me "Jocko," it was in good humor. A fine athlete, he was a star on the basketball team when it won the state championship.

He entered college and left it during the Korean War to become a navy frogman. Later, when pressed, he could talk about being dropped into cold water off the coast of North Korea, uncertain whether or not he would be picked up again. Home from the war, he finished college, married, and became a coach and teacher in California.

Welcomed into the Slaten family, I met another world new to me. They were a close-knit group, given to gathering for frequent big meals. I was never really keen for those family feasts, the women toiling too long to cook and serve them and clear the table and wash the dishes afterwards, while the men dozed through TV football games, but I always felt warmly received.

My own family was delighted with Blanche. Jim was taking charge of the ranch. A precarious and sometimes desperate enterprise during my childhood, it has grown more profitable under his management, new acres added and range practices improved. My parents finished their lives there with him, weathering the years better than most, comfortable and I think happy. Blanche and I drove out for frequent Sunday visits while they were alive.

People have sometimes asked why we still live in Portales, but I've never wanted to leave it forever. We've seen a good bit of the globe together, but we've always been glad to get home again. Our county is still a small community where everybody knows everybody else—though with my memory getting fuzzy and my mind often off in space, I see many friends whose names I can't call.

After a couple of years, we bought a lot and built a house of our own. It stands on the old Goodloe farm, where Blanche says she used to work in harvest, gathering tomatoes and crating sweet potatoes for ten cents an hour. I used my own small savings. We got a FHA loan—in those pre-inflation days the interest rate was 4½ percent and our beginning payments on a twenty-year loan were $56 a month. Willis loaned us $6,000 to finish the project. With no contractor, I took a few months off to work with the carpenters, driving more nails than they considered necessary. I know the place is solidly built.

Recently renovated, with new shake shingles, new furnaces, new kitchen, and retiled baths, it seems better than ever. The office-library-den was big enough for two squares in those old days when we were square dancing; it's crammed now with books and files and desks and word-processing gear. There's a large enough yard, which I still find time and energy to keep myself, with blue spruce and maple and aspen and pecan trees grown tall since we set them out. We're happy here, and we plan to stay as long as we're able.

Blanche likes people, and she enjoyed her business. Cheerfully—and wisely, considering the uncertainties of authorship—she kept it until ten years ago. It had grown before she closed it, from a very small beginning; as her young customers grew older, she bought larger and larger sizes for them.

Yet most of the time it was a one-woman enterprise, except for extra help during business seasons. When she couldn't leave at noon, I used to bring in a box lunch so that we could eat together. The tenth of the month, with all the bills to pay, was sometimes a budgetary crisis. I used to run errands and make showcards. When grandchildren began arriving, she outfitted them generously from the shop.

She had her own circle of friends, who generously adopted me. I remember frequent large parties on Saturday nights. For a time we were square dancing four nights a week. I learned to play bridge, though never very well; I couldn't help feeling that the time and attention might have been better spent with a book or at the typewriter.

She wanted to have more children for me. A generous offer, which I felt reluctant to accept. Keigm and Adele were becoming dear enough, and science fiction still meant so much that I was hesitant to give too many hostages to fate.

I enjoyed the newspaper job. It was yet another social stage, with another bit part for me to learn. Gordon was a fine teacher of journalism; far better, I think, than most college instructors. Many of his trainees have moved on to bigger papers and good careers.

After a few months, however, with the novelty of the job wearing thin, creation began to look more alluring than reporting. With my first real book in print and selling well, I was anxious to get on with the next. Though Gordon offered to raise my pay, I apologized and went back to science fiction.

24

BOOKS INTO PRINT,

1948–1950

The unfolding secrets of the atom were not all ominous. It promised peaceful power. Willard Frank Libby had turned from the problems of separating out weapons-grade uranium to revolutionize geology with his process for dating once-living objects from the carbon-14 they contain. Through the Marshall Plan, America was spending billions to revive Western Europe.

Oppenheimer had fought Edward Teller's campaign to develop the H-bomb, but Truman overruled him. The Cold War reached a warm climax with the Berlin blockade. NATO was established in 1949. The Communists were conquering China. Alger Hiss was convicted of perjury in 1950, and Joe McCarthy was running rabidly wild.

Science fiction had changed, grown far more somber since the bomb. The pulp world where it was born was dying, starved for paper during the war, later displaced by radio and TV and comic books and paperbacks. Science fiction survived, growing up to reach new readers and no longer merely pulp. Most of its first fans had been captured in their teens. They were older now, maybe wiser, grown perhaps too critical of technological progress since Hiroshima.

Slowly winning new recognition, SF was getting into books. Hardcovered science fiction had been limited to occasional novels by such mainstream figures as H. G. Wells and Aldous Huxley and Arthur Conan Doyle. My own pulp work had seemed consigned to oblivion, destined to disappear with the crumbling magazines that contained it. Now, certainly to my surprise, fans who remembered those old pulp serials began reviving them.

Even before the war, such eager fans as William Crawford and Conrad Ruppert had produced a few books, Crawford devotedly setting his type by hand. August Derleth and Donald Wandrei founded Arkham House in 1939 to launch their reverential collections of the *Weird Tales* star, H. P. Lovecraft. Their first volume, *The Outsider,* did poorly at first, through surviving copies are rare and valuable now.

Donald Wollheim, one of those dynamic former Futurians grown up to become giants in the genre, followed them more successfully with a paperback science fiction anthology in 1943 and *Portable Novels of Science* in 1945. Raymond J. Healy and J. Francis McComas broke more ground in 1946 with *Adventures in Time and Space.* The same year Groff Conklin began his long series of anthologies with *The Best of Science Fiction.* Two thick books, the contents of both mostly reprinted from Campbell's *Astounding.* To the astonishment of nearly everybody, they became best sellers.

Serious critics had been deriding science fiction when they noticed it at all, and publishers had kept the science fiction label off the few classics that did reach book print. Now such barriers were falling. Grown-up fans had money to buy permanent editions of the pulp yarns they recalled with love. They weren't turned off by hostile critical opinion or the wood-pulp stigma. With the big publishers still cautious, a handful of venturesome fans made science fiction an accepted category.

Bill Crawford pioneered again, with his Fantasy Publishing Company. Rivals soon followed, Shasta Press and Gnome Press and Fantasy Press among them. My own book adventures began with Fantasy Press, founded in 1946 by Lloyd Arthur Eshbach. I remember being pretty skeptical when he wanted to reprint my early serial *The Legion of Space.* He could offer no cash advance.

Only half persuaded that it could ever sell copies enough to make it worth revising, I sent him my carbon copy, with only the worst spots in it hastily patched. A pretty dim carbon on cheap yellow paper; he had to retype parts of it himself. Amazingly, he got advance orders for more than four hundred signed copies of the book. Published in 1947—with a lovely two-copy slipcased leather-bound special edition for Lloyd and me—it sold out quickly, earning me nearly $750, a good bit more than he had promised.

That modest success helped persuade me to return to writing as a full-time thing. With Lloyd planning to reprint my old stories at the rate of two books a year and the new humanoids serial well received, my hopes were running strong again. The next book was *Darker Than You Think.*

Only 40,000 words in the magazine version, but I liked it well enough to do a full-dress revision. Spending months of spare

The author, age probably 39.
This picture was printed on the jacket flap of THE LEGION OF SPACE,
my first book. It must have been in 1947.

time on it before I left the newspaper, I rewrote it to 90,000 words. Though it did no better at Fantasy than the first book, it has enjoyed a good many better-paying reincarnations in paperback and translation. The surviving first-edition copies, with their lovely covers and endpapers and illustrations by Edd Cartier, have appreciated nicely. It's still one of the books I'm happiest about, perhaps because of what it had enabled me to say about myself and the analysis.

Though Lloyd was never able to do those two titles a year, he did publish two more of my books. The Legion sequels, *The Cometeers* and *One Against the Legion,* were too short for separate publication; we put them together in a single volume and made another of two unrelated novelettes, *The Legion of Time* and *After World's End.* Sadly, he was running into problems by then, due largely to the growing competition, and the royalty payments slowed to a trickle.

Most of the early competition came from Marty Greenberg's Gnome Press. (As Isaac Asimov is careful to note in his autobiography, this Marty was a very different person from Martin Harry Greenberg, active now as a very busy academic scholar and anthologist.)

Gnome published several books of mine, beginning in 1950 with *Seetee Ship. Star Bridge,* my joint work with Jim Gunn, followed it in 1955. Reported royalties from each came to some $700, but collecting them took legal aid. Fred Pohl sold Marty our first three collaborations, the Undersea series, for which we were paid even less.

What I recall most clearly about Marty is the extraordinary difficulty of getting money from him. Perhaps my recollections are unfair. Fred knew him better than I did and seems to have kinder feelings for him. I know he had money problems of his own, due largely I suppose to the pressures of competition with the major publishers that scrambled into the field as soon as the fan publishers had proven the market.

Simon & Schuster first. Fred sold them three of my books, beginning with *The Humanoids.* A good friend since our meeting at that first WorldCon in 1939, he was my first literary agent, and a fine one. He and "Dirk Wylie" had printed letterheads and set up the Dirk Wylie Agency in 1947, with Fred at first a silent partner. Dirk—born with the more commonplace name Harry Dockweiler—was another of Fred's fellow Futurians, also just back from the war. He soon died from a wartime injury, and Fred took over the agency.

Science fiction was booming by then, and Fred's agency boomed with it. He has always known science fiction better than nearly anybody; he's an inventive creator of new opportunities in fiction or out of it; he can be a most persuasive salesman. His clients, for a few exciting years, were writing most of the best science fiction, and he sold it well.

Until his agency failed. The big reason, I suppose, is that he was too generous with his clients; he has always cared more for friendship and for good science fiction than for money. He advanced funds on too many unsold stories to keep his clients alive and writing, and I think his office costs got out of hand. The failure was a jolt to me, because of more than merely money. His debts to me and I think to everybody were finally paid in full, but I missed him as a reader.

Over all the years, we've collaborated on a good many novels. My work with him has often come more easily than things I was doing on my own. I think I know why. I like to look at writing, or any other art, as communication.

The first problem in any act of communication is to find the right voice for it. That involves a feeling for the audience and attention to language and response. Without a common language—a system of symbols and conventions shared between the speaker and the listener, between the artist and his public —no communication happens.

Without response—some sort of feedback to convey a sense of how the audience feels and what it understands—the writer, the artist, is fumbling in the dark. As agent and later as fellow writer, Fred had enough in common with me to make him the fortunate sort of audience John Campbell had been a few years before. I felt at ease in writing first drafts for him to read because I knew him, because we understood science fiction in much the same way, because I felt confident of his responses.

Though *Astounding* was still my best market, I had begun to have problems there, I think because Campbell and I were slipping apart. *Seetee Shock,* my next serial for him, took a long year of false starts and new beginnings before I got it done. He seemed happy with it then, and Fred sold book rights to Simon & Schuster. It did so poorly for them that the editor commented on my shrewdness in putting the pen name on it.

The jacket picture, I think, was partly to blame. A nearly meaningless pattern of planetary blobs, it has nothing to catch the eye or suggest dramatic interest. Yet the novel has a flaw. That's the ending, a problem I never really solved. Neither, I'm afraid, has anybody else.

In the story, seetee becomes a metaphor for the unlocked atom. Struggling to control its terrible power, my people are trying to cope with unlimited energy and absolute weapons. The title is meant to have a double application.

"Seetee shock" is first of all radiation sickness, which nearly kills Nick Jenkins. It is also nuclear war, threatening to kill whole planets. The upbeat ending shows Nick cured by a new medical discovery, war wiped out by the "Fifth Freedom" created by free power. I'm afraid our nuclear dilemmas will never be dealt with quite so neatly, in books or out of them.

There must have been moments when I wondered if I shouldn't have stayed with the newspaper. It might have paid me more. My writing income for 1947 was only $1,865, most of it from the serial for Campbell. In 1948 it was even less, $1,793. Down still again in 1949, to $1,439. Yet Blanche and I were happy together, and life as I recall it was good.

We both worked hard, but we were used to that. She spent long days in the shop, which was earning more than I was. I did most of the shopping and shared the cooking and household chores. We had energy left to give parties and attend them. No sports fan, I sometimes went with her to watch Keigm's mostly victorious ball games.

In 1949, I took Blanche to her first science fiction convention, the WorldCon at Cincinnati. It was a small one, at least by comparison with the modern monsters, with fewer than two hundred attending, but big enough to make an impression on her. We enjoyed it. She recalls meeting Forry Ackerman and George O. Smith, who was there at the top of his unforgettable form. He led us on a memorable expedition across the river into Kentucky to sample its distillations.

We built the house in the fall of 1949. The months of carpenter work were a welcome break from writing; I enjoyed them so much that I wondered if I shouldn't try building as a new career. Science fiction, grown harder than ever to do, was paying too little.

At Blanche's urging, I had bought my first electric typewriter. Though I kept at it pretty steadily, the stories came no faster. The $992 Campbell paid me for the seetee serial was half what I earned in 1948; the advance from Simon & Schuster on *The Humanoids* was half the rest. The book did fairly well, what with a Grosset & Dunlap one-dollar reprint and then a paperback reprint that sold 71,000 copies, but the advance had been only $500, and it was 1950 before any additional royalties began to trickle in.

Fred Pohl had sold my first paperback: *The Green Girl*, the serial I had written for *Amazing Stories* back in 1929. Don Wollheim bought it for Avon Books for $500—$450 for me. He printed 101,000 copies and sold 65,600. The royalty was half a cent a copy, which never paid out the advance. Big business!

Most of 1949 went into redoing *The Humanoids* and *Seetee Shock* for book publication. When Simon & Schuster didn't take *Seetee Ship*, Fred gave it to Marty Greenberg. It has done well enough in later reprints and translations to justify the work of revision. I've always recalled it with love, and such people as Jerry Pournelle have spoken well of it, but Marty's initial advance of only $100 was a bitter disappointment then.

By 1950, exciting things had begun to happen in science fiction. A new boom was on, but I couldn't help feeling left behind.

25.

SF IN TRANSITION,

1950

Not quite so violently as the bomb, science fiction had been exploding. It had burst into book print. With *Destination Moon* and *When Worlds Collide,* it captured a beachhead in film. With *Captain Video,* it invaded TV. In the magazines, now no longer pulps, it escaped John Campbell's dozen years of dominance.

Christmas, for Blanche, was always the year's climax, demanding all her energies. Christmas merchandise for the shop had to be bought many months in advance from salesmen who called or sometimes on buying trips to Dallas or Denver. It had to be paid for, displayed and advertised and sold, most of it gift-wrapped. Most of what was left after the holiday season had to be marked down, often sold at a loss.

More of her time and care went to the family. Gifts for children and grandchildren and other relatives and friends had to be found and wrapped and often mailed. Kids were easy. Grown-ups were apt to have everything, or not to like anything. Yet, with sentiments enduring, customs of gift exchange were difficult to break.

Too, there was an annual round of parties and dinners, culminating for many years with a drive out to the ranch as soon as Blanche could get out of the shop on Christmas Eve, for dinner with my parents and Jim and the Williamson tribe. Eager grandchildren were always on the phone too early next morning, calling us for the ceremonial opening of gifts. Friends invited us for eggnog on Christmas Day, and we commonly had dinner with Blanche's parents and a troop of Slaten kin.

My war diary ends in 1945, but our Christmases are recorded in an album Keigm gave Blanche, along with a large candle, in 1944. Nearly every Christmas, she has lighted the candle for an hour while invited friends and family signed the book, leaving space for snapshots. The yellowing pages offer a trip back through time; returning to the present, you see trees and children growing, cars and buildings changing, friends appearing and vanishing again, us oldsters aging.

It's Christmas of 1947 when I first appear, dark-haired and looking remarkably youthful. Keigm is seventeen and a high school senior. Blanche is charming in a chenille housecoat, standing in the snow on the front steps of our first home. Our grandson Neil appears in 1948, grinning happily out of his walker. Keigm is in navy uniform by 1949, in boot camp in San Diego. Christmas Eve of 1950 finds us in the new house on South Globe, the yard still naked and piled with dirt from the excavation.

Blanche's notes for that year comment that I'm still writing science fiction. In fact, however, I was falling out of step with its rapid evolution. Not quite alone; I think John Campbell had also been left behind. I believe he had got too serious. There's a liberating spirit of play in the best imaginative fiction. He'd been full of that; the life of *Unknown* had been its feeling of mind-stretching fun. By 1950 he had grown too sober.

The atom must have depressed him; besides my own downbeat stories, those about the humanoids, he had run too many others. His editorials, though still often brilliant, had become earnest evangelism for his own vision of the future, a pathway into progress the world was clearly choosing not to take. Maybe in search of some surer way to reach it, he fell for dianetics.

Dianetics. The brain-child of L. Ron Hubbard. To me, it looked like a lunatic revision of Freudian psycholoy—some of the basic notions seemed sound enough, but it extrapolated from them to make claims that struck me as incredible. Falling for it, Campbell let it cripple *Astounding.* He let Hubbard launch it with a long article in the magazine. Suddenly his letters to me are full of it. Instead of new story ideas, he's sending me case histories. If I have personal problems—or nearly any sort of problems—a dianetic auditor can solve them.

"Fifteen minutes of dianetics can get more results than five years of psychoanalysis. . . . We've got a set-up at the Foundation that involves a 10-day intensive therapy. We've broken homosexuals, alcoholics, asthmatics, arthritics, and nymphomaniacs with that 10-day processing."

He offers me contingent-payment treatment at his own center. To justify the thousand-dollar fee, he adds, "Incidentally, dianetics is not a money-making, commercial scheme, however much you hear to the contrary. I'm treasurer of the Foundation, and I KNOW.

"In the first place, it's a non-profit corporation. A lot of people get the idea that our $600 fee for 10-day processing is high; actually it involves full time for three auditors for 10 days. . . . You should see the sumptuous quarters we have; top floor in an old office building on a back street in Elizabeth, furnished with surplus army cots, surplus navy lecture-hall chairs, and some $20 sheet metal auditor's desks.

"A lot of the fans think I have gone Palmer one better, with a new Shaverism." (Raymond Palmer, one of my first fan correspondents and editor of *Amazing* through the 1940s, had gone farther off the deep end than Campbell ever did—if he actually believed the Richard Shaver "articles" he published as fact. In a crudely lurid hoax seemingly believed by legions of paranoid readers, Shaver was warning the world of the "deros," malevolent robots using sinister psychic powers to control humanity from a hidden underground world. In the grip of dianetics, Campbell seemed equally credulous.)

The skeptics, he continues, "haven't seen a raving psychotic snapped back to sanity in half an hour; I have. (She'd spent 16 years at St. Elizabeth's; Ron broke her back to sanity in 30 minutes.) They haven't seen a navy veteran come in with a calcified right hip, arthritis of the spine, ulcers of the stomach, eyes down to 2/20 and failing—and go out, eight months later, with no ulcers, no arthritis, eyes 18/20 and improving—perfect, full, physical and mental health. I have. "I KNOW dianetics is one of, if not the greatest, discovery of all Man's written and unwritten history. It produces the sort of stability and sanity men have dreamed about for centuries. And a sort of physical vitality men didn't know they could have!"

I declined to be audited, partly because of what I recalled of Hubbard when I saw him at Heinlein's party in Philadelphia before I went overseas. Hubbard was just back from the Aleutians then, hinting of desperate action aboard a navy destroyer, adventures he couldn't say much about because of military security. I recall his eyes, the wary, light-blue eyes that I somehow associate with the gunmen of the old West, watching me sharply as he talked as if to see how much I believed. Not much.

Earlier, he had been one of the top writers in the pulp field, reputed to hammer his copy out on an electric typewriter, two thousand words an hour with never a revision. He had written such fine things as *Fear* and *Typewriter in the Sky* for *Unknown.* I respected his imagination more than his new psychology. The astonishing success of his recent space opera, *Battlefield Earth,* seems to show his old pulp skills still alive—or perhaps his better-paying skills in commercial exploitation. He is apparently living now in impenetrable seclusion, if in fact he is really still alive; his estranged son has claimed that he is dead.

There's a story I used to hear, about a little group of hungry pulp practitioners sitting around a table, drinking beer and discussing tactics for survival. As the story goes, Hubbard said that the best way to wealth would be to invent a new religion. That tale may well be false, but he did invent a new religion.

The history of "scientology" reads like his own fantastic stories about a super-competent future medic, "Ole Doc Methuselah." He coined the word in 1952. His new faith spread fast; by 1953 it had reached Australia and South Africa. Incorporated in 1955, the Church of Scientology fought dramatic battles with unbelievers.

No longer welcome here in America, Hubbard moved to England. Deported from the United Kingdom and later sentenced to a prison term for fraud in France, as Peter Nicholls reports in the *Science Fiction Encyclopedia*, he ruled the movement from a fleet of ships in the Mediterranean.

One early dianetic convert was A. E. van Vogt, who had ranked along with Heinlein and Asimov at the top of Campbell's team. Van's enthusiasm is understandable; his most popular stories—for example, *Slan*—had been about supermen evolving fantastic new powers of the mind. Hubbard promised to turn such fiction real. Involved in dianetics, Van was almost out of science fiction for the next dozen years.

To the cynics among us, Ron's new scripture had the look of a wonderfully rewarding scam, though he may well have been as sincere as any other prophet of a new faith. I'm sure Campbell and Van were true believers, like all the loyal adherents who still defend the church. Sometimes with excessive zeal. Now and then, expressing my own heresy too candidly, I receive an unexpectedly hot protest.

I try to understand. People need faith. With the old dogmas under fire, scientology seems to offer new ones. For those who can believe, the promise to liberate the superman trapped inside us becomes a sort of substitute for the Christian promise of eternal salvation.

Dianetics didn't kill *Astounding*, and Campbell's early faith must have waned, because he soon turned to other obsessions that looked no more rational to me. The Dean drive was one, a device for space propulsion presented as a clever end run around Newton's Third Law of Motion. Yet he kept a loyal readership. Transforming *Astounding* into the graver and sometimes duller *Analog*, he stayed on for another twenty years, a successful and respected editor.

I kept on writing for him when I could, though with diminishing interest and success. That shining stream of new ideas had ceased to flow, at least into suggestions for fiction; I think he was more concerned with his monthly editorials, which were always stimulating, though often called reactionary. We never fell out, but he was finding other writers more comfortable with his preoccupations.

His "Golden Age" had ended. While he was lost in dianetics,

rivals had been rising. The foremost was Horace Gold, who got European support to launch *Galaxy* in 1950. An early writer for *Astounding,* at first as Clyde Crane Campbell—he says because the editors of the time didn't want Jewish names—Horace knew the field and he spoke to a new generation. Phoning writers in the middle of the night to get stories tailored to fit his own innovative ideas and vigorous opinions, he took the lead with his first issue.

F&SF—The Magazine of Fantasy and Science Fiction—became an equal threat to Campbell's old order. Tony Boucher and Mick McComas, with the success of *Adventures in Space and Time,* persuaded Lawrence Spivak to bankroll a trial issue of *The Magazine of Fantasy.* Soon renamed to include science fiction, it has always held a higher level of craftsmanship and quality than anything else in the field.

Ian and Betty Ballantine transformed paperback science fiction a year or so later with the same sort of impact. In the bad old days, paperbacks had been mostly reprints, half the royalties going to the hardcover publisher. Ian began with simultaneous publication in both hard covers and soft, the hardback editions meant to earn prestige and get reviews, the paperbacks to earn income. He paid the authors generous royalties on both.

Star Science Fiction Stories, which he published, was another exciting innovation. It was a pioneering anthology of original fiction, ably edited by Fred Pohl. The rates were high—maybe too high, because the series soon faltered. My first *Star* story brought nine cents a word, three times what the magazines were paying then.

Yet, in spite of a few such sales, I had come to feel left out of the game. I don't remember even making any serious attempt to write for Boucher or Gold. Most of what they bought was written by bright young people, at a level of style and sophistication I felt I couldn't match.

F&SF seemed not to care for the serious sort of "hard science fiction" I wanted to write; mood and style mattered more. Though Horace and I were friends, I still felt more in tune with Campbell. The bad stories he printed were only boring to me;

I actually hated a lot of those in *Galaxy,* and I felt turned off by Gold's reputation for merciless editorial revisions. I had begun to feel pretty gloomy about science fiction and my own future in it.

Yet Blanche always encouraged me to keep on trying.

26.

GENETIC ENGINEERING,

1950–1951

In spite of Oppenheimer, Teller and his followers were probing further into the hazards of the atom. In 1952, they obliterated a Pacific islet with the first H-bomb. Using an A-bomb for a sort of trigger, it fused light elements and freed awesome energy. The Russians followed fast.

Though I avoided the dianetic trap, I caught myself in another of Campbell's fads that did me more harm than good. I'd read Rhine at his urging, to pick up the parapsychology he wanted in *The Humanoids*. Though my half-belief in ESP had soon evaporated, I went on to invent what I called psionics— another word, I think, of my own invention.

The psion, as I defined it, was the elemental unit of mental energy. It's massless and chargeless, a twin to the neutrino, which was still new enough to be mysterious. The nucleus of every atom contains psions as part of its binding energy—the creative force that holds the atoms together. Psionic science could therefore bridge the gulf between mind and matter. Psionic technology could give god-like powers to its masters and turn weaker minds into driven machines.

Campbell was ready enough to accept that sort of thing as "science." In *The Humanoids*, it had worked well enough, but now I lost months of time and toil on two projected novels in which I tried to take it too far. Both failed dismally, for reasons I couldn't quite grasp at the time. One of the problems

must have been that I lacked any real belief in what I was trying to write.

Lethal Agent was my title for the first. Months of the fall and
winter of 1950 were wasted on a draft of it. The manuscript still
exists, moldering in the bulky file of my papers in the university
library. I dug it out this morning: 256 sheets of cheap yellow
paper, crumbling around the edges, its disintegration no great
loss to anybody. It's typescript, with interlined pencil revisions.

There is no white-paper copy because it was never finished for
submission; yet, page by page, it looks tantalizingly competent.
The style is adequate. The narrative seems to move, reporting
the adventures of a hero meeting a beautiful girl and undertaking a hazardous mission. His opponents are powerful, mysterious, and suitably sinister.

Yet, for all that, I had completely forgotten what the story was
meant to be about—which might seem to hint that I didn't much
care—and I've no desire now to read it again. Such false starts
and failures have filled too many feet of shelf space over too
many years, and they always depress me with their evidence of
squandered toil and hope.

I've seldom even tried to go back to salvage anything useful
from those abandoned projects, because they feel so utterly
dead. The things I'm able to write and sell come from whatever
is currently alive in my mind. That misbegotten novel was one
more of the too many doom-shadowed things written in the
bomb's aftermath, and it can't have had much to express except
that nuclear gloom. Certainly I knew too little about actual international espionage to make my people live.

That should have been enough of psionics, but next year I
tried again with something I meant to call *The Mindsmith.* A novel
about "the feelies." Done right, it might have made a compel-
ling story—even now, from other hands, it might be readable.
As my notes put it, psionic science "makes it possible to pick up,
record, and broadcast thoughts, emotions, and sensations." My
scientist is a high-minded idealist, busy with an ambitious project to reach the beings of other worlds with psionic beams.

Here on Earth, however, his inventions have got into the
hands of ruthless power-seekers who have set up General Psionics and built the feelies into a new entertainment industry. Its

hapless actors have to play their roles for real, enabling the paying public to share every thought and joy and pain as they live and strive and die.

I'd been reading Frazer's *Golden Bough,* and the plot comes from the myths of those primitive priest-kings of the old fertility cults who won their thrones by murder and enjoyed the feasts and the priestesses only through a single season, until new killers arrived to end their reigns.

The idea was fresh enough then, and it looked so good to Orrin Keepnews, my editor at Simon & Schuster, that he gave me an advance on the book. Somewhat I think to Fred's surprise. Looking in the files for the manuscript, I found hundreds of pages of notes and outlines and new beginnings. One fragment runs to 87 pages, but the novel was never finished.

Again, I didn't know the trouble. Looking back from here, I see that my purposes were mixed and shifting. I was writing the adventure story of a desperate man trapped as an actor in the psionic broadcasts, with everything to win and then his life to lose. I was writing a satire on the cynical sins of the entertainment industry, exploiting the innocent for profit. I was writing a thematic novel about the scientist and society.

I suppose the truth is that I hadn't lived and learned and felt enough to write any of them, yet I tried too long. A letter to Campbell, dated November 27, 1951, reveals a new burst of enthusiasm inspired by the suggestions he had made when I spent a weekend at his home. Yet the novel never got written. Simon & Schuster finally reclaimed their advance from the earnings of another book.

Such failures did depress me, yet those years were far from lost. Portales was and is a quiet and friendly place to live. I enjoyed Blanche and enjoyed our home and enjoyed new friends. I joined Rotary. I kept the lawn and planted trees and laid cinder blocks to build a yard fence. We went to dinner parties and gave dinner parties, played bridge and went square dancing. Memorizing more of the secret ritual, I was passed and raised to become a Master Mason, though soon, with the rites grown monotonous, I stopped attending.

There were stories, too, that didn't fail, some of them even involving psionics. Those were the years of the flying saucer craze. People seemed to feel that science fiction writers ought to be believers, though hardly any of us were. Joining Fred Pohl in one investigation, I went with him to Socorro, where an honest-seeming state cop had seen a UFO taking off.

We found the prints of its landing gear and the brush its jets had burned—evidence that dimmed when we took a closer look. The prints formed an imperfect rectangle, the impressions displaced as if to avoid rocks in the way of a square-pointed shovel. The brush was burned close to the ground where there had been dry grass, but not at the top, where a hot jet might ignite it. With the School of Mines only a mile or so away, I'm convinced that enterprising students had arranged for the cop to be watching while they sent up a balloon equipped with lights and noisemakers.

Other minds on other worlds. An unsolved riddle, still fascinating. On the one hand, we have evidence that planets are common, that life and intelligence should evolve everywhere, that we may have innumerable neighbors scattered through uncountable galaxies.

On the other, there's our own geological record, which shows Earth's evolving species all grown on the same planetary family tree, all akin, never supplanted by space invaders. The answers may lie in the vastness of the universe and the limiting velocity of light. Perhaps we're simply too far apart.

What I did in 1950, suggested by all the clamor, was to work out a fictional scenario in which secret and superior observers could really be watching us. I doubt that all the odds of evolution would often create anything resembling us. To make my watchers human, I assumed them to be cousins of ours, descendants of people who left the prehistoric Earth to escape the old catastrophe that refilled the dry Mediterranean and erased all traces of their origins here.

Still writing for Campbell when I could, I sold him a series of shorts and novelettes about these ancient astronauts, who have achieved their own galactic civilization and returned to shelter our own fumbling progress, under the Covenants of Non-Contact.

Later, Fred Pohl bought two more stories about them, "The

Happiest Creature" for *Star Science Fiction,* and "Planet for Plundering" for *Galaxy.* The last one was a novelette, planned as a frame to unify the whole series as well as I could into something I could call a novel. Finally, in 1962, Donald Wollheim published that as an Ace paperback, *The Trial of Terra.*

Another 1950 project was a novel I first called *The Maker.* Under Fred's better title, *Dragon's Island,* Simon & Schuster bought the book. Moderately successful, it was reprinted by the Unicorn Mystery Book Club and then in several paperback editions—retitled once, without my permission, as *The Not-Men.* It's about genetic engineering.

In the real world, heredity has been manipulated since the domestication of the dog. The creation of new life has been a science fiction staple at least since Mary Shelley's *Frankenstein.* Heinlein described the work of "genetic technicians" in *Beyond This Horizon.* Others may well have used the term "genetic engineering," but it was new at least to me when I put it into the epigraph of *Dragon's Island,* where it is presented as a quotation from Charles Kendrew, my own genetic engineer:

". . . Now at last life has found its own secret springs in the structure of the genes. Man may now become his own maker. He can remove the fatal flaws in his own imperfect species, before the stream of life flows on to leave him stranded on the banks of time with the dinosaurs and trilobites—if he will only accept and use the new science of genetic engineering."

The novel was published in 1951, a couple of years before the announcement by Watson and Crick that they had broken the genetic code, and I've always been proud of that passage.

The book has flaws. For one, not yet aware of the double helix, I had to let Kendrew use psionics to rewrite the message of the genes. For another, I let him push his new science a bit too far. He designs a somewhat-too-wonderful tree, which bears a flyable spaceship as its fruit. That was meant to emphasize the unlimited potential of genetic engineering; I wish I had managed to make it more believable.

Because of such faults, and because the new techniques for transforming DNA had come so far since I wrote the novel, I came back a few years ago to write a vastly different and I think better book, *Brother to Demons, Brother to Gods,* about an updated science of genetic engineering, carried again as far as I could imagine it.

Back to 1951. In spite of occasional magazine sales and a few books in print, I felt depressed. Campbell had rejected *Dragon's Island.* Though Essandess had contracted for *The Mindsmith,* it had gone gravely wrong. I was sitting at the typewriter one afternoon, baffled by problems I couldn't solve, when the phone rang. Ama Barker was on the line. The editor, she said, of the Sunday edition of the *New York Daily News.*

She asked if I would come to New York to create a comic strip.

27

"BEYOND MARS,"

1952–1955

The Cold War on and Joseph McCarthy raging, Oppenheimer's career reached its tragic climax. He had known Reds and made enemies. To promoters of the H-bomb, his opposition looked like treason. In December of 1953, his military security clearance was canceled.

Doing better, Watson and Crick, describing the double helix of linked nucleotides that carry the blueprints of everything alive from each generation down to the next, had transformed genetic engineering from fiction into fact.

In 1955, fourteen years after John Campbell alerted me to "seetee," Segré and Chamberlain made real antimatter. Bombarding a copper target with high-energy particles from the synchrotron at Berkeley, they created antiprotons.

"Beyond Mars" was another child of technology. Television was remaking lifestyles, turning readers from hard print to the flicker of phosphors in the tube. The *Sunday News* had been the world's biggest paper, selling nearly three million copies. Suddenly, now, that proud figure began to slip.

Close to panic, the editors were grasping for anything. Their parent corporation, the News-Tribune Syndicate, distributed dozens of comics, all available to competing papers. Perhaps a few exclusive strips could give them an edge. Four were planned, mine the only one that got into print.

For me, a comedy of ironies. Twenty-five thousand unsolicited scripts are submitted to the syndicate every year, so I was told, all rejected. Instead of looking at them, Ama Barker turned to the book reviews in the *New York Times.* Through some happy chance, she found the notice about my own *Seetee Ship,* a comment not very flattering.

Meaning me no special favor, the reviewer said a few kind things about the novel, but then concluded, "It is a pity that the quality of Stewart's writing is such that this 'space opera' ranks only slightly above that of atomic strip adventures."

Those last three words must have made the unintended magic. Wanting somebody to write a science adventure comic, Ama Barker placed that call to me. I caught my breath and said I'd create the strip. She wired, "Am interviewing artists and should be ready to work with you next Wednesday. Letter and check for transportation follow."

By Christmas Eve I'm just back from a trip to New York to work out plans for the script with John Gardner, her editorial assistant, and Lee Elias, the able artist they had selected. The snapshots in the Christmas book show snow on the still-new house. Our first small trees have been planted around it. Blanche's mother is sitting on a sofa with Neil beside her, beaming proudly down at Karla, her newest great-grandchild, six months old and smiling from her arms. Two dozen neighbors and relatives have signed, invited for hot buttered rum.

Comics, to me, were one more strange new world. Though newspapers had been running adventure strips at least since "Buck Rogers" began in 1929, I'd never read them. Certainly I had never thought of creating one, but no such unlikely chance was apt to come again. I felt desperate to seize it, in spite of a good many hazards.

First of all, an attack of shingles. An ache in my side, before I left home. Just a muscle strained, I thought, but it got worse until one morning I fainted and fell on the bathroom floor in my New York hotel. When I got to a doctor, he told me what the trouble was, gave me antibiotics, and said I'd get better. In time, I did.

I stayed seven weeks in New York, working at first at a desk in the enormous city room in the *News* tower. I had always looked askance at the paper as a trashy tabloid, but I soon found a high admiration for most of the *News* men I came to know. They were superbly professional, informed and shrewd and unflappable, well in tune with millions of New Yorkers. Among them, I couldn't feel very competent. My total ignorance of the comic strip genre must have been visible to everybody. An equal hazard was my innocence about the covert warfare I suppose is waged inside every big organization. I found myself trapped in an unexpected battle between undeclared enemies.

The syndicate people had fought the project from the start, so Gardner told me, simply because it wasn't theirs. They saw it as an invasion of their own turf. I sensed that when one of their editors was called in to teach me how to write comics. Though she did answer questions and produce sample scripts for me to study, her enmity was obvious.

Better information came from Chester Gould, the creator of "Dick Tracy," when I was allowed to phone him. He explained how he built his scripts in linked plot sequences, each usually developing a conflict with some new villain in a story to run for a good many weeks. We followed his pattern.

The biggest thing I had to learn was how to tell things visually. In fiction, I like dialogue. Its open pages have eye appeal, and characters are more convincingly revealed by what they say than by what the writer says about them. But too many speech balloons on the comic page can spoil the effects of good graphic art. The ideal is to let the pictures tell the story.

Scabbed and blistered from the virus at work half around my middle, I tried pretty grimly to get a feel for the comic form and come up with something acceptable. The editors wanted the new strip set in the same background I had used for *Seetee Ship* —the asteroids that orbit the sun out beyond Mars.

That gave me the title. Looking for an aptly named protagonist, I invented Mike Flint. I see now that he was too much the standard pulp hero to be very memorable. A bold and able future spaceman, handsome enough as Lee Elias drew him, he lacked the faults and singularities that might have made him more appealing. He might even have had a sense of humor.

The star of the strip, to my own surprise, came to be Tham Thmith, Mike's worm-shaped, metal-eating Venusian sidekick, who has learned his English from a lisping Earthman. Tham got all the gags.

Everything about the strip had to be worked out in confer-

ences with the editor and the artist. Elias was a fortunate choice.
Working with Milt Caniff, the creator of "Steve Canyon," he had
mastered Caniff's clean, effective style. His spacecraft and future
machines looked workably real, and he had a fine flair for scenes
of spectacular action.

Though I recall him as a bitterly sardonic sort, convinced that
all the world was conspiring to do him in, he and I got on well
enough. To him, as to me, the strip looked like the way to a
rewarding lifetime career, and he devoted high talents to it.

John Gardner, the editorial assistant, was harder to deal with.
He seemed as close as a son to Ama Barker, loved as well as
trusted; she was half disabled with arthritis, and she let him
control everything. A keen-witted young man, he appeared as
cynical as Elias—I believe he had a difficult divorce in progress.
He was a strong ally against the syndicate, yet he struck me from
the beginning as an uncertain friend. The strip was his baby, and
he never seemed willing to leave much to me.

Our story conferences were hard bargaining sessions. Luckily
for me, my colleagues knew no science fiction nor even any
science. They had to depend on me for the space background.
I could suggest characters and plot sequences and action scenes.
Lee was a gifted craftsman. Working from hints and possibilities, he came up with vivid portraits—our minor characters and
our villains were generally more memorable than Mike Flint. He
knew what he could draw and what he couldn't, and he made
inventive suggestions.

Gardner thought he knew how to make the strip capture its
hoped-for ten or twelve million readers every week, and he kept
a close rein on all my own ideas. He wanted a certain sort of
humor and more suspense, a hint of sophistication and more
sentimentality. Our future world was filled with petty villains, yet
we had to keep it serenely free of anything gone seriously
wrong. When I came up with a sequence about food shortages,
and beefleggers thriving, the *News* ruled it out.

Looking back, I see how the strip could have been better. Mike
Flint might have been more complex and more engaging. So
might the women in his life and the enemies he fought; they were
all too simple, too starkly good or bad. I think we had too many women, all too nice. Mike might better have been more deeply in-

volved with some alluringly wicked interplanetary enchantress.

More might have been done with the whole promise of the space frontier. I had tried in *Seetee Shock* to look at the coming energy crunch and a possible solution. All the *News* cared about, however, was selling more copies, and I had to grapple with too many immediate problems during those first few hectic weeks to think much about long-term possibilities.

We decided to do three episodes a year, each to run some seventeen weeks. The *News* agreed to let me write the scripts at home in New Mexico, coming back to New York to discuss characters and plot action for each new episode. My pay was to be a hundred dollars a week.

A lot of money then, at least to me; far more than I had ever earned. Fred Pohl was still my agent. Though the *News* wanted nothing to do with any agent, I discussed the contract with him before I signed and gave him 10 percent of my checks for the first six months.

The strip began in the *Sunday News* for February 17, 1952, launched with an impressive display in the street-floor windows of the *News* building and a burst of publicity I enjoyed. Running on the back page of the color wraparound, opposite "Dick Tracy" on the first page, it was on sale everywhere, even in Portales. Only ten cents a copy.

At first it seemed a great success. Gardner told me that papers all over America were wiring to buy it. The syndicate was not allowed to offer it here at home, but it did appear in papers off the continent. Ten million readers a week!

A wonderful thought, until the time I watched one of those readers boarding the subway with her paper. A young black girl, she sat down across from me and leafed through it page by page from "Dick Tracy" on the front page to "Beyond Mars" on the back. There, with a single glance at that, she dropped the paper on the floor.

Socially, the strip made me more important to a lot of people than I had ever been before. Elias took me to a banquet meeting of his fellow cartoonists, among them such famous names as Milt Caniff.

I got to know Bob Sheckley. One of the many new stars in the field, he was writing for *Captain Video*, earning a hundred dollars an episode. I renewed old friendships with the Futurians: one night, talking science fiction with Cyril Kornbluth, I walked him back to his hotel; instead of going in, he walked me on to mine.

At Horace Gold's Friday-night poker parties, I always lost my few bucks on the first few hands, but stayed to visit with Horace and the other writers there. Horace was confined to the apartment by agoraphobia; he used to retreat even from his own living room, peeping at us now and then from the hall.

Blanche came with me on one trip to New York. Willy Ley took us home for dinner with Olga. She was a trained ballet dancer, radiant with an exotic-seeming charm; she made Stroganoff for us. John Campbell and Peg had us out to spend a day at their New Jersey home. George O. Smith and Doña, Campbell's first wife, entertained us. Blanche says we took the Smiths and Leys to a restaurant dinner, and we attended one of Horace's Friday-night poker sessions.

I found more friends at Chicon II, the 1952 world convention. Hugo Gernsback was guest of honor. I must have seen him and probably heard him speak, but what I recall is meeting Cliff Simak and Jim Gunn. I had known and admired Cliff's work for many years. Recently, digging through old files, I discovered a fan letter he wrote me back in 1940.

There, sitting with him in a Chicago hotel room, sipping a little good whiskey and talking about ourselves and our worlds, I really got to know and love him. The writers of good science fiction are nearly always bright and interesting and likable, but Cliff has a genuine humanity, something calmly wise and warm that is all his own. I wish I could see him more often.

Jim Gunn was not quite thirty then, just establishing himself as one of the gifted young people who were selling to Horace and transforming the field, displacing most of us old hands. He knew science fiction—he had done his master's thesis on it at the University of Kansas.

He liked my work, and we found so much in common that he agreed to collaborate on a revision of *Star of Empire*, that stalled project I had abandoned back in 1941 when Campbell turned me toward seetee. We retitled it *Star Bridge*, and Jim replotted it from my unfinished draft. I made suggestions. He rewrote it, brilliantly, I think. I supplied more material about such matters as the energy tubes that link the stars to bring all interstellar traffic through a single central planet.

He finished the final draft in December, 1953, sending it to Harry Altshuler, his new agent. Events soon wilted our high hopes for it. The bubble had burst.

The magazines were dying. They had peaked in 1953 with nearly forty titles. Far too many. Though scores of such able new writers as Jim had come into bloom, they were nearly all slanting their work toward a handful of great editors, Horace Gold and Tony Boucher and still John Campbell.

Other editors had to buy too many rejects from the three at the top. Some paid too little; some aimed too low or didn't care. Damon Knight and a few others did care, but they failed to stay long enough to build readerships. Along with many newcomers, *Planet* and *Wonder* and *Startling* were dead by 1955.

The book market too had dwindled. The fan firms that pioneered it were nearly all out of business or in trouble by then, and the bigger publishers were turning cautious. Failing to find a better home for *Star Bridge,* Altshuler let it go to Marty Greenberg, the advance another stunning hundred bucks.

Our reviews were a good deal better than the royalties, but they bought us no butter. Marty passed along five hundred more for an Ace paperback. Others got the book for less. It was plagiarized by Spanish pirates, cover and all. Though fans in Spain still seem to recall it fondly, we got never a peseta. I heard rumors of other translations, never reported or paid for.

In a series of more recent reprints and foreign editions, it has made a more profitable splash. Only a few years ago, the good, gray *New York Times Book Review* went so far as to conclude a flattering review of a new edition with the comment that it reads "like a collaboration between Asimov and Heinlein."

My long series of collaborations with Fred Pohl began in much the same way. When his agency failed, I went over to Harry Altshuler, but Fred and I kept in touch. I sent him another unfinished novel, a long-stalled epic about the future colonization of the oceans that I called *The Conquest of the Abyss.*

I think it had died for me because too much of my own creative drive had gone into elaborating a background for it, complete with technology and history and maps of the submarine

*Keigm Harp, Navy frogman in
South Korea, 1952.*

world and sketches of the characters. That's how teachers tell
you novels should be written, but such systematic approaches
have seldom worked for me.

Fred rewrote it as *Undersea Quest* and we turned out two sequels, *Undersea Fleet* and then *Undersea City*. Marty published all
three a year apart, the royalties trifling even when at last they
came. Yet the effort had not been wasted: all have done far
better in later reprints, here and overseas.

Without "Beyond Mars," those would have been lean years.
Even with it, I ran into problems. John Gardner wanted it all for
himself, perhaps with some justice. I suspect that the whole
notion of comic strips to fight TV had come from him. Certainly,
at least at first, he knew the comic form better than I did, and

he worked from the first to take complete control, retyping all my copy, often with revisions I felt weren't always necessary.

When my first one-year contract ran out, he persuaded Ama Barker that he could turn my plot outlines into finished scripts himself, with no more help from me. The new contract they offered me was to pay only five hundred dollars each for three new plot sequences to run through the year. A confidential arrangement, Ama Barker wrote; my name would stay on the strip and Elias wouldn't know unless I told him.

A bitter pill, but when she agreed to pay my expenses for three trips a year to work out the new sequences with Gardner and Elias, I signed. Gardner did the scripts from my outlines through the first half of 1953, until he died of a heart attack.

Ama Barker wired the news. I expressed regret, not without a certain secret sense of justice done, and agreed to turn the accepted outline into finished scripts. So I did, even though the *News* refused to make any extra payment for the extra work. They did raise my pay again with the next contract, back to that regal hundred a week. Worth Gatewood became my new editor. A fellow New Mexican, he was another veteran *News* man of the well-seasoned sort I had learned to admire, and luckily less ambitious than Gardner.

We worked well together, and the Christmas book records those years as good. On the way home from New York in 1952, Blanche and I stop in Kansas City to celebrate her birthday with Berwyn and Harvey; he is now in dental practice there.

There's a picture of Keigm, made in Korea that year, naked to the waist in his frogman gear, looking handsome and intrepid with a knife at his belt and the skull and crossbones tattooed on his arm. By 1954, he's back from the war, back in college and married to Donna Barnes. The trees around our house have begun to grow.

Gatewood and I kept "Beyond Mars" alive through 1954. Long enough to convince the *News* that it would never become the final reply to TV. In January of 1955, Ama Barker wrote that it was being discontinued. Shrunk from that full page on the wraparound cover to a half-page buried inside, it expired in the issue for March 13.

My heart was broken.

28.

BACK TO SCHOOL,

1956–1964

Sputnik I began beeping across the sky on October 4, 1957. In frantic pursuit, the American *Explorer I* was launched in the following January. Yury Gagarin got into space in April of 1961. Alan Shepard followed in May. Still far behind the Russians, but John Kennedy promised that our *Apollo* spacecraft would reach the Moon "before this decade is out."

X-ray astronomy began in 1962, when Geiger counters carried into space found unexpected radiation from toward the center of the galaxy. The same year saw *Mariner II* launched toward Venus on the first successful interplanetary mission. The first quasar was discovered in 1963.

Elias and I had no appeal when "Beyond Mars" was sentenced to death. The syndicate owned all rights in the strip, but nobody there wanted to carry it on. It was reprinted for a few more months in England, Australia, and Sweden. That was the end.

It had taken most of my creative energy through the few years it lived. Now, with that comfortable five thousand a year abruptly cut off, I felt pretty desperate. Science fiction, of course, was still alive and growing, but I felt more than ever out of the picture.

In search of a new income, I turned to teaching. While the strip was still running, I had begun taking spare-time courses at our hometown college, now Eastern New Mexico University. Electronics first, for a better science background. Then analytic geometry and calculus, because math was still so much a mystery to me, and the essential language for descriptions of the universe.

With credit for my army schooling, I was soon ready to begin the M.A. The math courses had been more fun than toil, and I thought at first of teaching math. When I inquired, however, the math department had no graduate assistantship open. The English department did, and I asked for that. A fortunate choice.

Even though most academics still took a dim view of science fiction, as too many still do, a few seemed impressed by my long apprenticeship in authorship. Grady Moore, the department head, displayed an open mind in spite of his scholarly reverence for the classics. Debs Smith, another good faculty friend, had been publishing Western fiction until the pulps faded away. Thanks to them, I got the job and found myself happy with it: the courses I taught and those I took, my learned colleagues, my students most of all. It was a fine thing, I soon decided, to be paid to read and talk about great literature.

A friendly graduate committee let me do my thesis as "A Study of the Sense of Prophecy in Modern Science Fiction." I've always felt that the overriding appeal of science fiction rises out of its probing into the new futures where advancing technology may take us, and the thesis reviews eighteen classic novels in terms of their optimism or pessimism about the shape of things to come.

I received the B.A. in the spring of 1957, the M.A. that fall. Luckily a little ahead of the flood of graduates who would be looking for jobs a few years later, I found a place as "Captain Williamson," teaching high school English at New Mexico Military Institute—the military rank by courtesy only, intended to impress cadets. I was there two years.

Good years, in a great school. Great, at least, for students who could accept and benefit from military discipline. Besides the basics, they learned social poise and leadership. We always had a few rebel souls who resented everything and occasional problem kids who might otherwise have gone to the reformatory, but even they generally became my friends.

The school is in Roswell, only ninety miles from Portales. I lived on the campus during the week, eating with the cadets in the dining hall, "walking the stoops" to supervise the evening study hours, and making bed checks after lights-out. Most week-ends were free; I could drive home to Blanche.

I didn't like being away so much of the time, but the school itself was another small world with a culture of its own, traditions I could respect, and challenges enough to keep me fully occupied. I enjoyed my students and the new friends I made among my colleagues, and I enjoyed learning to teach.

Luckily for me, the school had hired me without the forbid-ding list of education courses commonly required. I did have to make up a couple of them by correspondence, learning nothing useful I recall. I think our country was better off before teaching became a bureaucratic monopoly. In spite of fine and well-meaning friends in monopolies ranging from education to the army to the post office, I can't help concluding that all such organizations tend to put interests of their own ahead of what-ever function they were created to fill.

Blanche says she missed me. She recalled somebody asking why she didn't move with me to Roswell. Her answer was "He doesn't want me to. He wants me to stay here and take care of the house."

Which was true, though I think she had the same pride in our home and the same determination to keep it. I doubt that she had much time for loneliness. She still ran the shop, which kept her as busy as I was. She had relatives and good neighbors all around her. Her parents were near. Keigm and Adele were beloved and important to her. Our grandchildren had begun arriving. Leon and Bernice, her brother and his wife, lived on the next block.

For both of us, the weeks went fast.

In 1956, our annual Christmas reception is on December 23. Three dozen guests sign the book. There's a shot of Blanche at the table in the embroidered squaw dress she wore to square dances. Keigm and Donna are there with Valerie, their first daughter. Gorden Greaves is standing in front of our fireplace, Betty sitting on the hearth with their three daughters, Becky, Judy, and Tish. Tish, the youngest, is our first godchild—Kim Forbes became the second.

On Christmas Eve we have dinner at the ranch with my par-

*My family in our living room, 1958. My parents are seated. Sherry, Don,
and Larry Littlefield are kneeling. In the back row, Bud Littlefield on the left,
Katie beside him, Jim, myself, Blanche, my sister Jo, and Fred Harvey.*

ents and Jim. Katie, my younger sister, is there, married during
the war to her girlhood sweetheart Bud Littlefield, who fought
his way from Salerno to Munich as an antiaircraft machine gun-
ner with the Forty-fifth Division and got back alive. Their three
children are peering out of snapshots, Donnie with a gap in his
teeth, Larry grinning through his freckles, Sherry breathlessly
intent on something beyond camera range.

Kids with remarkable aptitudes, as their later lives have
shown. Don is now maintaining heavy machinery and delight-
edly scuba diving somewhere in the Caribbean. Larry learned
Russian and spent a year in the air off the coasts of Siberia,

eavesdropping on the U.S.S.R., before he came home to earn degrees in computer science and go to work for Hewlett-Packard. Sherry and Allen are running a busy commercial print-shop in their basement.

On the pages for 1957, there's a shot Gordon Greaves took of Blanche and me standing at the table set for serving the hot buttered rum. I'm in the uniform I wear as a captain by courtesy at the Institute—a grave faux pas, as I learn later, at least in the eyes of a couple of army reserve colonels among the guests. Jim stands by the fireplace grinning happily, his arm around his new bride.

He has been snared as deftly as I was. Nancy was a Cleveland girl, in love with horses and opera; she spent three years on a government job in Japan and stopped at a ranch near here on her way home to visit a childhood girl friend who taught her how to nab New Mexico cowboys.

Committed now to teaching, I decided to work toward the Ph.D. Nearly too late. I was fifty in 1958, when I began inquiring. Too old for most schools. Several rejected me. The University of Colorado did admit me, but even there my application for a fellowship was turned down because the graduate committee was "doubtful about the man who decides on an academic career late in life."

I spent a few summers at Boulder, and one whole year. Gene Fox was with me there the first two summers. An instructor at the Institute when I went there, he had come to head the language department at Eastern. We'd met when he signed up for a writing course I taught. A genial, wide-minded man with a doctorate from the University of Mexico.

Something of a fan, he was a great friend for the rest of his life. His vigor seemed boundless then. I remember the New Year's morning we were trying to get home from a New York convention of the Modern Language Association. When the taxi drivers were all preying too avidly on drunker revelers to pick us up, we walked from our hotel to the West Side bus terminal, carrying our bags.

He had done research on Santa Anna, the colorful and dashing Mexican general who took the Alamo. We collaborated on a bit of historical fiction climaxed with that battle; it was sold to a magazine that went out of business and lost the manuscript before they got it into print.

The summers with him in Boulder were almost holidays. It's a beautiful spot at the foot of the Rockies. That was before the rebel generation vandalized the campus, and I had great teachers, the best of them noted scholars there in the summers as ·:isiting professors.

The graduate school was one more stimulating field of stern challenge and high reward. I've always enjoyed such spells of concentrated effort. We students were a small, hard-driven group, living from one crisis to the next with little time or money for anything but study. I made new friends; we shared hopes and trials and battle-plans. Though they were all younger, my advancing age turned out to be no real handicap.

I've never worked harder, but nearly all the courses were absorbing. Chaucer. Shakespeare. Ben Jonson. I chose the novel as my field, following it from Rabelais and Cervantes and Defoe down through the eighteenth century and the great Victorians and on to James Joyce. Though Anglo-Saxon became a year-long ordeal, Middle English was mostly fun.

Professor Colgrave taught it. He was a humane scholar there from England for the summer; I audited a fascinating course he taught on British antiquities, ran his slide projector, and earned a happy A in Middle English. Though the words may look odd, you know they're English; my reading method was to attack as if I were facing an ill-spelled and grammatically erratic freshman paper.

Crisis after crisis. Residence requirements. Tests in every English course. French translation test. German translation test. Comprehensives. Dissertation. Final oral. Each a forbidding mountain ahead, diminishing to a little hill as it fell behind. Somehow I got by them all, even when younger people slaved and failed. Unexpectedly asked to teach a freshman section, I even became a part-time faculty member.

I was lucky enough to find a science fiction fan on the faculty. A. L. Soens, who became chairman of my graduate committee and approved the topic for my dissertation, "H. G. Wells: Critic of Progress." Writing it, I picked up the thread of my master's thesis, looking into Wells's career as the chief creator of modern science fiction and his use of it to satirize science and the dream of future human progress. Later, a little rewritten, the dissertation became a book.

I owe more to Leslie Lewis, a humane scholar on the committee who took me over when the hard pinches came and saw me through to the end. There was a sticky moment in my final oral, when somebody was unhappy with all I didn't know about deism, but when the verdict came in I had passed.

Blanche had stayed with her shop and our house in Portales, and we were together only during school vacations. Woody and Theda, her youngest brother and his wife, were living in Denver. I saw them often, and she came up with her parents on Thanksgiving for a happy visit. I was back in Portales for Christmas, but our festivities must have been limited. The Christmas book has only a handful of signers. Blanche's notes report that Keigm has moved to California, where he has a high school coaching job and a new son, Nikki.

Though we didn't like living apart, we endured these separations cheerfully enough. Blanche says they were never great problems. She was busy with her business and the family and happy, I think, to be keeping our home alive in Portales. My own goal was more security for both of us, and we always looked forward to being together again.

I doubt that I minded living apart as much as she did. The university was its own rewarding world. I enjoyed most of the people I came to know. Some of my fellow students were women, friendly enough and attractive to me, but I was never offered any actual temptation to break my faith to Blanche. My classes were far more seductive.

I've always enjoyed being totally involved in something new: meteorology, linguistics, the technique of the comic strip, the new universe of a new novel in progress. Absorbed in meeting the challenges of such new worlds, rewarded with the sheer joy of learning, I can forget most other things most of the time. Computer science tempts me in the same way now.

The history and the classics of English literature claimed me so completely that I might have enjoyed spending another year at Boulder finishing the degree. Luckily, however, a position opened unexpectedly on the faculty at Eastern, here at home. Blanche insisted that I apply.

Adele Lovorn, our daughter, 1962.

I got the job and came back to Portales in the fall of 1960 with the rank of assistant professor. The beginning pay was $6,800, with long summers free. The death of the comic strip was no longer a total tragedy.

Researching and writing the dissertation and winding up the final bits of academic red tape took a couple more summers, but at last, in the spring of 1964, the battle was won. Blanche went with me back to Boulder, the commencement speaker took his text from Fred Pohl's "Midas Plague," and I walked across the stage to receive my academic union card.

The first years at Eastern were nearly as strenuous as working for the doctorate. Our teaching load was fifteen hours, a demanding burden. Preparing lessons, making audiovisual materials, meeting classes, grading papers, committee chores. Altogether, the job often took sixty hours a week.

All of which left little time or thought for science fiction. I did keep up my magazine subscriptions and somehow got a very few short stories done, but my fiction income had fallen to a few hundred dollars a year, most of that from foreign sales. The

single novel I managed to finish was an utter failure. That was
The Mechanical Ants, based on another idea from John Campbell.

A good enough idea; what I did with it was no fault of his. The
ants were small, self-replicating machines; they swarmed like
actual ants, spreading to set up new factory-colonies where they
built more ants to swarm and spread and build again. The trouble for humanity came when they began stealing metal to make
into ever more ants.

I wrote the first draft of it on weekends at home while I was
teaching at Roswell, and finished it perhaps too hastily in the
early summer of 1959, before I went to Boulder. I'd hoped for
it to pay for my degree, but Campbell disowned it when he saw
it. Harry Altshuler looked at it and decided it wasn't fit to be
offered anywhere else. With no time to try revision, I retired it.

I haven't looked at it since, and I've forgotten nearly everything about it. The ants were there, I know, but perhaps no
human beings worth recalling. Perhaps I was trying to work
through too many distractions, or perhaps the ants were simply
small humanoids, so much like their older cousins that I found
no more to say about them. Whatever killed the story, I have no
heart to go back for an autopsy now.

Better things grew with help from Fred Pohl. *The Iron Collar
Man* was my title for an ambitious serial I had begun and failed
to finish while the comic strip was running. The idea came from
Fred Hoyle's theory of the steady state universe and Webb's
Great Frontier.

Webb saw all our most precious freedoms in danger now,
since the closing of the Earth's frontiers. The reefs of space,
formed between the stars by the steady creation of new matter
as the universe expands, could open endless new frontiers, rich
with limitless freedom.

With four hundred pages written, the project had finally become too much for me. We revised the plot, and Fred rewrote
it, or part of it, into *The Reefs of Space.* There's a body bank where
social misfits are held until the Plan of Man finds uses for them,
organ by organ. The story took so long to do that I was afraid
the real-life surgeons would beat us, but Fred got it into *Galaxy*
in 1963, four years ahead of Christiaan Barnard's first heart
transplant.

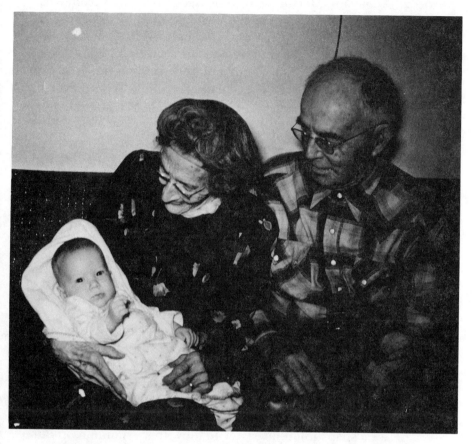

My parents with Stewart, their first grandchild, on the last day of my mother's life, 1960.

Acting as an unpaid agent for our joint works, Fred sold book rights to Ballantine. We followed it with *Star Child* and *Rogue Star*. I found time to do first drafts that he rewrote. They've been our most successful novels, frequently reprinted, most recently in a single volume, *The Starchild Trilogy,* now near its second hundred thousand copies in the book club and paperback editions.

The Christmas book records the long flow of years. The trees in the yard have grown taller in 1958, and Keigm has a second daughter, Carol. By the next Christmas, he has moved to California. Adele and Melvin have come back to Portales from Roswell, where he had been supervising salesmen for a bakery.

My mother dies in 1960, quite suddenly. There's a snapshot taken on the morning of her last day. She's sitting with my father on the living room couch. They are both smiling down at the baby in her arms, Stewart, their first grandchild. When she was stricken, Nancy rushed her to the hospital. She was already lifeless when I carried her inside. Born in 1874, she was eighty-six.

My father, six years older, survived until 1964, when he was ninety-six. Remarkably vigorous, he was alert and active till the end. In the hospital through his last few weeks he was sometimes confused, once in the middle of the night so bent on getting out that I was called to sit with him, but often lucid. When a nurse asked him what he thought about the fall of Khrushchev, he had to reply, "I'm not up on that."

The last words I recall were an uneasy question: "What's supposed to happen now?" I still feel bad because I was slow to understand and had no good answer ready.

There is no candle-burning on Christmas of 1960, because Blanche is sick in bed. Exhausted, I suppose, after the Christmas rush. She's well again in 1961, though the guest list is limited to kin. Jim and Nancy are there with two children, Stewart and Betty Jane; Gary arrived the following year. My father signs the book, legibly if unsteadily.

There's a snapshot of my sister Jo, now Joan, standing on our front steps with Fred Harvey, whom she married during the war. Fred had survived a grim and rootless Depression childhood to grow up unspoiled by hardship; cheery, original, and creative, he discovered a talent for art. He and Jo seemed happy together and good for each other. He cared for her tenderly through her long final illness in 1974 of something diagnosed at last as multiple sclerosis.

The receptions grow less elaborate as the years go by, the guest lists shorter. The pages for 1963 contain a shot of Keigm and three happy-looking children in front of their La Habra home; Dawn is yet to come. In 1964 there's a Christmas card from "The Williamson Tribe," Jim and Nancy's three on a spotted pony. Two students of mine sign the book that year, Ben

My parents, Asa and Lucy Williamson, sometime in the 1950's

Chang from Taiwan, and "Saifuddin Dirk W. Mosig" from Crdoba, Argentina.

A devout Moslem convert then, born in Spain of German parents, Dirk had come to Eastern from Argentina because he'd read my science fiction. English was his third language; perhaps the fourth, counting Arabic. A brilliant student, he finished his degree in less than three years, married a local girl, earned his black belt in karate, and went on to become a professor of psychology and one of the top scholars on H. P. Lovecraft. He was recently back, when I last saw him, from a Lovecraft symposium in Italy.

Though I sometimes felt that the university was too much the ivory tower, shielded too well from the irrational nuts and flying bolts of life, it became a pleasant haven. Even those rigidly traditional academics who saw no good in science fiction were commonly too kind to say so. The school was smaller then than it soon became, and even friendlier. Faculty and students still gathered in the Student Union for coffee; you could know them nearly all. Walking across the campus, everybody smiled and spoke to everybody else.

Too long too much of a loner, I enjoyed forging new social links. On the campus, I talked shop with my colleagues and met my quota of committees and sponsored the student group that published the literary magazine. Downtown, I came back into Rotary, which I'd had to drop. I joined NEA and AAUP, but with reservations. I can't help feeling that they exist not so much to work for excellence in education as to pry salaries up and protect the tenure rights of incompetents.

In the National Council of Teachers of English I felt more at home. Their conventions were maybe less fun than science fiction cons, but planned to advance the arts of teaching. I heard such people as Noam Chomsky revealing dimensions new to me in modern linguistics.

Boulder, I discovered, had left an enormous gap in my education. All those grueling hours with *Beowulf* had taught me nothing at all about the new science of language, with all its exciting insights and unresolved controversies. I had to know more about it. For what I could teach, for what it might reveal about the art and craft of writing, most of all for its own fascination.

In the summer of 1964, my doctorate barely earned, with no protest that I recall, Blanche let me go back to school.

29.

LINGUISTICS,

1964

The genetic engineers were mastering the language of the gene. In March of 1963, Robert W. Holly deciphered the structure of a transfer RNA, one of the vital molecules that follow the genetic blueprints of DNA to shape new generations of living cells. By 1967, RNA had been synthesized in the laboratory.

When I discovered modern linguistics, it fascinated me completely. Transformational grammar, tagmemics, semantics, psycholinguistics, sociolinguistics, language and culture, language and the computer, language and philosophy—they promised exciting new keys to understanding nearly everything human. I was burning to learn all I could.

The Linguistics Institute, was the great annual gathering of language scientists, sponsored each year by some host university. Indiana University at Bloomington in 1964. Some sixty of the top linguists in the free world were there, either teaching through the summer or as visiting lecturers. We lived in a complex of our own, complete with dorms and classrooms and dining hall and library. A fine environment for the total dedication to some fresh field of learning that I've always enjoyed. It let us do linguistics day and night.

Needing to take no courses for credit, I sampled most of the classes and found only a handful of truly outstanding teachers among all those scholars. I stayed through most of the summer with that inspiring few. Noam Chomsky, there for only a week, was easily the most exciting to me and to nearly everybody.

His transformational grammar was still new then. Though he used to deny that it had grown out of computer science, it does assume that our minds work much like computer programs, using regular rules to form all the sentences we say from a few kernel patterns, which are themselves determined by inborn aptitudes we all inherit.

Edward O. Wilson and sociobiology were still to come, but I think the theories overlap. We know our world through models, mathematical models for many of the sciences, verbal models for nearly everything else. If the genes shape language and program the way we learn it, linguistics has to underlie all philosophies. Our genes themslves would seem to dictate and limit what we can know and what we can think about our universe.

Breath taking notions, hotly debated then, perhaps even more controversial now. That summer was full of intellectual drama, with Kenneth Pike and Charles Hockett and others coming with their rival ideas to challenge Chomsky. Most of them, as I recall them, tending to beards and belligerence. I felt sorry for Pike; facing Chomsky, he seemed to be surrendering too abjectly.

All sorts of other issues seized me. Computer translation: a possibility that tantalized me, something beyond the reach of computers as they were then, but already beginning to reveal unsuspected complexities in language structure. Stylistic analysis. Bilingual education. Even the seeming promise of linguistics as a better way to teach freshman grammar.

I imposed somewhat on one inspiring scholar who didn't want me in his class because I hadn't enrolled for credit. I found him so gripping I couldn't stop coming, and he was too much of a gentleman to toss me out. Speaking about the origins of language and culture, he said more than I had ever known about the theories of human evolution.

With a modest apology to the women in the class, he began with when we first walked upright. Physical changes allowed sex contact face to face, instead of from the rear. The female breasts consequently fattened far beyond any lactic need as they took on something of the form and function of buttocks as sex lures for the male.

Body hair was lost, and the female's facial hair. Thus more baby-like, she could inspire the male with something of the tenderness first evolved to ensure the survival of the human infant. With the estrus cycle modified for year-round sex, transient lust could be transformed into more enduring love. Such changes made for lasting families and more complex societies, which in turn required better verbal communication. Evolving with our bodies, linguistic aptitudes made civilization possible.

Back at Eastern, I read more linguistics, joined linguistic societies, and wrote up courses for the college catalogue. Basic linguistics, transformational grammar, teaching English as a second language. Debs Smith was departmental chairman by then, and willing to approve them.

I taught all three for a good many years. Most of my students were teachers or training to be teachers. I'm afraid they didn't always find linguistic answers to all their classroom problems, but a good many of them seemed to share my own enthusiasm for a new, exciting science.

Some of those early promises have failed. When last I looked, the old question of how to teach English grammar still had no final answer. Though better computers are coming, computer translation still works better in prospect than in fact.

Bilingual education has gone sadly wrong. Students who comes to school with no English or poor English need teachers who respect their native language and their native culture, who understand their hard problems well enough to give effective and sympathetic help. But in the hands of politicians and job seekers, bilingual education is tending now to hamper and delay mastery of English, isolating the students who need it most in permanent minorities, crippling them and dividing the nation.

Language and the mind will never be precisely what Chomsky tried to make them. The problem is a gap between the mind and reality. Besides perhaps astronomy, linguistics and meteorology are the sciences I've worked hardest to master. Studies of human behavior and air-mass behavior, they're about as far apart as possible, yet oddly alike.

Each constructs those essential mental models that sometimes allow understanding and prediction and control, but such models never equal nature. They have to be simple. Reality isn't. Always, probing deeper, we find more and more complexity.

Even in physics, searching for the simplest and most basic sort of matter, we find its molecules dissolving into atoms. Atoms, no longer "uncuttable," come apart into electrons and protons and neutrons. These in turn split and split again until we reach the quark, which itself defies simplicity with such aspects as color and flavor and charm, all without apparent end.

We have to seek simplicity, choosing patterns we can grasp. Models in abstract math or maps or art or everyday language. Good models enable us to cope, but they never fit any ultimate reality. Not entirely or exactly, because we must sacrifice detail to get some comprehensible simplicity. If our genes do in fact leave a gulf between reality and the ways we can know it, the far frontiers of every science may always be mysterious.

Though linguistics was perhaps the most exciting, Eastern let me undertake several other such adventures beyond my share of freshman English and types of lit and technical writing. In a larger university, I would have been confined to some single specialty. Eastern was small when I came, but still growing vigorously. My colleagues seemed to trust me. When a new course was wanted, I was often allowed to collect a new library shelf and explore something new along with students as trusting as Debs.

I'm grateful to him for that. Grateful to Donald Moyer, the president who hired me, and to Charles Meister and Warren Armstrong, presidents who kept me on. Grateful, also, to all the other colleagues who let me do my thing, even those traditionalists, specialists in a few hallowed writers of the receding past, who felt that our departmental mission was to initiate a few selected students into their own esoteric mysteries.

Deb's field was general semantics, a doctrine more akin to philosophy than to the classics and almost as suspect to the old school as science fiction was. We were fellow dissenters. Looking at possible jobs for our graduates, we saw very few academic opportunities for new experts in Samuel Johnson or Edmund Spenser.

Once, in a spirit of mischief, I stepped into a colleague's Milton class to quote Housman, "Malt does more than Milton can to justify the ways of God to man." She seemed to forgive me. Most of our graduates were going out to teach high school English. I felt that our true mission was to prepare them as best we could for that difficult but worthy endeavor.

Gene Fox and I set up a freshman honors program. I taught creative writing and technical writing and the Russian novel. With no very impressive background for it, I was allowed to teach the history of literary criticism. Later, when enrollments for traditional courses began falling off, I was able to find students for a course in modern mystery fiction. Even for one in the history and techniques of film.

I enjoyed them all, but one I loved was called "Literary Figures." A wonderful way of self-education, it let me pick one or two inviting writers and explore them with a little group of curious students. Melville, Twain, Hemingway, Faulker, Ibsen, Shaw, Joyce. Faulkner and Joyce became my favorites among them.

Best of all, I was allowed to teach science fiction. When a newspaper described the pioneer course that Mark Hillegas taught at Colgate in 1962, I proposed one of my own. Though some of my colleagues considered it "fluff," the department approved it, and I taught it for a dozen years, from 1964 until I retired.

A three-hour course at the junior level, based largely on my own writing experience. Treating science fiction as a new and legitimate literary genre, we considered origins and definitions, history and types, techniques and critical standards, even how to write and sell it.

The readings were chosen to illustrate the history and the widening scope of science fiction, but also as briefs from the unending debate over the values of science and the usefulness of technology and the possible shapes of things to come. Pessimism, from Swift or maybe Aristophanes down to Harlan Ellison. Optimism, from Plato to Arthur Clarke's magnificent visions and Asimov's robots and the Heinlein juveniles.

Intellectual questions that ought to interest anybody. I enjoyed the course. I think the students did. Most of them tried writing their own. A good deal of what they wrote made our literary magazine. Few of them have gone on to fame, but I've been cheered now and then to hear from one who seems grateful for what he learned.

30

SUMMERS OVERSEAS,

1965–1970

Apollo 11 reached the Moon in 1969. On July 20, Neil Armstrong and Edwin Aldrin landed the Lunar Module on the Moon, and Armstrong climbed down first to take that "one small step." Robert Oppenheimer died in 1967. Of throat cancer. Or was it really from his despair over the future of mankind and the untamed atom?

Nobly, in the summer of 1965, Adele took charge of the shop for eleven weeks so that Blanche and I could get away together for our first trip abroad. Another enchanting chapter of education. We had reservations on a freighter, but it took so long to load that we had to go by air.

First to Madrid. Continental breakfasts with *café con leche* in a luxury hotel where the Beatles were staying. The Prado, with all its haunting centuries of art and history. The bullring; old Toledo; Segovia. Sun-baked Spanish landscapes and gloomy cathedrals. The Fourth of July at an American air base.

Hot hops across African deserts to Cairo. The Nile and the pyramids. Teeming millions, reeking streets, the mind-bending panorama of Egypt in "Sound and Light." I hired a plane for a flight upriver to see the Aswan High Dam and the Valley of the Kings, but had to cancel that when we woke up ill. Both feeling better next day, we went on to Greece.

My first glimpse of the Acropolis, a moment I won't forget. Sad relics of old magnificence, drowning in time and people and industrial pollution. A whiff of tear gas in Athens, a modern subway to Piraeus, a bus to old Corinth and Argolis. Ouzo and archeology. Greek islands, bright and dry as New Mexico.

Italy, and more millennia of history. Romans weary of tourists, yet grasping for tourist lira. The Colosseum and the catacombs and the old Roman roads. Capri, and a boat into the Blue Grotto. Red-tiled Florence, and Milan's magical cathedral.

Lucerne and the Swiss Alps, natural beauty we saw nowhere else. A search in Zurich for James Joyce's grave; there was no monument then, and we failed to find it. Munich; a pen pal of Nancy's became our gracious guide there.

A steamer down the castled Rhine. By rail to Paris. Our hotel was near the Arch of Triumph; we saw the Louvre and Versailles and the Eiffel Tower. The métro and Notré Dame. Names that echo in history and romance and my own imagination.

London, with all its monuments to the history of our race. The Thames and 10 Downing Street. Big Ben and the British Museum. The Tower, a cruel relic of the Norman conquest and hard oppression. Piccadilly Circus. Bus trips out to Stonehenge and Stratford and Canterbury. Haunting relics and reflections of all the English literature I'd been trying to learn.

Russia. To Leningrad on a Russian steamer, with an evening ashore in Helsinki. Back overland on a Belgian bus, with stops in Novgorod, Moscow, Smolensk and Minsk. Ghosts of Napoleon and Peter the Great. Blacker shadows of Hitler and Stalin. Red Square and the Kremlin walls. Reverent thousands trooping through Lenin's tomb, and empty cathedrals decaying. The Cold War had barely begun to thaw; except for our efficient Intourist guides, no sober Russian dared talk to us.

One of our group had a bad time from buying black market rubles, but to me the trip was fascinating. The Russians seemed more Russian than Red. The war had scarred them all, twenty million dead. Understandably, they were almost paranoid about outsiders. Less intent, I thought, on world conquest than on their own absolute defense.

Across the Bug into Poland we all relaxed a little. Life there must have been better then than now, certainly better than it had seemed in Russia. Richer farmland, better food, the people friendlier—they nearly all seemed to have kin in America. In

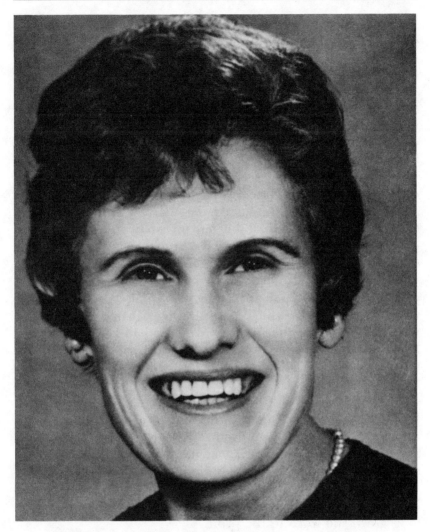

Blanche, from her passport picture when we went overseas, 1965.

rebuilt Warsaw they showed us Stalin's gift tower, not much appreciated, and the ironic victory monument. Standing in the rubble-cluttered emptiness where the ghetto had been, it was built of black marble Hitler planned to use.

The two Berlins and the appalling wall between them. The Hook of Holland and a short night at sea. Wonderful kippered herring on the boat train that got us back to London just in time for the World SF Convention. Though I found old friends and new ones there, I had slid a long way out of the game; most of the people I saw were strangers.

Dublin. We drank Guinness beside the Liffey, Joyce's "riverrun." Recalling *Ulysses*, looking for spots where Leopold Bloom had been on his celebrated day, I found the rocks of Sandymount and the Martello Tower. A museum now, closed that Sunday morning, yet it brought Joyce back to life.

By air across sweet green landscapes to Shannon. Ruined castles that recalled bitter history. We drank Irish whiskey, ate a medieval banquet, kissed the Blarney Stone. Limerick, Cork, Killarney. Best of all the genial Irish people, the friendliest we'd met. They have more American relatives than even the Poles.

Rich with new recollections, we got back to Eastern with our quotas of whiskey in time for fall registration. The trip had taken us back to the wellsprings of civilization, let us touch a wider world and glimpse the future stirring. It had been a wonderfilled makeup for a lot of early education I had missed; I used to wish I could have made it while I was younger, but it was still high adventure.

On the pages of the Christmas book for 1965, the card from Jim and Nancy shows them sitting with their kids on the cowcatcher of the little locomotive that pulls the narrow-gauge train along the scenic route from Northern New Mexico into the mountains of Colorado. In 1966, Neil is a cadet at NMMI, where I began teaching. Jim's son Gary has learned to write his name by 1967, and Karla is a high school senior, tall and lovely in the long gown she wore to the prom.

There's no candle-burning in 1968, because Janet, Blanche's mother, has had a stroke. Next year she's better, standing in our living room between Keigm and Donna, but her trembly signature is barely legible. Willis, Blanche's father, died in 1969, ailing with arthritis but mentally sharp to the end. Janet lived into 1970. Blanche assumed the responsibility for their care.

We went back to Europe in 1970 for the Heidelberg convention. Science fiction, so-called, began as something American. It stayed American for many years, even when British and over overseas writers were doing some of the best of it, because the highest-paying markets were here. Identified with the pulps where it was named, and always distinct from occasional bits of science fiction recognized as mainstream literature and therefore not called science fiction, it first got overseas in unsold magazines, sometimes used to ballast ships.

Under that American label, it had found a widening welcome everywhere that new technology had begun to challenge old ways of thought and life. The attendance at Heicon was over six hundred.

Landing at Heathrow, we toured England and the south of Scotland before the convention, pleased to be so near our ancestral roots again. I recall the bare stone splendor of old Edinburgh, and the tragic relics of Mary, Queen of Scots, kept in the old castle on its dead volcanic plug. England was alluring, with all its literary links, even with the place names I saw from the tour bus.

We got to Vienna after the convention, to stay a few days in a pension in an old palace, our third-floor room at the top of a magnificent marble stair. Our reserved bath turned out to be exactly that, a shower stall in the corner, the toilet down the hall but clean enough.

We took a boat trip on the not-so-blue Danube, and I had a real Vienna schnitzel at a Rotary meeting—Rotarians are seldom science fiction fans, but most of them are interesting. Successful businessmen, they're often leaders in their communities, all of them pledged to ideals of international service and always ready to welcome visiting members.

We spent a few more fine days in Salzburg, with Walter Ernsting and Uschi. Walter had been my German agent, even once a collaborator, when he rewrote my old novelette, "The Sun Maker," into novel length. He had survived most of the war years in Russian prison camps, his wry sense of humor still intact.

As Clark Darlton, he was one of the founding editors and writers of the Perry Rodan series. We found him a genial host.

Snapshots in the Christmas book for 1970 record our ascent of a Bavarian Alp with him and Uschi, who was a memorable blond.

The convention itself was good fun, though what I remember best about it is all the good friends we made there and on the way home. Waiting in Amsterdam for our return flight, we got to know Dan and Carmel Galouye. Dan had been a brilliant writer, though by then he was already losing ground to the war injuries that finally killed him. He and Carmel were natives of New Orleans, and we had a fine visit with them later when I was at a TESOL meeting there.

Through nearly ten years of preparing and beginning to teach, I'd been a long time away from everything else. Yet science fiction still held wonder. Now, knowing at least a little more about literature and life and language, I was keen to try writing again. As the first step, I decided to change literary agents.

Harry Altshuler had done well for me. Now, however, with more sales abroad than at home, I was uncertain about his foreign connections. Even here, he no longer seemed very active; Jim Gunn and other friends of mine had left him. I went over to Scott Meredith and stayed with him for many years.

Scott's a top agent. I've found him honest and efficient and respected; he stays in business and he has good connections all over the world. When I decided to leave, only a few years ago, it was because his agency sometimes seemed too big for me. The time we had dinner, he was on his way to Boston to get more for Norman Mailer.

I was a far smaller fish. Most of my sales were made through others on his staff, not through Scott himself. I had worked happily for years with such able people as Bob Hoskins and Anton Tibbe. They knew my work and did well for me. The problem was that they always left the agency.

Somebody, of course, always carried on. Yet I had come to feel so lost in his huge mill that I changed in 1979 to Eleanor Wood. Not, I should add, because of any falling out with Scott; we're still friends, and the checks for sales he made keep arriving.

Trying to whet my somewhat tarnished skills, I had begun attending Damon Knight's Milford Conferences. These were week-long annual workshops that Damon Knight and Jim Blish had been conducting since 1956 at Milford, Pennsylvania. Our groups were limited to about twenty-five, a mix of proven professionals and talented newcomers. Each of us brought a manuscript to be criticized by everybody else.

Over the years I attended four Milfords, following Damon and Kate—Kate Wilhelm, herself as lovable as her work—on their moves to Florida, Michigan, and finally to Oregon. Each was a week of hard labor and exciting stimulation. For me, precious retraining. The story critiques were sometimes too savage and sometimes wrongheaded, but generally honest and revealing.

Besides Damon, I met a lot of writers new to me, a new generation of people I came to like and admire. Harlan Ellison, who always brought his rock music and his typewriter and hammered out a new story while the rest of us were sleeping. Gene Wolfe, just finding his astonishing stride. Ben Bova and Gordy Dixon and Keith Laumer and Larry Niven and Norman Spinrad and more others than I can name.

Outsiders used to mistrust the "Milford Mafia," but I think the conferences were a fine thing for all of us. Science fiction writers are an independent lot, and earlier efforts at organization had all come to nothing. At Milford, we got to know each other, got on well enough to set up the Science Fiction Writers of America, launched in 1965 with Damon as the leading founder and first president.

Such gifted teacher-critics are very seldom gathered to look so hard at any sort of writing, and I'm grateful for all I gained. The conferences gave me at least a keener feeling for what science fiction was becoming, and they helped me begin edging back into the game.

For several more years, however, another sort of project took most of my free time. Science fiction had been escaping the old pulp ghetto ever since the war, creeping toward intellectual respectability. Libraries were collecting the working papers of writers ranging from Asimov to Zelazny. Critics had begun to pay attention, and faculty fans wanted to teach it. My own course had gone well.

In 1970, I set out to do what I could to help science fiction find its place in the classroom.

31.

SF INTO ACADEME,

1970–1977

The computer came of age in 1971 with the introduction of the microprocessor. Integrated circuitry on a silicon chip, it brought machines a long step closer to thinking. Actual genetic engineering began in 1973, when methods were devised to produce recombinant DNA. Smallpox was finally eradicated in 1977.

By 1970, I'd heard of a score or so of people offering college-level courses in science fiction, and of others who had run into problems with unsympathetic curriculum committees when they wanted to teach it. At a meeting of the newly formed Science Fiction Research Association, I handed out a request for information about courses taught.

That brought a surprising blizzard of responses. Within a couple of years, I had descriptions of some 500 courses taught at the college level in the United States and Canada. Summarizing them, I began publishing the results in a series of little offset booklets, which got more attention than I had dared hope for.

Phone calls from *Time* and *Newsweek* and *The Wall Street Journal,* as well as from book publishers keen for new markets. Ace Books bought 125 copies for their distributors. *Publishers Weekly* asked for an article, which ran in 1971.

I carried the campaign on for a few more years, keeping the course descriptions in print and speaking when I could to academic groups, trying to muster support for teachers in conflict with all the skeptics who saw no good in science fiction.

Skeptics do remain. Science fiction hasn't remade academe.

Yet it lives and thrives there. Libraries still collect it. The courses have proliferated, in the high schools as well as the universities, offered in departments ranging from English through the hard sciences to philosophy and religion. Publishers have issued shelves of special texts, and longer shelves of criticism.

For the academic critic, under sentence of "publish or perish," all this has opened new doors to tenure and promotion. Chaucer and Shakespeare and Milton had been dissected, down to the ultimate comma. So had a lot of lesser lights. Suddenly, now, scholars were doing critical monographs on Edgar Rice Burroughs.

Inside science fiction, all this has excited mixed reactions. Recognition is sometimes wonderful, but maybe not always beneficial. Such people as Ben Bova have been afraid of dusty classroom approaches that might kill student interest. In the critical arena, the old guard is not yet vanquished.

My own attitudes are a little bit mixed. I read a good deal of criticism, and I've published bits of my own. I belong to SFRA. I enjoy the annual meetings and all the friends I see there. I'm deeply appreciative of the Pilgrim Award given me in 1973. I'm grateful to my academic friend Professor Robert Myers, for doing his "primary and secondary" Williamson bibliography, for the reader's guide he has in progress, and for asking me to lecture on his campus.

Yet I can't help a certain wariness toward criticism in general, an attitude more emotional than rational and hard to clarify. A successful story is a thing in itself, unified by its own internal consistency and purpose, existing to communicate feeling and idea to some specific audience. I like the kind of criticism that can help the reader find and read new work, as a good many scholars helped me into James Joyce.

The criticism I suspect is the sort that takes the work apart in search of items the critic wants to use in some new construction of his own, with no intention to illuminate it, though his purpose may be consistent with the ideas of Freud or Marx or some other high authority and perhaps admirable enough in the critic's own dimension.

For a case in point, I might cite the demolition of that old novel of my own, *The Legion of Time,* in an article Brian Aldiss wrote in the 1960s for the pioneer critical journal *SF Horizons.* The story had been published back in the 1930s. Aldiss dissects it as an artifact from our pulp past, exploring its various failures to fit the standards of his own new era. The article is half the length of the novel. Perhaps I should have felt flattered that he had chosen a story of mine for dismemberment, yet I couldn't help feeling that he was using a sledgehammer to flatten an unsuspecting gnat.

Not that I felt any trace of malice. Brian is a critic I admire, and also a friend. I respect his *Billion Year Spree* as perhaps the best history of science fiction. Yet I couldn't help a sense of violence done. A fully felt story remains part of the writer, alive as he is. Even the fairest criticism, reducing it to a minor item in the critic's other frame of things, can be painful.

Or perhaps I've let such occasional pain overwhelm my own objectivity. We're all sometimes critics: the writer when he pauses to plan or revise his own work, the appreciative reader when he is moved to find a place for it within his own chosen horizons or to recommend it to his friends.

The critics I enjoy—Algis Budrys among the best of them—make up for others whose purposes I can't share so fully. On balance, I'm happy with the widening critical and academic recognition of science fiction and delighted to find it in the classroom. In our age of TV, when too few students really read anything, those who do are often first turned on by science fiction.

"With very few taboos," to quote myself from *Publishers Weekly,* it can deal "with nearly every social and moral and technical problem that the human race must meet, from nearly any point of view."

My own class led to a guidebook, *Teaching Science Fiction: Education for Tomorrow,* which I edited for Owlswick Press. Carl Sagan was persuaded to write the foreword, back when he wasn't quite so busy. Other contributors include Le Guin and Asimov and Gunn. Published in 1980, it got heartening reviews. I hope it has been helpful.

Snapshots in the Christmas book for 1971 show Blanche and me on the sidewalk under the neon sign that read "Blanche's," with a "Quitting Business" legend in the shop window. After thirty years there, she's retiring. The page records an early and very small family gathering here at home. Afterwards, we went to Kansas City for Christmas with Berwyn and Harvey and their offspring, Kraig, Kim, and Jeff.

On December 14, 1972, my James Joyce class comes for Irish coffee. Most warmly, I recall three young women among those who sign the book, Helen Tabaco from Pukalani, Maui; Tilani Lelealley from Pago Pago, Samoa; and Bobbie Ferguson, back home from years in Morocco. Our Christmas Eve reception is larger that year, and Larry Littlefield heads the page with a greeting in Russian.

The guest list for 1973 is brief again, but the Forbeses are with us. The book reports that we went to Roswell for Christmas dinner with the Stanley Slatens; Stan is Blanche's nephew. On the card from "The Williamson Tribe," Stewart and Betty and Gary are riding their cow ponies.

The mid-seventies were sad years for Blanche. Leon, her younger brother, was stricken with Alzheimer's disease. Keigm contracted cancer. Nikki, his young son, developed a brain tumor and died in July of 1974. Leon died that August. The candle wasn't burned that Christmas, because Blanche was in California at Keigm's bedside. The proud athlete and former frogman, who had always felt tough enough to defy anything, he fought with stoic courage until his death that January.

Jo, my own sister, died in March of that year. She had a fine mind, and I've always felt she deserved better breaks than she got. Yet I do admire her courage and her cheer in enduring those endless illnesses. In some sense, her life was well spent.

In the face of such bad times, Blanche and I had good ones, too. Every summer through the seventies we traveled somewhere. On a fine Asian tour in 1971, we made made new international friends. Sachito Shibano met the plane when we landed in Toyko, with red roses for Blanche. Hayakawa-shobo, the science fiction publisher, hosted a banquet for us that night. I received gift copies of my books in Japanese—books I didn't know had been translated; I was told that books in English print for ten years were unprotected by Japanese copyright. The warmth of our reception almost made up for my unhappiness with that.

We toured Tokyo with the Takumi and Sachito and Kiochiro Noda, a Japanese TV director who had translated some of my novels. More fans were waiting to greet us us in Kyoto. One of them, Kouichi Yamamoto, is still a loyal friend who sends me copies of my work in translation. Robin Johnson came from Melbourne to meet us in Sydney, and Jack Chandler entertained us.

There were other Rotarians in the group. We had fine make-ups in Tokyo and Hong Kong and Bangkok, where the king was a member, and on around the Pacific. We took off our shoes to wade ashore on a tiny Fiji islet and enjoy a Polynesian feast cooked in a pit. A memorable day, even though there was no long pig.

That tour was sponsored by Carl Parker, one of my colleagues at Eastern and a great travel guide. With students working for academic credit, we looked into problems of cultures in contact and too often in conflict: East Indians in Fiji, Chinese in Malaysia, Maori in New Zealand.

Visiting schools, watching able young people everywhere fighting so hard to master new technologies, I thought I could see trouble to come for America. As a nation, we've lived too long and too easily on our rich heritages of European culture and the untapped wealth of the new frontier. Far too sure of our own superiority, we've come to expect more than we have earned.

In 1972, we spent two weeks in Mexico. An enchanting glimpse of a rich sister culture, with a giddily quick review of its history and a glance at growing troubles that will doubtless come to trouble us.

I had joined TESOL, the organization of teachers of English to speakers of other languages. Grappling with all the difficult issues of language and culture, we attended their 1973 convention in Puerto Rico, with side trips to St. Thomas and then to Haiti, where lovely tropic settings failed to veil aching need and tragic history. Haiti seemed an ominous glimpse of the whole human future. Too many people trapped on too little worn-out land, with nowhere to go.

With Carl Parker guiding us again in 1974, we had another wonder-filled month overseas. Istanbul, with all its echoes of old empires. Afghanistan, not yet overrun; when I got lost in the Kabul bazaar, friendly natives pointed my way. India; the Taj Mahal on a blazing midsummer day when Blanche stayed on the air-conditioned bus.

Believers bathing in the Ganges, and a vulture on the swollen body of a water buffalo floating down it, picking out the eyes. Calcutta and Bombay; arrogant wealth and heartbreaking poverty. Sri Lanka; I had hoped to see Arthur Clarke, but he was gone to Europe. The Holy Land, as harshly arid as New Mexico. Relics of Jews and Romans and Crusaders; Israelis and Arabs, religions at war. Greece again; this time I got to Delphi and saw the navel of the world.

Alaska, in 1975. By luxury steamer up the inside passage from Vancouver to Skagway—wonderful enough, yet not quite so thrilling as my first ocean voyage so long ago in steerage. By narrow-gauge to White Horse, along the gold rush trail. By jolting bus up the dusty Alcan Highway through the Yukon and on to Fairbanks. A jet flight to Point Barrow; permafrost beneath the tundra, and ice floes in the Arctic Ocean. By rail again, to Mount McKinley and Anchorage. By air again, to Nome and all its gold rush recollections. Hawaii in 1976, and a glimpse of its relics of Polynesian culture drowning under all the tourist hordes.

Those summer trips were the best sort of education, yet I found another school, nearly as rewarding, in the New Mexico Humanities Council. Thanks to Gordon Greaves, I was invited in when it was formed, and I served until 1980.

The Council is a child of the National Endowment for the Humanities, which had been set up to give humanistic studies the same sort of support that science was receiving from the National Science Foundation. In theory, at least, a fine idea. We were to find public problems and solve them with federal funds. The members were a mix of interested academics and such wide-minded laymen as Gordon.

Meeting three times a year, we discussed and sometimes funded proposals meant to involve the academic humanist in the discussion of public policy issues. Illegal immigration, minority rights and women's rights and labor rights, the aims of education, problems of crime, of urbanization, of vandalism on archaeological sites, the depletion of our precious geologic water, the preservation of our rich mix of Indian and Spanish and Anglo cultures—those issues and others were grave enough, and now and then we did draw interested audiences. A few films we funded got national attention.

Yet I'm afraid too few of our projects repaid the tax dollars they cost. The humanists in their ivory towers were generally content to stay there, and the people we were trying to enlighten seemed happy in the dark. All that aside, however, the Council was a fine thing for those of us on it. We got to know one another. Selected scholars from all across the state, and leaders from every class and group we could reach. Wonderful people; the friendships we made and the insights we shared were a high reward for all the time the Council took.

Though teaching took most of my time, with travel and my evangelism for the academic image of science fiction biting deep into the rest, I kept on writing when I could, trying hard to keep and cultivate whatever skills I had.

In 1973 I'd turned sixty-five, the normal retirement age. Eastern kept me on for a few more years. Reluctant to quit, because I liked teaching so much, I knew that in time I would be left with nothing I really wanted to do except write science fiction. I tried hard to stay in the game.

Algis Budrys says there are two kinds of stories, those felt and those constructed. Ideally, I suppose, good work needs both: sound construction in the planning, deep feeling in the writing. Trying all my life to learn construction, I've found that no structure works unless the feeling comes.

The Moon Children is a story almost lost when efforts at construction blundered, saved when feeling finally entered. The plot germ came from an early Milford. While we were demolishing a Tom Disch story, I was hit by an idea that looked alluring: a novel about people lost in the midst of spectacular cataclysm, unable ever to learn what's obliterating their world.

Not a hopeless idea, necessarily, but when I tried to write it, about people trapped in nightmares of totally inexplicable disaster, my plots all died. Only one stray notion survived, the idea that an interstellar culture might try to make contact with us by changing our genes.

At work with Fred Pohl in my office at home on my birthday,
April 29, 1971.

The novel came from that. Three astronauts touch black crys-
tals they find on the Moon, objects from an interstellar missile
that fell there long ago. Their sperm is transformed. Back on
Earth, they father the moon children: a girl and two boys, not
entirely human. The book is their story. They grow up, learn
who they are, reach for their interstellar parents.

In structure, the book is far from perfect. It sprawls across too
many worlds and too many years. It lacks any very original
meaningful theme. Yet it worked for me, and I think for a good
many readers, because I came to feel it very deeply. The children and their world came to be so real that afterwards, every
time I drove through the Tijeras Pass, down out of the mountains into Albuquerque, where the climax happens, the whole
story came back.

The Power of Blackness, my next novel, was planned as a sort of thought experiment in theme: a test of primitivism at odds with progress. The setting is Nggongga, a semidesert planet whose long-isolated colonists have sunk back to savagery. It has just been rediscovered by the advanced galactic culture. My young Nggonggan warrior meets a sophisticated girl from outside, and the story grows out of their cultural conflicts.

The idea is still appealing, but the book came out flawed because of the way I had to write it. Using scraps of time left over from teaching and everything else, I did it as a series of novelettes. Some of them worked well enough because they were fully felt, but I was never very happy with the concluding story. It's a difficult trick, to provide half a dozen minor endings in the course of a novel without some harm to the total effect.

Fred Pohl and I had embarked on another series. We borrowed a notion from the astronomer Freeman Dyson, the idea that searchers for interstellar cultures should look for sources of infrared radiation. Dyson had suggested that beings with a truly high technology would trap and use all the radiation from their star, letting only waste heat escape.

The Dyson sphere poses interesting engineering problems. If it spins, centrifugal force would support the equatorial zone, but the poles would fall in. Our solution was a multilayered network of frictionless rings, spinning in different planes to support the whole superstructure, an immense hollow globe with a sun at the center.

I designed the sphere. We discussed plots. I wrote drafts and sent them to Fred. The actual stories came harder than the engineering, perhaps because the concept of the sphere was too big for most of the beings and events we were able to invent. "Doomship," a novelette about the discovery of the sphere, was published in 1973, "Org's Egg" in 1974. Rewritten in 1975, they became *Farthest Star*.

At that point, the unfinished series stalled. We discussed more plots. I wrote new drafts. Fred began what was meant to be a final revision that died halfway through. I revised that and carried it once more to the end. Fred's next attempt balked again. Our publisher gave us a better contract, and more years passed. I taught my classes and turned to other projects. Fred was doing such superb things as *Man Plus* and *Gateway*. A whole decade was gone before we got it finished and into print in 1983 as *Wall Around a Star*.

In 1977, I was retired from teaching. Again, overage. I missed and still miss my classes. Though writing is another social thing, it's lonely, the responses long delayed. In the classroom, what you say and do gets instant feedback. And you belong. You're accepted, commonly respected, sometimes even loved.

All that was over.

32

SFWA,

1977–1980

The last *Apollo* astronauts reached the Moon in 1972. *Pioneer 10,* launched that same year, crossed the orbit of Mars and the asteroid belt to fly by Jupiter and climb on out of the solar system. Here at home, in the aftermath of such triumphs, our space programs were underfunded, slowly winding down. Yet the Europeans and the Russians kept forging toward space, and the whole exploration of our universe pressed on. Einstein's old dream of a unified theory had crept a little nearer by 1978, with the forces of electromagnetism linked to the weak nuclear interaction.

A fine thing happened in 1977, the year I found myself out of the classroom. I was invited to be Guest of Honor at Suncon, the World Science Fiction Convention, held that year in Miami Beach.

Such conventions are unique to our field. Fans enough exist for a dozen other sorts of writing, but they lack the dedicated enthusiasms and the sense of belonging to a special community that has distinguished sf fandom since that long-ago beginning when our numbers were so few.

Each is organized and run by a new group of fans, though the leaders are commonly experienced veterans of successful earlier affairs, and the "world conventions" are governed by a permanent constitution. Besides these American-dominated "world cons," independent international conventions have sprung up in Europe and Japan and sometimes elsewhere. There are regional cons and local cons, fantasy cons and horror cons and comics cons. Half a dozen may be happening, scattered all across the country, on any weekend. The largest have become big business, supported by membership fees, huckster rooms, and auctions. Attendance is often in the thousands, the budget in the hundreds of thousands.

Being GoH has been a great thing for both Blanche and me, not only at Suncon but at Rivercon and Westercon and Norwescon and Bubonicon and Leprecon and Philcon and Windycon and Deep South Con and Aggiecon (twice) and more others than I have space to mention. The committee pays all expenses, commonly meets the plane when we land, puts us up in luxury. People say flattering things, applaud talks and panels, ask me to autograph books. All this may have nothing to do with writing the next book, but it's heady fun.

Certainly for me. Blanche has often gone with me. She has enjoyed being on such panels as "The Care and Feeding of a Big-Name Pro," and she has found good friends among writers and editor and fans, but she has never read much science fiction besides mine, and except for the chance to renew friendships she has limited interest in the field. Sometimes she encourages me to go alone because she feels that looking after her would take me away from too many of the activities I came for.

We were together at Suncon, with Donald Lundry the chairman and our chief host. With a suite at the Fontainbleau, the convention hotel, we were entertained royally. Certainly I was honored enough. An impressive portrait by Vincent DiFate on the cover of a magnificent program book and a fine cartoon of me and my humanoids by Kelly Freas inside. Flattering appreciations by E. Hoffman Price and Fred Pohl. A bibliography. Pages from *Beyond Mars* and a gallery of illustrations for my stories.

Who am I to say that I am undeserving?

In these recent years, with our parents gone and siblings scattered, Christmas celebrations are no longer so large as they used to be. The candle and the book are sometimes neglected,

The author, with Samuel R. Delaney and Arthur C, Clarke, about 1978.
(Photo by Jay K. Klein)

but Fred Pohl signs in 1978, a few days late—coming to the
sunny Southwest to escape the Eastern winter, he got here in the
middle of a January cold snap, with the thermometer down to
−7°F.

Earlier signers had been Peggy Tozer and Mary Jo Walker
and other good friends from the Golden Library at ENMU,
when we took them out to dinner by way of thanks for a fine
reception they had staged for me in recognition of the fiftieth
anniversary of my first story in print, "The Metal Man" in that
1928 *Amazing.*

Gene Fox is there too, writing his own name and Margaret's,
but time is overtaking them. Our very dear friends. Margaret
had been a lovely person, gracious and sensitive and generous,
but by then she was already slipping into the confusion and
distress of Alzheimer's disease.

Gene's enormous bright vitality was failing. He had retired
early from Eastern with health problems of his own that he hated
confessing. One morning when I went by his place to take him

out for coffee, I found him dead on the floor by his bed. Margaret's body is still half alive, cared for tenderly by their son Steve
and his good wife Jo, but her mind is gone.

Losses hard to take. A grim condition of advancing age is that
so many old friends are falling around us, but Blanche and I try
not to dwell upon it. We've been lucky, weathering the years and
finding good things to do.

Since 1965, when Damon Knight got the Science Fiction Writers of America afloat, I had been a member, never very active,
though immensely flattered in 1976 to be awarded the Grand
Master Nebula, the honor I value most highly. The regular
Nebulas are bestowed at an annual springtime affair staged to
recognize those publications of the previous year selected as
most worthy by a vote of the membership. The Grand Masters
are "for lifetime achievement." Bob Heinlein received the first,
in 1975. Mine was the second. Cliff Simak, Sprague de Camp,
and Fritz Leiber have followed.

I've always felt a vast pride in being admitted into such a
company of respected and beloved peers. We all of us, whoever
we are, need very deeply to be loved. The Grand Master is the
sort of recognition I'd longed for ever since I first thought of
writing science fiction.

The catch to such an honor is that you can do so little about
it. What you have written is part of yourself. To the degree that
people ignore or find fault or reject it, you are hurt. If the right
people love your work, and thereby you, the best you can do is
love them in return. If they praise it and you, all you can do is
try to express your thanks.

There's an ironic upshot. Though most writing may be done
in hope of earning approval in terms of editorial acceptance and
royalties paid and kind comments from loyal fans and their
requests for autographs, the processes of creation can ultimately
mean even more. If you are living what you write and like what
you have finally written, doing it can come to be even more
rewarding in the long run than even the best things that may
happen to it afterwards.

Not that I slight the Grand Master. Few rewards could matter
more. SFWA is filled with friends of many years, people I respect

The author, looking intoxicated with the honor of it, with the Grand Master Nebula Award, 1976.

and sometimes love. It's part social club, part mutual aid society. Together at the parties editors and agents stage at the convention, or together anywhere, we enjoy one another, sharing drinks and market information and writing know-how. We promote science fiction and attempt to recognize the best. Publishers, I think, have come to respect us as a group, and members with problems can commonly get help.

It's sometimes hard to find people with free time enough to serve as officers. While I was still teaching, Fred Pohl had asked

me to run for the presidency of SFWA. Now, with time to do my
bit, I agreed.

Elected in 1978 and again the next year, I undertook the job
with a good bit of apprehension. We then had some five hundred members, including most of the writers of English-lan-

The author as atronomer, about 1978.

The author, with Jim Gunn and Fred Pohl, standing in front of the Liberal Arts Building on the ENMU campus. Jim and Fred were here as the first speakers at the Williamson Lectureship, established when I retired from the faculty in 1977.

guage science fiction and fantasy, many of my best and oldest friends among them. Individually, I admire them nearly all, but I had found them remarkably contentious at meetings I attended. I expected difficulties.

They were surprisingly kind to me, and generously helpful. I needed the help. There were more problems than will ever be solved. With Peter Pautz, our executive secretary, our only paid employee—and he not highly paid—our machinery sometimes stalled. Our dues were minimal, our solvency in question. Legally, we were still in a shadowland, our tax status uncertain. A good many members were unhappy with our annual Nebula Awards, afraid of unfairness or some of them protesting we shouldn't be giving awards to ourselves at all.

We were just emerging from the "Lem affair"—we had given an honorary membership to Stanislaus Lem, the distinguished Polish author of *Solaris,* and then withdrawn the membership when he expressed contempt for American science fiction. Lem is a best-seller in his native Poland and widely published. In view of what he says he thinks of us, I doubt that either action touched him, but many of our members became hotly concerned.

My first resolution was neither to make nor to unmake honorary members. With strong aid from Heinlein and Pournelle and other old hands, we raised the dues enough to keep us afloat and hired Alex Berman as attorney to look into our legal status and offer members legal aid. The Nebula Awards go on, though doubtless still debated—judgments of literary excellence are so subjective that total agreement will never be likely. It's true that not many of our members have time to read and judge all the recommended works. Yet I think the awards have generally gone to writers who have earned them.

The job took about half my working time for those two years, but I found it well spent. People in science fiction are a self-directed lot, most of them brightly original and well worth knowing. Once I had known nearly everybody writing or editing science fiction, but their numbers have grown amazingly. The job let me meet new people and renew old friendships. With more unity than I had expected, with so many people so generous with time and unpaid effort, SFWA is still alive and thriving.

With more free time, Blanche and I were traveling again. To Scandinavia in 1977, and on to Russia for another look. Our Intourist guide was a charming young woman, and we found tensions somewhat eased since 1965.

To Brighton in 1979 for the world convention. Julius Kargalitski was there, a Russian scholar I knew. Though Russian science fiction flows in a channel of its own, separated from the American sort by barriers of language and censorship, H. G. Wells is the chief source of both, and Kargalitski is the great Russian Wellsian, editor of the fifteen-volume Russian edition of his works and author of a fine modern study. When he spoke at Brighton, I felt honored to be allowed to introduce him.

That winter I went to China with Gordon Greaves. During the war he had been flown over "the hump" from Burma to spend several years there as an air forces radio technician. With Americans welcome again, since the fall of the Gang of Four, he was anxious to go back.

The author on the Great Wall of China, 1979.

By happy accident, we were on a Yugoslav flight, which gave us an unexpected two-day stop in Belgrade on the way out to China and another three days in Zagreb on the way back. Fred Pohl had been there. With tips from him and help from the American embassy, I got in touch with the Yugoslav science-fictioneers.

They gave us a wonderful welcome. Meetings with science fiction clubs. A gift bottle of slivovitz—which is powerful stuff. A reception by the Serbo-Croatian writers association. A taped interview for national TV, the morning we left. Best of all, new friendships.

Science fiction there was more Western than Russian, and its popularity surprised me. *Sirius,* the sf magazine, had a circulation of 30,000. It had begun with reprints—I was happy to find a reprinted story of mine on the newsstands, duly bought and paid for—but half its authors are now Yugoslavs. Krsto Mažuranić, one of those new friends, has since translated *The Humanoids* into Serbo-Croation, publication pending.

The people we met were mostly young professionals, physicians and journalists and engineers, a good deal more serious than the typical American fan. Their freedom of speech surprised me, and the way they saw science fiction as a medium for serious discussion of social and political issues. It seemed to carry none of the wood-pulp stigma we in America have never entirely escaped.

The flight itself, from Belgrade to China, was another great adventure. From Karachi to Peking, we flew across the Himalayas and the Trans-Himalayas and the snowy plateaus of Tibet in clear daylight, getting magnificent camera shots of the raw welter of glaciered summits soaring nearly to our flight level, ice-scapes and rock-scapes that looked as remote and cruel as Mars.

The People's Republic of China. Our guides were bright, likable young people. They lodged us well and fed us well—the food came cut into bite-sized bits; I seldom knew exactly what it was, but we ate it with chopsticks and enjoyed it thoroughly. Very efficiently, they showed us old China and new China, all we could absorb in two crowded weeks.

A grade school in T'ai-yüan with primitive facilities and levels of achievement that amazed us. A fish-farming commune, and Shih Huang-ti's terra-cotta army. Mao serenely half-smiling in his crystal sarcophagus, and the old Ming tombs. The Great Wall winding forever along sharp mountain ridges, and posters on "democracy wall" the week before it was abolished.

Men and women ladling fertilizer into neatly weedless fields out of honey buckets, and gifted artists at work in a jade-carving commune. We watched people moving earth in baskets, building hills to hold up the arches of a stone bridge under construction, removing the hills as the arches were finished. We spent three nights on better passenger trains than run in America.

China's people. We loved the children. Clean, their clothing in bright contrast with the uniform drabness of the grown-ups, well disciplined but seemingly happy about it, always waving and smiling at us. Everywhere outside of Peking (Beijing, officially) we were stared at, as strange to the people as they were to us. Silent people, curious but friendly. Crowding close around us, they always parted courteously to let us pass.

I left China with a vast respect for them, an awe mixed with pity. A billion of them in too little space, their problems all but hopeless. Yet they do compel hope. In spite of Mao and the Red Guard, they're still more themselves than Marxists, as I thought the Russians were.

They've been surviving unfortunate governments and intolerable times for many thousand years. Their brains and skills and hardihood demand admiration. They are doing more than any other nation to curb population overgrowth, which I see as the world's great danger. There's at least a chance they may survive again when stronger-seeming rivals die.

Later that same winter, Blanche and I spent two weeks in Kenya. A very different world, one I had been anxious to see before the poachers finish the game, before hungry people burn all the forests for cooking charcoal and turn the exhausted soil to naked laterite, before the whole continent topples too far toward famine and chaos. I try to hope that doesn't happen, but I'm grateful that we got there when we did.

On a camera safari, we stayed in lodges on game reservations. Watching waterholes or cruising off the roads in Volkswagen minibuses, we found lions lazily asleep or waking to blink idly at us. Cheetahs, sleekly elegant, one overtaking a frantic impala. We found it later in a thicket with the kill.

Elephant herds, regally ignoring us. Warthogs and waterbuck and buffalo. Fearless baboons, raiding the "treehouse" from which we watched. Fat zebras grazing and giraffes reaching high. Black-maned wildebeest, hippo yawning in their pools, hyenas as ugly as their names. Apprehensive ostriches, and a few cautious rhinos. Except for leopards, nearly everything we looked for.

Landscapes and people as fascinating as the game. The endless wall of the Great Rift Valley, towering termite nests, volcanic cones and jungle-covered lava fields, the awewome loom of Kilimanjaro. Proud Masai herding their cattle and shaking spears at incautious photographers. Mombasa. Ancient and half Asian, fringed with modern luxury hotels building all along its endless coral beaches. I swam in the Indian Ocean.

The clashing contradictions of Nairobi, stark poverty lapping all around the parks and towers at its modern-seeming core. Too many people, bright and likable people, striving hard to finish their emergence from old tribal divisions into democratic unity and the richer future almost in their reach.

We found science fiction in the bookstores there, and another friendly fan, Rashid Mugal. A feature editor on the national newspaper, he was writing science fiction of his own. I was happy to find it spread so far. A cheering hint of wonder alive, of the urge to learn, of the zest for science that can open new horizons.

In times that sometimes disturb me, I try to see the international appetite for science fiction as a sign of widening awareness, at least a spark of hope that our threatened world can somehow sense its dangers in time to save itself.

33.

RETURN TO WRITING,

1980—

Space remains the most exciting new frontier. Though manned efforts have been lagging, robot probes have mapped the planet Mercury and landed on Venus and Mars to send precious data back. Pushing farther out, the *Pioneers* and then the *Voyagers* have explored Jupiter and its moons. *Voyager 1* went on to reach Saturn in November of 1980. *Voyager 2* got there in August of 1982. Flung farther on by the planet's gravity, it should reach Uranus in 1986, maybe Neptune in 1989.

Jerry Pournelle, once on the NASA staff, had been able to persuade his old friends there that science fiction really does support the space effort. Thanks to him, Blanche and I were among those waiting at the Jet Propulsion Laboratory in the hills above Pasadena with press credentials to watch the *Voyager* flybys of Jupiter and Saturn.

Each event gave us a week of high-space drama. The *Voyagers* are robot explorers, computer-run, guiding themselves, reporting all that their electronic senses see and feel. What they found is dazzling wonder.

Those planets are giants. Each has its own satellite system, formed by the same processes that shaped the whole solar system and made our Earth itself. Their far moons had been no more than points of light in the best telescopes, but the *Voyagers* took us close.

Breathtaking wonders flashed across the monitors, faster than we could drink them in. Jupiter's belts of giant-sized storms, Io's

253

The author, 1982.
Hair getting pretty thin, pretty white.

sulfurous volcanoes, four billion years of cosmic history crater-carved into the outer satellites. The incredible complexity of Saturn's rings, the mysteries of Titan, the puzzles of the other icy moons. Always more new riddles posed than old ones resolved.

Panels of scientists briefed the press formally every morning, in smaller circles every afternoon. They showed us enhanced images, discussed new data, gave us new perspectives, grappled with new bewilderments, all revised from day to day in the light of still newer revelations.

We saw scientists doing science, and science fiction coming true. Watching those cratered moons looming larger in the monitors, we were space explorers coming in to land. Their long history, decoded from all the *Voyager* data, is also the history of the early Earth. The flybys recharged my own imagination.

Though I'm retired from teaching, Eastern has been good to me. Maybe too good. An annual lectureship has been named in my honor, the first speakers Jim Gunn and Fred Pohl, Bob Silverberg here more recently. I'm still on the payroll, a research professor at a dollar a year. In 1981, I was given an honorary doctorate of "humane letters" and invited to make the commencement talk.

My working papers are preserved, along with Ed Hamilton's and Leigh Brackett's and manuscripts from many others, in the university library. My fan friend Woody Wolfe had an outstanding collection that was bought after his death. Thanks to Stan Schmidt, there are many years of copy-edited manuscripts from *Analog.* Items have come from many other sources. In 1983, the science fiction collection included 7,000 books, 6,500 individual issues of 230 different magazines, and 130 cubic feet of manuscripts and personal papers.

In 1982 it was named the Jack Williamson Science Fiction Library. Mary Jo Walker is the librarian, and a special friend. My thanks are due her and her staff and her historian husband, Dr. Forrest Walker, for a great deal of help with the research for this book.

The dedication was a rather elaborate affair, with scores of my local friends and science fiction friends invited. They were asked to write letters for a volume that was presented to me. I felt rather awkward about this solicitation of testimonials when I learned about it. I can't thank all those who wrote, and I try not to take all the generous words too seriously, but the letters light a glow of warmth every time I look through them. I am deeply grateful.

Though I miss my students and my academic colleagues, it's nice to be writing full time again. Science fiction has been generous to me. In 1977 I was guest of honor at Suncon, the world convention held that year in Miami. Though our trips overseas seem to have ceased, I still attend conventions, Blanche sometimes with me.

We have good friends scattered far around the globe, many I've never met. In Italy, Ugo Malaguti has retranslated many of my books and published them in handsome hardcover editions.

The author at the dedication of the Jack Williamson Science Fiction Library, 1982.

Annamaria Ferarri has written a thesis on my work at the University of Turin. Piero Giorgi has done a book that is awaiting publication.

Writing again, I've been trying as hard as ever to keep up with my able and often brilliant peers. Sometimes lagging, but happy to be still in the race. The craft has aspects that can be taught and learned, and aspects that can't. I've never felt that doing one story makes the next one easier. Sometimes it seems more difficult, because the most urgent things, those closest to the heart, have been expressed.

Yet that long return to academe must have left me with at least a little more to say. Perhaps the encounters with the classic masters gave me better grasp of what words can do and a clearer sense of how to make them do it. I've been delighted, anyhow, to find that the springs have not gone entirely dry, that writing science fiction can still yield exhilaration.

First of all, out of school in 1977, I finished *Brother to Demons, Brother to Gods*, which I had begun as series of connected novelettes. Genetic engineering had come a long way since 1951 and *Dragon's Island*. Taking a new look, in the light of all the progress since, I tried to push the future possibilities as far as I could imagine them.

My genetic engineers are the Smithwick family, each generation redesigning the Smithwick genes they pass down to the next. They create four new races. The trumen are bright and beautiful people, designed for citizenship in an engineered utopia. The mumen are mutant humans specialized for war or space or anything. The stargods are the immortal and nearly omnipotent rulers of the planets—Ben Bova, my editor then, urged me to make them more godlike. Finally, there is the fourth creation, created to supplant the too-tyrannic gods.

In the time of the story, only a few of the Smithwicks' kind, our own kind, have survived. They're the hopeless premen, confined to reservations. Two lone members of the fourth creation live among them, naked kids when the story begins, ignorant of who they are and hidden there from the jealous gods, who don't intended to be supplanted. The story follows their effort to learn what they are, to escape the jealous gods, to realize their destiny.

With science fiction booming then, publishers were offering good contracts for unwritten books. I had always refused to attempt a sequel to *The Humanoids*, but Fred Pohl, serving an editorial hitch at Bantam Books, offered me a contract so tempting I couldn't refuse. Adele Leone, then at Pocket Books, tendered another, for a new novel about Giles Habibula and the Legion of Space. I signed both.

Neither book came easy. The humanoids, perfect machines built to guard us from the worst in ourselves, do their work too well. The original stories were based on the premise that, being perfect, they can't logically be corrupted or diverted. In *The Humanoid Touch,* grappling again with the same dilemma that baffled those earlier protagonists, I tried to set up a fresh fictional experiment with men and machines.

Two planets, Kai and Malili, were settled long ago by fugitives from the humanoids. Kai is a cold and barren little world where men without machines could not survive. The settlers on Malili were compelled to learn to live without machines because of native microorganisms that crumble most metals into useless mud.

When at last the humanoids overtake these refugee worlds, they assume control of Kai at once because they find its people using machines in warlike ways to attempt the conquest of Malili. It is this old and tragic habit of violence that they were created to restrain. The natives of Malili are luckier: evolving to become less aggressive, possessing no dangerous machines, they require no humanoid care.

The Queen of the Legion gave me problems of a different sort. I'm no longer the same eager young man who set the series going in 1934. Those first stories, with their headlong pace and their desperate tension, were written with emotions and enthusiasms not easy to rekindle. The book took nearly a year to do, but I think it finally went well. The background was worked out with more care than I'd had time for before. I feel pretty happy with the novel in its final form, and several veteran fans have spoken well of it.

Most of it was written on a word processor, a little TRS-80 computer. A Model I, already obsolete yet still wonderful. On the typewriter, I used to hammer out several thousand words a day to be printed pretty much as they came, but I've learned through the years to do more and more revision.

The computer makes that sometimes too easy. I can try a dozen versions of a sentence if I need to, with no penalty in erasures or marked-out passages or drafts to be retyped. This ease can become seductive, tempting one to keep on tinkering with beginnings when the story might better have been carried straight on to the end.

Howard and Pearl Campaigne are signers of the Christmas book in 1980. A fine new friend, Howard came to Portales to teach computer science at Eastern. Not quite my own age, he was a wartime Navy cryptanalyst and later chief of research at the National Security Agency. Now retired, he jogs, rides his bike, flies his own plane, instructs student pilots, writes computer programs, solves cryptograms, and sometimes reads science fiction.

He has been my mentor in computer science. Fascinated with it, I've bought books and subscribed to the magazines. No expert yet, I've written a few BASIC programs that really work, one to compute travel time for spacecraft moving between planets at uniform accelerations. The little I've learned was useful in doing my 1982 novel, *Manseed*.

It grew from an idea that captured my imagination: another way to sow the human seed on the worlds of other stars. The seedships are tiny fusion-powered spacecraft. Unmanned, they carry computers loaded with the human genetic code. They can fly forever. When one of them nears a suitable planet, it is activated to land and retranslate the code into living men and women.

As the first step in the re-creation of humanity, each ship creates a Defender. My editors call him a cyborg. He's human-shaped but more than half machine, his computer-brain loaded with the know-how he'll need to care for the ship and the infant colony, know-how recorded by an imperfect process from the brains of a team of specialists.

The Defender in the novel is imperfect, awakened on a ship damaged by a micrometeor and adrift a million years. Half his memory banks were lost. What he does recall is a jumble of special skills and fragmentary recollections from the minds of his creators. His nature shaped the novel, and the shape it took delighted me.

Lifeburst is a new book, one I hope to see in print in 1984. It came from things I learned at the *Voyager* flybys, about the Oort cloud. Jan Oort is the Dutch astronomer who established the rotation and the dimensions of the galaxy. The cloud is a suggested swarm of ice planetoids, "dirty snowballs" of star stuff left over from the formation of the solar system, millions or even billions of isolated objects scattered along orbits reaching out perhaps a light-year from the sun. The comets, Oort suggests, are members of the swarm that happen near enough to the sun to be vaporized and visible.

These objects are a mix of water ice, ammonia ice, methane ice, and assorted cosmic dust. The same elements that make human beings. They contain a lot of hydrogen. Fused, that could yield nearly unlimited energy. With the right technology, we could colonize this solar halo. The "lifeburst" of the title is the evolutionary jump that gets us there. A limitless new frontier, it could offer new room for new freedoms, well away from all the hazards of military accident or technological miscalculation that might wipe out our not-quite-civilized Earth.

An idea that delights me. Yet, still at work by trial and error, I ran into trouble with the first attempted draft. Working out a background in the next two centuries of history, and tempted to try a three-volume epic, I began the planned first volume too near today. When that stalled, I turned to this book, which Jim Frenkel had encouraged me to try.

Not without hesitation. I wasn't sure how much I could recall, or how much would be worth recalling. I felt another hazard, maybe graver. If it is published and people read it, they'll know me far better than I know them.

Now it's written. Like any book in progress, it took on a shape of its own; no set of symbols can ever be entirely true to anything outside them. I enjoyed the months of work, and I think the long confession has been good for me. Hard as I tried to be candid, the "I" of the book has always tended to become another persona, nearly as far as some story character from the formless flicker of image and impulse that's all I know of the mind of the actual me. I've come to see him with a certain detachment. Knowing him, I think I know myself a little better.

Writing about these recent years, I've been concerned about dramatic interest. Drama comes from conflict, hope of victory and fear of failure. For most of my life, that has been the pattern: the struggle to sell another story, the search for some sane place in the scheme of things and the means to stay alive.

That pattern has changed. Though each story still offers ample chances to blunder and big risks of failure, the consequences aren't so harsh as they used to be. Our social roles seem firmly fixed, and we have little urge or opportunity to change them. Money troubles no longer haunt us, what with retirement benefits and a modest income from writing.

Yet, beneath a deep contentment, life is still dramatic. Counted out by heartbeats or atomic clocks, time runs on. In no haste for it to stop, I feel the future nudging. Once unlimited, horizons keep closing in. Hoping for no survival except in whatever brief way such words as these may live, I try to face events I can't control with a decent stoicism, untroubled by doubts or fears of any supernatural hereafter.

The years are telling. Blanche has had both hip joints replaced. She gets about with no pain, but we neither one go so fast or so far as once we did. Faced too squarely, the future can look ominous. Yet, here and now, we still have brighter things to look for. Still absorbed in science, I try to keep up with its revelations of the nature and the history of our universe. I enjoy the people I know and the friendships I feel.

With this book and *Lifeburst* now on their way into print, Blanche and I have reservations to leave winter in New Mexico for a long-dreamed-of cruise around South America. From Florida to Puerto Rico and across the Caribbean to Cartagena and the Panama Canal. Down the west coast, with a side trip to see Machu Picchu, the "lost city of the Incas." The Strait of Magellan, and a day ashore in Patagonia. Buenos Aires, and a glimpse of the pampas. Montevideo. Finally, a flight home from Rio.

Those names are still magic to me. We'll see at least the fringes of one more continent, with a quick review of its dramatic history and a glimpse of its peoples and their critical current problems. I hope to come back recuperated from a long stint of steady work and ready to attempt another project.

We're excited about the adventure, and I trust it won't be our last. Nobody is likely to invite me for a flight in the shuttle, but at least we're hoping to get back to Australia next year for the world sf convention in Sydney.

Not that we're unhappy here at home. We've fallen into an easy routine.

Blanche cooks breakfast while I shower. Sitting at the table, we watch bits of the morning news shows. I work at the computer an hour or so, then drive downtown to the post-office box and sometimes shop for groceries. We read the mail when I get back and drink a cup of coffee. I work again till lunch.

After lunch, we nap. I work awhile, ride my bike three miles along streets where the traffic is light, and perhaps work again till time for the evening news. I get more magazines and books than I can read; writing my own fiction seems to satisfy most of my need for that; what I read is mostly science and current events, with bits of biography and history.

Blanche is active in Faculty Dames and Altrusa. She keeps the house and reads proof when I have something ready. Reading for recreation, she has almost abandoned TV. I see a good many news and documentary programs. We have a drink before dinner; I have one bourbon and Coke. She drinks tonic without much vodka. Sometimes we see friends in the evening; when we have dinner guests, we commonly take them out to eat. Adele lives near and watches over us lovingly, phoning every morning.

An interviewer inquired not long ago what I felt I had accomplished. A sticky question, but I suppose what I feel best about is simply having been able to stay alive so long in science fiction, from the "scientifiction" in Gernsback's *Amazing Stories* to these amazing days when science fiction films break attendance records and Arthur Clarke and Isaac Asimov and Robert Heinlein and Frank Herbert make the best-seller lists.

Overage for many things, I've been elated that writing is still great fun to do. The wonder's still alive, and I rejoice that these words aren't yet actually the end—

INDEX

263

Mathematics studies, 39, 204–205
Maugham, William Somerset, 134–135
Mažuranić, Krsto, 250
Mechanical Ants, 212
Mehrens, Leona, 170
Leister, Charles, 220
Menninger Institute, 101, 148
Menninger, Karl, 101, 109
Meredith, Scott, 228
Merritt, A., 52; influence of, 50–51, 56, 58, 60–61, 64, 66–67, 73, 146; meeting with, 110
Merwin, Sam, 131
"Metal Man, The," 52, 55, 73, 243
"Meteor Girl, The," 66
Meteors, 38–39
Methodism, 5–6, 7–8, 9, 30, 163
Mexico, 19, 20–22; trips to, 21, 58–60, 132, 235
Milford Conferences, 229, 237
Military service, 136, 137, 143–150, 151–156, 159–160. *See also* Weather forecasting
Mindsmith, The, 190–191, 194
"Minus Sign," 136
"Miraculous Gift, The." *See* "Star Bright"
"Mist, The," 72
"Mistress of Machine-Age Madness," 72
Modern Language Association, 208
"Monster-God of Mamurth, The," 73
"Moon Bird, The," 60
Moon Children, The, 237–238
"Moon Era, The," 78, 83
Moon Is a Harsh Mistress, The, 61
Moon Pool, The, 50, 52, 55, 146
Moore, C. L., 129
Moore, Don, 68

Moore, Grady, 205
Morang, Alfred, 122
Morey, Leo, 58
Morojo. *See* Douglas, Myrtle
Mosig, Dirk W., 215
Moskowitz, Sam, 1, 118
Mosley family, 6
Motion pictures, 38, 64
Moyer, Donald, 220
Mugal, Rashid, 252
Music, 68, 100. *See also* Dancing
Myers, Robert, 232

Narrative Technique, 64
National Council of Teachers of English, 215
Nature, 31–32
Nebula Awards, 247–248
New Castle, Pennsylvania, 92
New Fandom, 117–119
New Mexico, 10, 30, 111
New Mexico Humanities Council, 236–237
New Mexico Military Institute, 205–206
New Mexico Quarterly, 84
New Orleans, Louisiana, 76, 228
New York City, 108
New York Daily News, 194, 195, 196–199, 203
New York Times Book Review, 201
Newspaper work, 166, 167, 171, 174
Niven, Larry, 229
Noda, Kiochiro, 235
"Non-Stop to Mars," 112, 113
Not-Men, The. See Dragon's Island
Novak, Michael, 18
Novels (*See also* Characters, in novels); advances for, 121, 125, 181, 191, 201; income from,